SOUTHWEST ARK

3 8430 00150396 5

MW00359156

HEMPSTEAD COUNTY LIBRARY
HOPE, ARKANSAS

THIS WAS THE LIFE

THIS WAS THE LIFE

Excerpts from the Judgment Records
of Frederick County, Maryland,
1748-1765

By Millard Milburn Rice

93 - ~~970~~ 969

GENEALOGICAL PUBLISHING CO., INC.
Baltimore 1984

Copyright © 1979 by Millard Milburn Rice
Frederick, Maryland
All Rights Reserved
Reprinted by Genealogical Publishing Co., Inc.
Baltimore, 1984
Library of Congress Catalogue Card Number 84-80270
International Standard Book Number 0-8063-1077-4
Made in the United States of America

PREFACE

This book is composed of extracts from the Judgment Records of Frederick County, Maryland from its establishment in 1748 to 1765. I hope readers may find its contents as fascinating as I have; such a hope is my reason for its publication.

Since the Frederick County Court was the sole governing body of the County, as well as its civil and criminal court, the record of its actions covers every phase of Colonial life. Here is reflected not only laws and customs, but also humor and tragedy, compassion and cruelty.

The English influence is very evident, and because that influence pervaded all the original colonies, the record is of much more than local interest. This is especially true since laws and customs were uniformly English and government at the local level differed primarily only in nomenclature and detail.

The records of the proceedings (the Judgment Records) of the County Court, now in the office of the Clerk of the Circuit Court, are contained in sixteen huge volumes. Only one volume, covering the years 1763-1766, is an original record. The other volumes are photostatic copies of the originals now kept in the Hall of Records at Annapolis. The records are not entirely complete from 1748 to 1765, as the reader will notice. And records for November 1771 to November 1779, inclusive, are missing, resuming again in March 1780 and ending with the year 1783.

Since the records are so voluminous, selection is an obvious necessity. In making the selections forming the text of this book, I have tried to record the interesting and the significant as well as occasional items of purely genealogical interest.

I believe readers will be surprised and intrigued by the number of items in these records which are inviting spring-boards for further research — to which, actually, there is probably no end. In order to achieve an ending, however, I have resisted this temptation here, but I hope many readers will not.

Because the sessions of the Court follow a rather well-defined pattern, a most serious problem has been the avoidance of repetition and monotony. Indeed, the decision to end this transcription with the November Court of 1765 was strongly influenced by a desire for such avoidance. And since the repudiation of the Stamp Act in 1765 was a highwater-mark in Frederick County history, it has seemed especially appropriate to end with the record of that act of the County Court.

In the text which follows, where direct quotations from the records are made, the spelling of the original has been retained, but not the peculiar capitalization within sentences. Where sentence structure is faulty, a clarifying word or two in brackets has occasionally been inserted. In general, however, quotations are unedited. As a result, it may not always be quite clear whether English typical of the times is being reproduced, or the carelessness or ignorance of some unknown scriveners is being embalmed.

Punctuation in the Judgment Records is remarkable for its absence. A few commas, semi-colons and an occasional period have been inserted. But here also, with those exceptions, the original is quoted as it appears in the record.

In all cases, whether in direct quotation or paraphrase, proper names are spelled as they appear at the point in the record. While spelling of such names varies widely throughout the records — frequently in the same paragraph — no attempt has been made to standardize by imposing personal preferences.

Except for an occasional footnote or explanatory reference, truly interested readers are left free to do their own clarifying research.

I am indebted in varying degrees to several members of the Frederick Bar, assistants in the Office of the Clerk of the Circuit Court, and numerous other friends, to all of whom I now express my gratitude and thanks. I am particularly indebted to Mr. Charles C. Keller, Clerk of the Circuit Court, and to Mr. Frank W. Rothenhoefer, Sr., for their most valuable assistance. My deepest debt, however, is to Mr. John P. Dern, 950 Palomar Drive, Redwood City, California. As I said of him in the preface to my book New Facts and Old Families (1976), without his massive collaboration and counsel, this book would not exist.

MILLARD MILBURN RICE

INTRODUCTION

The Frederick County Court was an extension of the Prince George's County Court, which was itself an extension of the County Courts of Charles and Calvert Counties, from which Prince George's County was formed in 1696. As a result of the Protestant Revolution in England in 1688, Maryland became for a time a Crown Colony, and the Prince George's County Court of 1696 was held in the name of William III and Mary.

But by 1748, when Frederick County was formed from Prince George's County, the Proprietorship of the Maryland Colony had been restored to the Lords Baltimore and its first Court was held in the name of the Lord Proprietor, Charles Calvert. Cases were transferred to it from the Prince George's County Court just as cases from Calvert County (there was none from Charles County) had been transferred to the Prince George's County Court in 1696.

The first recorded session of the Frederick County Court is dated December 13, 1748. It opened with the reading by Nathaniel Wickham, Jr., of a proclamation issued in the name of the Lord Proprietary by Samuel Ogle, "Lieutenant General and Chief Governor of our said Province of Maryland." The purpose of the proclamation was to appoint justices, define their duties and establish the limits of their jurisdiction.

In civil cases, jurisdiction was limited to suits involving not more than £100 sterling or 30,000 pounds of tobacco.

In criminal cases the Court held the power of life and limb over Negroes and other slaves, though apparently always subject to review by the Provincial Court, the next higher Court in the State. In criminal cases involving Caucasians, punishment by the Court was limited to the pillory, the whipping post, fines or imprisonment.

Of the twenty-three "Gentlemen" appointed as Justices by the initial proclamation, only ten ever served on the Court. Twelve were identified as "Esquires" (lawyers), but only one of these, Daniel Dulany, who was the first Chief Justice, served.

During the seventeen years covered by this record, forty-two Justices served as members of the Court. Attendance by the Justices averaged approximately ten per Court session.

The 1748 proclamation is long and repetitious, covering about four and a half closely written pages of the record book. Because of its length, it is reproduced in Appendix "B" (page 279), rather than here.

At the conclusion of the Reading, those Justices present were sworn. Court was then called. Present were "The Worshipful Nathaniel Wickham, Jr., Thomas Beatty, Henry Munday, Thomas Prather, William Griffith, Gentlemen, Justices...."

John Darnall was appointed Clerk of the Court by order of Edmund Jennings, Secretary of the Province. John Thomas qualified as Sheriff, and James Dickson, later to be named a Justice himself, became Undersheriff.

The Justices ordered the Clerk to prepare commissions for the Constables and Overseers of the highways "which were appointed by the Justices of Prince George's County at their last November Court."

"The Court then adjourned to the third Tuesday in March next," at which time the routine business of the Court began.

The next entry in the Record is a MEMORANDUM of a Court of Election, dated February 25, 1748. This seemingly prior 1748 date, referring to a Writ of Chancery directed to John Thomas, Sheriff, who according to the record above didn't qualify until December 1748, need not be mystifying if it is remembered that until September 1752 England and her Colonies were still using the Old Style Calendar. With that calendar the year did not end until March 24th of what we now consider the following year, so that, allowing also for an 11-day correction when the New Style Calendar was finally adopted, the February 25, 1748 O.S. date was the equivalent of March 7, 1749 N.S. in today's reckoning. To eliminate the possibility of similar confusion in the sequence of Court sessions, wherein March Courts in a given year seemingly follow all other Courts of that same year, I have adopted in the text which follows the common practice of adding the new year to the old for the March Courts, e.g., March Court of 1748[/49].[1]

The Writ of 1748[/49] directs the Sheriff to call at least three Justices together and have them issue a proclamation setting a day for all freeholders of the County to meet at the Court House and elect delegates to the General Assembly to be held in Annapolis on the following 9th of May. They met "at Mr. Kennedy Farrell's, there being no Court House in the County," and set "the 7th day of March, next" for the election.

Qualifications for voting were ownership of 50 acres of land or "a visible estate of 40 pounds sterling." The election was held "at Mr. Thomas Baker's in Frederick Town," and those elected were:

Capt. Henry Wright Crabb
Joseph Chapline
Daniel Dulany, Jr.
Capt. Thomas Owen

With this preliminary work completed, the Judgment Record then turns to the record of individual Court sessions, and these follow.

---

[1] I am indebted to Mr. John P. Dern for this explanation of dual datings resulting from change in the Calendar.

The March Court of 1748 convened on the third Tuesday and twenty-first day of March. Present were the Worshipful Justices Daniel Dulany, Chief Justice, Nathaniel Wickham, Junior, Henry Munday, William Griffith, John Rawlins, Thomas Prather, Thomas Beatty, Thomas Cresap, Joseph Chapline and George Gordon.

One interesting thing about this list of Justices is the fact that only one of these men, Thomas Beatty, was listed in 1733 among the taxables of Monocacy Hundred of Prince George's County, which was essentially that part of Prince George's County which is now Frederick County. This indicates that these men were in a sense imposed upon Frederick County by the Government of the Proprietary.

Present also were John Thomas, Gentleman, Sheriff, and John Darnall, Clerk.

The members of the Grand Jury were as follows: Foreman David Linn, Edward Owen, Samuel Magruder III, Ninian Magruder, Junior, Benjamin Perry, Aaron Prather, James Perry, John Swearingen, William Murdock, John Lamar, Joseph Wood, Charles Higginbothom, Elias DeLashmutt, William Beatty, John Perrin, Abraham Alexander and Moses Chapline.

The Grand Jury made numerous presentments for various purposes, but the page containing these presentments is so badly blurred that it is almost impossible to read them.

Of interest from a legal standpoint, the following men qualified themselves as attorneys before the Court: Henry Darnall, Daniel Dulany, Junior, William Cummings, Stephen Bordley, Edward Dorsey and Richard Chase.

What is apparently the first petition to the Court for a license to operate a tavern is made by Cleburn Simms, who presents the following petition: "That your petitioner, having provided himself with accom-

1

modations fit for travelers and others, humbly prays that Your Worships would be pleased to grant him a license for ordinary keeping, he complying with the Act of Assembly in that case provided and he as in duty bound will pray."

"Upon reading his petition and consideration thereof had, it is ordered by the Court here that the petitioner have the effect of his prayer on giving security according to law." Later evidence indicates that the Simms tavern was in Frederick Town.

"Simon Harden, an orphan child aged (as 'tis said) about eight or nine years, is by the Court here bound to Charles Higginbothom until he arrives to the age of twenty-one years and the said Charles Higginbothom in Court here promises to teach or cause the said Simon to be taught to read and write and at the expiration of his time to give him a decent suit of apparel."

"William Luckett agrees with the Court here to keep ferry over the Mouth of Monocacy until the last day of November next, for which he is to be allowed in the next County levy twenty-two pounds current money and the said William obliges himself when the boat or scow cannot pass by reason of low water to provide a cart to carry tobacco and other things over and the Court orders that the said William do not demand nor take more than four pence for carrying a man and horse over and four shillings for wagons belonging to non-residents."

"Edward Wyatt is appointed to keep ferry at the mouth Conococheague until the last day of November Court next, for which he is to be allowed in the next County levy at the rate of ten pounds current money for the time he keeps the ferry and has his boat or scow ready to convey persons over; and ordered that the said Edward do not demand or take more than four pence for carrying a man and horse over and three shillings for wagons belonging to non-residents."

The Court purchases of Daniel Dulany, Esquire, six volumes of the Statutes and Nelson's Justice in two volumes and orders that the said Daniel Dulany be allowed forty pounds, fifteen shillings current money in the next County levy for the same.

The Court likewise agrees with the said Daniel Dulany to send to England for the succeeding volumes of the Statutes, Hawkins' Pleas of the Crown, Hale's History of the Pleas of the Crown and Hale's Pleas.

Henry Ballenger contracts with the Court to keep a ferry over the middle ford on the Monocacy and to provide a boat or scow and an able hand or hands to work it until the last day of next November Court for which he shall be allowed ten pounds at the next County levy.

"At the request of Mr. Nathaniel Wickham, Junior, the Court appoints Mr. Edward Beatty, Joseph Ogle and Joseph Wood to lay out a road from Captain Joseph Ogle's ford to John Biggs' Ford on Monocacy and from thence to Frederick Town."

"William Wilburn is by the Court here appointed to view the road from Frederick Town to the top of Kittocton [Catoctin] Mountain and if any amendments are wanted to make such as he shall think necessary."

"George Gordon, Junior, is by the Court here appointed to buy a standard weight for this County and ordered that he bring in his amount thereof at next Court."

"Ordered by the Court that George Gordon and John Rawlins, Gentlemen, adjust the weights at Rock Creek warehouse."

The Justices of the Court here settle the rates of liquors and other accommodations vendable in this County as follows:
Hot dyet for a gentleman with a pint of small

3

beer in the country	£0/ 1/ 0
In town	0/ 1/ 3
Rum per sealed quart and so pro rata	0/ 4/ 0
Hot dyett for a gentleman's servant with a pint of beer	0/ 0/ 9
Lodging in a bed per night	0/ 0/ 6
Syder per gallon	0/ 2/ 0
Maryland good strong beer per gallon sealed	0/ 3/ 0
A bowl of punch made with a sealed quart of rum and loaf sugar and so pro rata	0/ 6/ 0
Stabling and good fodder for an horse per night	0/ 1/ 0
Corn and oats per bushel and so pro rata	0/ 4/ 0
A sealed quart of maderra wine	0/ 4/ 0
Good small beer per quart sealed	0/ 0/ 4
A cold dyett	0/ 0/ 8
Maryland spirits distilled from grain per gal.	0/ 9/ 8
Peach brandy per gallon	0/13/ 4
All other European wines	0/ 5/ 0

Joseph Wood presents to the Court a petition which is of modern interest because it is apparently the forerunner of the present Maryland Route #194 which is a main road from Frederick to Hanover and other points in Pennsylvania. This is the petition: "Whereas the road from Monocacy Ford where John Hussey lives that leads to Lancaster is very much used by travelers as well as by this inhabitant and the road being very crooked and stopped up by trees falling across the same and whereas the road might be laid out a shorter way and to less damage to the settlements that lays near the said road, your petitioner therefore humbly prays Your Worships that there may be a road laid out as aforesaid and three overseers to clear it, one from Monocacy crossing my Lord's Manor and one from my Lord's Manor crossing Little Pipe Creek to Great Pipe Creek and one from Great Pipe Creek to the temporary line of ye province."

"Upon hearing which petition and consideration thereof had, it is ordered by the Court here that Nathaniel Wickham, Junior, Thomas Beatty, and Joseph

4

Wood lay out the road as prayed for and that they make return thereof to the next County Court."

Mary Thacker prefers to the Court here the following petition: "May it please Your Worships, I, a poor child named Mary Thacker, my father and mother both dead, I having no family, I was bound at Anne Arundel County Court to a certain William Hayward of the said County. He never gave me no schooling according to the rules of Court. From thence he removed up back in the woods, from thence down to Monocacy, he being there in debt to a certain Joseph Hill in Monocacy and had not the money to pay him. When he came up the country last July, I was sold a servant to the said Hill for three years to pay the debt. Your humble petitioner prays Your Worships to consider me if I must be continued a servant or whether I may be at liberty to provide for myself, being now about fourteen years of age and your humble petitioner is ever bound to pray."

The Court ordered a summons issued returnable to the next County Court for the said Joseph Hill to answer the above complaint.

In the June Court of 1749 Mary's case came to the attention of the Court. The record there states: "Mary Thacker, aged (as it is said) fourteen years the twenty-fifth day of October next, is by the Court here bound to Joseph Hill till she arrives to the age of sixteen years and the said Joseph Hill promises to learn her to read distinctly in the Bible and to give her at the expiration of her time of servitude a gown and petticoat made of linsey woolsey, a pair of shoes and stockings, an apron of white linen, two white hats and two shifts, one of brown and the other of white linen."

And then in the same record it was "Ordered by the Court here that Mary Thacker her petition for freedom preferred last County Court against a certain Joseph Hill and which was referred to this Court be rejected."

"Ordered by the Court here that the Clerk thereof make out advertisements notifying that the Magistrates of this County or the major part thereof intend to meet on the 8th day of May next at Frederick Town to contract with any person or persons to build a court house for said County, which advertisements the Sheriff is ordered to set up in the most convenient places of this County."

The Justices established the following Hundreds and named the Constables for each as follows:
Upper Potomac Hundred. Constable James Offutt, Junior.
Lower Potomac Hundred. Charles Jones, Constable.
Newfoundland Hundred, to extend to the lower end of the County. William Waters, Constable.
Rock Creek Hundred, Middle part. John Bean, Constable.
Sugarland Hundred from the mouth of Senecar to the mouth of Monocacy to the southwest of Main Road that leads from Monocacy Ferry to Seneca Bridge. Thomas Fletchall, Constable.
Sugar Loaf Hundred to lie between Senecar, Monocacy and twixt the old Main Road and the new Main Road. John Norris, Constable.
Linganore Hundred to begin where the new road crosses Monocacy and so run up to the mouth of Linganore and with Linganore to the Main Road that leads to Annapolis till it intersects with Anne Arundel County so as to take in all the taxables and to join with Newfoundland Hundred. Thomas Maynard, Constable.
Manor Hundred to begin from the mouth of Linganore, up the Monocacy to the mouth of Pipe Creek and up Pipe Creek to the fork and up Little Pipe Creek to William Farquhar's Ford and from thence with a straight line to Linganore Main Road Ford. John Martin, Constable.
Pipe Creek Hundred to begin from the mouth of Pipe Creek up with the Monocacy to the temporary line and with it to the dividing line between Baltimore

6

and this County and with the dividing line to the wagon road that leads from Monocacy to Annapolis. Joseph Wood, Constable.

Kittocton Hundred to begin from the end of Kittocton Mountain up the river to the end of Shenandore Mountain and with the top of Shenandore to the temporary line and Kittocton Mountain till it comes to the southwest end of same. John Johnstone, Constable.

Andietum Hundred to begin on the end of Shenandore Mountain to the mouth of Andietum and up with Andietum to the temporary line and with that to the top of the South Mountain otherwise called Shenandore Mountain and with that [to point of beginning]. Moses Chapline, Constable.

Marsh Hundred to begin from the mouth of Andietum to the mouth of Conococheague and up that to Vulgamot's mill and from thence with the road that leads from Vulgamot's mill to Stull's mill. Nathaniel Tumbleson, Constable,

Salisbury Hundred to begin from Vulgamot's mill up with Conococheague to the temporary line and with it to Andietum and down Andietum to Stull's and from thence to the beginning. Robert Downey, Constable.

Conococheague Hundred to begin from the mouth of Conococheague up to the mouth of Big Tonoloways and with it to the temporary line and with that till it crosses Conococheague and down the same to the beginning. William Ervin, Constable.

Linton Hundred to begin in the mouth of Tonoloways Creek up Potomac River to the fountain head thereof and from thence to the meridian line till it intersects the temporary line and down the same till it strikes Tonoloways Creek. Edmond Martin, Constable.

Monocacy Hundred in three parts, the Upper Part divided by Fishing Creek to the dividing line. Joseph Farys, Constable. The Middle and Lower Parts divided by Henry Ballenger's Creek. Constable, Middle Part, Stephen Julian. Constable, Lower Part, Joseph Wilson.

7

JUNE COURT OF 1749

The June Court of 1749 met on the third Tuesday, the twentieth day of June in the 35th year of His Lordship's Dominion. Present were the Worshipful Nathaniel Wickham, Jr., Captain Thomas Prather, William Griffith, Thomas Beatty, George Gordon and John Rawlins, Gentlemen, Justices.

The Grand Jury was composed as follows: Foreman Thomas Stoddert, William Wilburn, Charles Cheney, John Adams, John Johnson, Isaac Baker, William Boyd, William Shepherd, Samuel Ellis, Nathaniel Magruder of Ninian, Hugh Conn, William Pritchett, William Gray, Thomas Boydstone, Buckner Evans and William Nicholls.

The first presentment by the Grand Jury is of six women for bastardy. In this connection as I leaf through these records, it seems to me that the women involved in such matters always seem to bear the brunt of the legal opprobrium. I know of only one or two cases in which a man is presented by the Grand Jury for bastardy. Merely to indicate how this is done, I shall here list the women. I feel some hesitancy in doing this, but since they were presented to the Grand Jury by the several Constables of their Hundreds, it seems to me of some interest merely to see how the presentments were made. Certainly enough time has elapsed since this period so that no opprobrium should rest on these folks or their descendants:

Presented by Charles Jones, Constable, was Johanna Jenvers, servant of William May. Anne Russell, presented by Joseph Wilson, Constable. Rebecca Wise, servant of Robert Wells, presented by Nathaniel Tumbleson, Constable. Jane, the servant of Thomas Waller, presented by the same Thomas. Penelope Pane, presented by John Norris, Constable. And Anne Cape, presented by Stephen Julian.

The second presentment reads as follows: "We, the Grand Jury, do present Van Swearingen, Junior, Samuel Swearingen and Robert Fells, Junior, on the information of Nathaniel Tumbleson, Constable, for refusing to carry before the magistrate the body of George Parker taken by him with a warrant for debt."

Martin Earnest presents a petition to the Court wherein he states that "your petitioner has had the hard fortune to have four children born blind and so continues and your petitioner finds a very great hardship to maintain them with the bare necessaries of life. Therefore, your petitioner humbly prays Your Worships to allow me levy free which will be some help for me towards their maintenance, and your petitioner shall forever pray."

"Upon reading which petition and consideration thereof had, it is ordered by the Court here that the petitioner be levy free for the future."

Another petition to the Court: "Abraham Decart, old above sixty year, and Jacob Fouer, old sixty-three year, cannot do no work come to bray the Court to be levy-free and will be danksfull in their lifetime for it. Upon reading which petition and consideration thereof had, it is ordered by the Court here that the petitioners be levy-free for the future."

This use by the Clerk of the German phonetics, bray for pray and danksful for thankful, is perhaps illustrative of the condescending English attitude toward the Germans.

The Grand Jury was discharged from this present service and allowed four hundred pounds of tobacco in the next County levy.

Basil Bealle takes the oath, "In relation to the suppressing the exportation of tobacco not inspected as required by Act of Assembly."

9

"John Reislin, aged 16 years as it is said, is by Court bound to John Hufman til he arrives to the age of twenty-one years and the said John Hufman promises to learn or cause him to be learned to read and write and at the expiration of his time to give him a coat jacket and breeches of drugget, a castor hatt, a pair of shoes and stockings, two white linen shirts and a handkerchief."

"To the Worshipful Justices of Frederick County, the petition of Matthew Richards, most humbly sheweth that your poor petitioner is now and has been these four years past most grievously afflicted with what is called the Cuntrey Distemper and has employed doctors so long (though of no purpose) that your poor petitioner's small substance is expended and gone already and nothing left to maintain my wife and six small children for I am so word away and so weak that I am not able to do any individual thing for their support and without some relief must certainly come to suffer greatly myself and my wife and children come to poverty and want which they do already in a great measure. Therefore, your poor petitioner most humbly prays Your Worships look upon me with the eyes of pity and with tender and compassionate hearts and allow me what Your Worships in pity thinks proper and your poor petitioner shall forever pray."

Ordered by the Court that the petitioner be allowed 800 pounds of tobacco in the next County Levy for his support to next November Court.

John Cramphin [today: Crampton] petitions the Court for a license to keep a public house in Frederick Town, and the Court grants him permission.

John Mitchall petitions the Court for a license to keep a public house or house of entertainment "on the Main Road near Volgomot's Mill," and the Court grants its permission.

William May of Tonoloway Hundred presents a petition as follows: That for sixteen years he has been "More often taken with the fitts sometimes senseless and falling into the fire to the hurt of your petitioner and falling into dangers which prove hurtful and troublesome to house and family insomuch that they are obliged to take care of both person and affairs, being now about fifty-three years of age and uncapable to travel or labor to maintain a family or be without tendance or be at any time alone without someone to support your aforesaid petitioner when in sore extremity. Hoping Your Worships will be pleased to take such pittiful condition into consideration your most humble petitioner shall as in duty bound forever pray."

"To the Worshipful Justices and Court now sitting, we whose names are hereunder written do certify that your petitioner William May has been ever since he lived in our settlement very troublesome to his family and is growing worse in his disorder to his hurt and disadvantage which we testify to Your Worships. Signed by several persons. Upon reading which petition, it is ordered by the Court here that the same be rejected."

A petition to the Court reads, "Your petitioners humbly sheweth that they are in great want of a road from Nelson's Ferry to Frederick Town and pray that an order of Court may be had for a bridle road fitt to ride from the said Nelson's Ferry [near Point of Rocks] to Frederick Town and your petitioners will ever be bound in duty to pray." It was signed by Arthur Nelson, Jr., Elias DeLashmutt, Notley Thomas, James Dickson, James Hook, John Jacobs, Christian Kemp, John Hook, Thomas Morris, John Cramphin, Benjamin Piburn, Samuel Duval, John Nelson Sr., Arthur Nelson, Sr., and John DeLashmutt. "Upon reading which petition and consideration thereof had, the Court appoint Mr. William Griffith and Elias DeLashmutt to lay out the road as above prayed for." This is now known as the Ballenger Creek Road.

11

HEMPSTEAD COUNTY LIBRARY
HOPE, ARKANSAS

Elizabeth Weaver presents a petition to the Court which "sheweth that your petitioner on the 23rd day of November 1748 did by ind[entu]re bind her two sons named William and Jonathan Neall to a certain Matthew Edwards of the County aforesaid. But your petitioner not knowing how to read and not intending to bind her children to the said Matthew Edwards and his assigns, the said indenture was before she signed it read to her not mentioning assigns and therefore she voluntarily signed it. Your petitioner humbly conceives that as the indenture was not read to her as it was wrote, notwithstanding that is she signed it, it is not her act and deed, therefore prays Your Worships to take the same into your consideration and make such orders as shall be thought by you most necessary and she will pray."

The Court ordered that bench warrants issue returnable to the next County Court for Matthew Edwards and a certain Thomas and John Fletchall to answer this complaint and likewise ordered that the Fletchalls bring before the Court the two children mentioned and that these children be mentioned in the warrant. The Court also ordered that summons be issued for John Allen to testify on behalf of the petitioner.

This case reached its conclusion in the August Court of 1749, where the Court issued the following judgment: "Whereupon the premises being seen and by the Justices of the Court here fully understood, it is considered by the same Court that the aforesaid William and Jonathan Neall be absolutely free and discharged from the services of the said Matthew Edwards, Thomas and John Fletchall."

The case of Mary Ryan, a servant to Benjamin Harris, who had been presented by the Grand Jury in the March 1748 Court, came to trial in the June Court. The charge against Mary Ryan was for having a mulatto child. She appeared before the Court and "says that she is nothing guilty of the premises, that she will not contend with the Lord Proprietary, but submits herself to the Grace of the Court here."

The Court's judgment was "that the said Mary Ryan is guilty of general bastardy only. It is therefore considered that the said Mary Ryan be fined or suffer corporal punishment according to Act of Assembly in such cases made and provided and because the said Mary Ryan does not pay the fine aforesaid nor procure anyone to pay the same, it is ordered by the Court here that the said Mary Ryan by the Sheriff to the whipping post be taken and there receive on her bare body five lashes well laid on and it is further adjudged that the said Mary Ryan serve her present master Benjamin Harris nine months exclusive of her present time of servitude for the trouble, expense and loss of time occasioned by the bastardy aforesaid."

John House, Sr., who had also been presented at the March 1748 Court for assault "on the body of Mary Divelbess," says "that he will not contend with the said Lord Proprietary in and about the premises but submits himself to the Grace of the Court here." The judgment of the Court was "that the said John House, Sr., be fined, forfeit and pay to the said Lord Proprietary five shillings current money for his offense aforesaid."

"And hereupon Michael Divelbess of Frederick County, farmer, in his proper person in Court here undertakes for the said John House that as well the fine aforesaid as the fees due for the officers of the Court here by occasion of the premises shall well and truly be paid and the said John House, Sr., is dismissed."

One Staffel Bernard who had been presented also at the March 1748 Court is now brought into Court to answer for an assault and battery committed on the wife of George William Lawrance "by information of said Lawrance. The said Staffel Bernard in Court here comes and says that he will not contend with the said Lord Proprietary in and about the premises but submits himself to the Grace of the Court."

13

"It is considered by the Court that the said Bernard be fined, forfeit, and pay the said Lord Proprietary one shilling current money for his offense aforesaid."

"And John Long of Frederick County, farmer, in his proper person in Court here undertakes for the said Bernard that the fees due to the officers of the Court here by occasion of the premises shall well and truly be paid and the said Staffel Bernard be dismissed."

A case originating in Prince George's County in 1746 was transferred to Frederick County and was heard in the June 1749 Court. It was a suit of Col. Thomas Cresap against Evan Shelby, Sr., for fees for surveying land in 1746. In support of his suit, Col. Cresap itemizes his bill, which amounted to 1,595 pounds of tobacco. Here is the itemization:

The resurvey of part of "Hazard"		
original 100 acres	400	lbs. of tobacco
Plats and certificates on the same	45	"
The addition of 140 acres	120	"
Plats and certificates on that	60	"
Plats and certificates on the whole	75	"
Journey fees	40	"
The resurvey on "Hunts Cabin"		
original 50 acres	400	"
Plats and certificates on same	45	"
Survey the addition of 260 acres	165	"
Plats and certificates on that	75	"
Plats and certificates on the whole	90	"
Journey fee	80	"
	1,595	lbs. of tobacco

The outcome of this case is unknown. Its interest lies in Cresap's charges for surveying. Moreover, since Evan Shelby was a pioneer settler in the Hancock area, it would be most interesting to identify, in present-day terms, the two tracts surveyed for him.

14

AUGUST COURT OF 1749

The August Court of 1749 convened on the third Tuesday and fifteenth day of August, 1749.

The Justices present were Daniel Dulany (Chief Justice), Nathaniel Wickham, Jr., Thomas Beatty, Henry Munday, George Gordon, Thomas Cresap, Joseph Chapline, Thomas Prather and William Griffith.

The Grand Jury included Thomas Stoddert again as foreman, William Beall son of Ninian, Ninian Beall son of Ninian, Biggar Head, Gary Davis, William Hickman, Jeremiah Hays, Arthur Nelson, Patrick Mathews, Edmund Rutter, John Moore, Peter Rench, Peter Stull, John Carmack and John Richards.

As appears to become customary in the Court, the first presentments by this Grand Jury were of seven women for bastardy.

The Jury indicted "Thomas Brown for stealing a bell and collar off the neck of a horse belonging to the estate of Henry Crampton, deceased.

Elizabeth Weaver (see June Court) was indicted for stealing a sheet, "the property and by information of Alexander Lamar."

"Jonas Hammond, an orphan child aged one year the fifteenth of July last past, is by the Court here bound to Elizabeth Hickman until he arrives to the age of twenty-one years."

The Court heard a number of petitions, some of them filled with pathos and some with bathos, the purpose of which was to be excused from tax levy. Some of these petitions were granted and some rejected. In no case were reasons given.

The Grand Jury was then discharged and allowed

four hundred pounds of tobacco in the next County levy.

Thomas Fletchall, Constable of Sugarland Hundred, "certifies to the Court that Andrew Cottrell in his presence swore 26 oaths for which this Court has adjudged him to pay £6/7/6 current money according to Act of Assembly in such cases made and provided."
"Thomas Thompson in like manner is adjudged to pay £1/7/6 current money for swearing six oaths" and Arden Evans £0/12/6 for swearing three oaths, both in the presence of Thomas Offutt, Jr., Constable.
Obviously oaths were not cheaper by the dozen, for the 26 oaths cost 4sh., 11d each, the six 4sh., 8d, and the three only 4sh., 2d a piece.

The Court appoints Thomas Ma[y]nard and Moses Chapline as deputy rangers for the County.

"Ordered by the Court here that the overseer appointed to lay out the road from Frederick Town to Mr. Dulany's Mill alter the same and carry it through the back of Francis Wise's plantation and Christian Thomas' land without going through his enclosure, the nighest way to the mill."

John Mitchall petitions the Court to be permitted to continue to keep a public house of entertainment at his plantation near Volgamot's Mill. The Court allowed this petition.
Kennedy Farrell petitions to be allowed to continue to keep a public house of entertainment in Frederick Town and the Court allows him to do so.
Elizabeth Reynolds, wife of Thomas Reynolds, petitions the Court to keep a public house on Monocy [sic] which the Court allows.

The remaining time of the session of this Court was occupied with many suits for the recovery of debts, most of them small. The largest was for £44.

NOVEMBER COURT OF 1749

The November Court, held on the third Tuesday and twentieth day of November, opened with the reading of the Commission which was first read when the Justices were installed. The Justices present were: Daniel Dulany, Esquire, Chief Justice, Nathaniel Wickham, Jr., Henry Munday, George Gordon, John Rawlings, Thomas Cresap, Thomas Prather, William Griffith and Hugh Parker.

The first presentment by the Grand Jury was against Francis Wise "for cutting down and destroying the land of John Van Metre, an orphan."

The second presentment was of three women for bastardy.

Elias DeLashmutt was presented "for keeping a tippling house on the information of James Hook." In addition, "the Grand Jurors present the following persons for keeping tippling houses, namely Jacob Baney, Conrad Cross, Martin Adams, Bartholomew Jesserong and John Cramphin. Thomas Schley for keeping a tippling house by the information of Kennedy Farrell. John Carlton and Abraham Miller for keeping tippling houses by information of Thomas Stoddart. Isaac Jardy on the information of Nathan Beach. Isaac Elting on the information of Nathan Beach."

"The Grand Jurors present Nathan Tomlinson, Constable, for taking two sheep as security for George Lawrence's levy and not returning him in his list of taxables." They also present Tomlinson for not returning in his list the following taxables: Henry Prather, Thomas Lucas, two of his brothers and his father-in-law. That was on the information of Van Swearingen.

The Grand Jury also presented William Waters,

Constable of Newfoundland Hundred, for not returning several taxables in his list. They further indicted Tomlinson for permitting a prisoner to escape. The Grand Jury returned indictments against Moses Chapline, Constable, for failure to return certain taxables.

There were contract overruns in November 1749 as well as today. Edward Bewsie petitioned the Court to the effect that "he hath built a good bridge over Rock Creek by agreement for £14/10/-, but as the aforesaid bridge is something longer than it was expected to be and better built than work of this kind is commonly done, it is humbly prayed Your Worships will take it in consideration and allow your petitioner £5/10/-, which will be agreeable to the work and your petitioner and in duty shall ever pray. Upon reading this petition and consideration thereof had, it is ordered by the Court here that the same be rejected."

Dr. Orlando Griffith petitions as follows: "that as your petitioner hath a good parcel of fresh medicine and imagines Your Worships may employ some doctor to have the care and cure of the County patients, your petitioner therefore most humbly offers his services and will engage himself to give contentment and satisfaction.

"Upon reading this petition, it is ordered by the Court here that the same be rejected."

The Court again set the prices for various accommodations and since apparently there had been no inflation, the prices set were the same as those of March 1748.

"John Myers prefers to the Court here the following petition, to wit, to the Worshipful Court of Frederick County in Maryland the petition of John Myers humbly sheweth that whereas your petitioner labors under a great difficulty by reason about or near six years ago your petitioner sold his land in Maryland to

18

Neal O'Gillion and took ye said Neal's note of hand for 100 gallons of licker and removed up to ye south branch of Potomac and ye winter following his wife came down from ye said branch to see her children and in ye Spring after sent up to her husband, your petitioner, for ye note to receive ye 100 gallons of licker which accordingly he sent her in order to receive ye licker aforesaid for his use. But she being a very weak woman and by ill advisers sold ye said note to Evan Shelby of ye County above said contrary to your petitioner's will or order which when your petitioner heard of he came down ye same Spring and forewarned ye said O'Gillion not to pay ye note to Shelby and sold two mares to Neal O'Gillion for £15. One of them of £7 he offered ye said O'Gillion that he might have his licker without trouble for he was old and could not go to law which the said O'Gillion promised to do. But ye note being in Shelby's hands, ye said O'Gillion refuses to pay any part of ye sum or sums due to your petitioner by reason he says ye note lies in force against him by Shelby's attorney in said County which your petitioner humbly desires Your Worshipful Court will take in consideration for his relief and your petitioner shall ever pray.

"Upon reading which petition and consideration thereof had, it is ordered by the Court here that the same be rejected."

One wonders what the purpose of the following petition could be. It seems so much out of character from the usual petition to the Court. But we let it speak for itself: "Several of the inhabitants on Conocochneague and others prefer to the Court here the following petition, to wit, to the Worshipful the Justices of Frederick County November: The motive of your humble petitioners addressing themselves by way of a petition which we humbly lay before you pray for your inspection into the same for had we not sufficient grounds and reasons we should not trouble the Worshipful Bench but taking a general review of our dis-

abilities and calamities and labors we struggle under
to pay unnecessary expenses and particularly this one
that we think and which is the opinion of many others
that it is superfluous and that there is no necessity of
a ferry to be kept at the mouth of Cannogige excepting
it be to support idleness and run the County to charges
and whereas the inhabitants of this County are so seldom obliged to make use that we hope it will be your
favorable oppinions and we doubt not but Your Worships will be convinced of the same for such extrava-
gant expenses doing no good but only impoverishing
poor people your humble petitioners doubts not but you
have inadvertently been influenced upon to grant and
appoint a ferry there and likely some will do their endeavor out of self-interest tho they know it to be no
benefit to the country to continue it. But when we consider Your Worships' worthyness in considering the
most properest methods for the easement and interest
of the County and in your rejoyceing to see these parts
flourish and not your petitioners to be in bondage by
such a multiplicity of needless charges such applications as shall be made in opposition we hope will have
no influence but rather appear to you that any endeav-
oring so to do is not for the good of the County. Your
petitioners as duty bound shall ever pray &c." [The
petitioners' names are not recorded.]

"Upon reading which petition and consideration
thereof had it is ordered by the Court here that same
be rejected."

A petition to the Court was presented by a number
of inhabitants living near Rock Creek, the terms of
which reflect the times rather interestingly. The petitioners state that sometime since a few inhabitants
had asked for a rolling road[2] to cross Rock Creek to
Mr. Gordon's house and that the Court in response to

---

[2] Hogsheads of tobacco were rolled to market. There
is still a street in Baltimore called Rolling Road.

that petition had appointed Samuel Beall and Edward Busey to lay out this road.

"But as it is humbly presumed that in such cases this Court never intended for a very insignificant difference (not above 300 yards at most) to a very few people to have a road run through the wheat and corn fields, pasture and tobacco grounds of sundry plantations to the great damage and expense of the owners without any necessity or adequate conveniencing to the public, it being a rule with all Courts that not to detriment particular persons in their interests or properties unless on most extraordinary occasion where a manifest and evident advantage accrues to the public which is not the present case and that the persons appointed are suspected by some of your petitioners to be actuated by prejudice and a desire of doing all in their power to their hurt and inconvenience...."

The petition goes on to request that the Court appoint "impartial, well-meaning men in the neighborhood" to examine the road and relocate it if thought desirable. The petition was signed by Daniel Carroll, Thomas Nickolls, Charles Williams, Sabrit Sissel [today: Cissel], John Adamson, John Ramsey, John Nicholls, Joseph Elde, Joseph Miles, William Nicholls, Joseph Belt, Jr., John Madding, James Beall and Benjamin Becraft.

In response to the petition, the Court ordered that the matter be referred to Mr. George Gordon, Captain Henry Wright Crabb and Mr. Nathan Magruder or any two of them.

Colonel Sprigg states in a petition that he has a plantation near the Sugar Loaf Mountain but no road fit "to convey his tobacco and other things to navigable waters" and asks that a road be laid out to the nearest public road. The Court orders that Charles Busey, Robert Constable and John Warford be appointed to lay out the road petitioned for.

"The Vestry of All Saints Parish prefer to the

21

Court here the following petition, to wit, to the Worshipful, the Justices of Frederick County, the petition of the Vestry and Church Wardens of All Saints Parish humbly sheweth, viz, your petitioners humbly prays Your Worships to assess this year three pounds of tobacco per taxable to defray the publick charge of this Parish and your petit oners shall forever pray." This is signed by Joseph Wood, Clerk Register.

"Upon reading this petition it is ordered by the Court here that the sum of tobacco per poll above prayed for be levied in this levy on the taxable inhabitants of the said Parish according to the direction of the Act of Assembly in that case made and provided."

"The Vestry of All Saints Parish prefers to the Court here the following petition, to wit, to the Worshipful, the Justices of Frederick County, the petition of the Vestry and Church Wardens of All Saints Parish humbly sheweth, viz, that your petitioners having neglected one year to petition for one half of the money allowed us by Act of Assembly for building a church and two chaples your petitioners therefore humbly pray Your Worships to levy on the taxables of this Parish this ensuing year £150 current money as it may be applied to the aforesaid use and your petitioners shall forever pray." This is also signed by Joseph Wood, Clerk Register.

"Upon reading which petition it is ordered by the Court here that the sum of money above prayed for be levied in this levy on the taxable inhabitants of the said Parish according to the direction of the Act of Assembly in that case made and provided."

Negro Peter, the slave of James Wardrop, was brought into Court and charged with stealing "a narrow axe and a hatt from Richard Smith, on the information of the said Richard Smith." The Court found him guilty and ordered John Thomas, Gentleman, Sheriff, to take Peter to the whipping post and lay on his bare body thirty lashes.

"John Smith Prather produces to the Court here his servant, namely John Egleston, to be adjudged for runaway time, and it appears to this Court by the oath of his master aforesaid that he, the same John Egleston, absented himself from his said master's service 74 days and the said John Smith Prather was at £8/13/6 current money expense in regaining him to his service. It is thereupon ordered that the said John Egleston serve his said master or his assigns four days for every one of the runaway time and six months more for expenses."

Osborn Sprigg, Esq., contracts with the Court to keep a ferry at the mouth of Monocacy until the end of next November Court. The Court agrees to pay him 7,200 pounds of tobacco for the service. "And said Osborn Sprigg obliges himself to give good attendance at the said ferry at all times, nights and days, Sundays not excepted and also to provide a cart or wagon to carry tobacco over said ferry when the boat or schow can't pass."

Anthony Smith agrees with the Court to support Joseph Baker until November Court and to supply Baker with sufficient apparel and other necessities for which he is to receive 1,200 pounds of tobacco.

Elizabeth Chew presents a petition to the Court in which she says, "that your petitioner, being desirous to keep a house of entertainment for travelers and others at the mouth of Monocacy opposite Mr. William Luckett's," asks permission of the Court to keep such a house, and permission is granted. This petition is of some interest, apparently locating William Luckett's place of residence.

There were three petitioners seeking permission to keep taverns or ordinaries in Frederick Town. Among them was Thomas Schley, who had previously been presented (cf. p. 17 above) for keeping a tippling house. Schley was convicted on the indictment in the following March Court and fined 40 shillings.

The Vestry of Prince George's Parish [now Montgomery County] petitioned as follows: "The petition of the Vestry of Prince George's Parish prays that Your Worships would please allow them five pounds of tobacco per poll on the taxables that are in the said County belonging to the said Parish toward defraying the charges of the aforesaid Parish." The Court ordered the levy to be made as petitioned in the current levy.

"Joseph Hardman, bricklayer, and John Shelman, carpenter, in Court here engage themselves to build the hull of a Court House in Frederick Town and offer Messrs. Thomas Beatty, Abraham Miller and Patricke Matthews as their security, who the Court approved of, and the same Court appoint Nathaniel Wickham, Jr., William Griffith and Henry Munday or any two of them to agree with them, the said Joseph Hardman and John Shelman for the same, and the said Gentlemen are desired to lay before the Justices of the next County Court the bond and articles of agreement for the building the hull of the Court House aforesaid."

The Court appointed several overseers for roads in what is now Frederick County, which are of some interest. They appointed William Luckett to supervise the road from Monocacy Ferry to Henry Ballinger's Branch. Captain William Griffith was appointed overseer for the road "from the Main Road by Mr. William Griffith's to the top of Catoctin Mountain." John Kimbol was to supervise the road "from Henry Ballinger's to Hussey's Ford and the new road to the Middle Ford and from Frederick Town to John Biggs' Ford on Monocacy and from Frederick Town to the top of Kittocton Mountain."

Because of the interest in the early roads leading over what we now call South Mountain but what was

then called Shanandore, the appointment of Thomas
Swift as overseer for roads described as follows is of
considerable interest: "From the top of Kittocton
Mountain to the top of Shanandore and the road that
leads from the top of Kittocton to Shandore by Richard
Touchstone's, from the top of Kittocton Mountain to
the top of Shanandore that leads by John George's,
from the road that leads out of John George's road that
leads by Robert Evans' to the top of Shandore."

James Spurgin was appointed to oversee "the
River Road and Richard Touchstone's road."

"The Justices of the Court here appoint the following persons pressmasters of this County for the
ensuing year, to wit, Joseph Wood of Israel's Creek
and John West."

Shakespeare speaks of the "law's delay and the in-
solence of office." Delays are likewise evident from
the records here. Robert DeButts brought suit against
Patrick Halligan, but the notation here reads: "After
three imparlances, agreed." To imparle is literally
to talk over. Actually these were what are now known
in legal phraseology as continuances. Another case
immediately following the previous one is that of
George Moore, Jr., against Richard Touchstone, and
the notation after that case is, "Debt, after three imparlances, declaration filed; agreed." In still another
case, that of Gilbert Ireland versus William Snowden,
the notation is "After three imparlances ordered to be
left off the docket." Continuances seemed to pay off
then as they do now.

The case of Philip Wood against William Snowden
is of interest as illustrating commercial customs of
the day. The suit if for a debt of £5, but it is spread
over four closely written pages of the Record and is
entirely too long to record in full. However, the
phraseology is of considerable interest and some quotations follow: "William Snowden, late of Frederick

County, taylor, was attached to answer unto Philip Wood of a plea of trespass[3] upon the case. And whereupon the same Philip by Henry Darnall, his attorney, complains that whereas the same William on tenth day of May 1745 at Frederick County aforesaid, the same William then and there negotiated and using commerce made and with his proper hand and name subscribed his certain third bill of exchange in writing according to the custom of merchants from the time whereof the memory of man is not to the contrary used and approved bearing date the same day and year and the same bill to a certain Solomon Lonsdale at Green Town [Grinton?] in Swaledale near Richmon[d], Yorkshire, directed the same Solomon then and there residing and using commerce at Green Town aforesaid in the Kingdom of Great Britain, to wit, at Frederick County aforesaid and by the same bill requested the said Solomon at thirty days sight of that his third of exchange first second nor fourth paid to pay unto the said Philip the sum of £5 sterling for value received and to place the same to the account of him the said William, which said bill so as aforesaid made, subscribed and directed was by the order and for the use of the said Philip after the making thereof, to wit, the 25th day of August 1748 at Green Town aforesaid exhibited and shown a certain Mathew Wilkinson and Jane his wife who was the widdow and executrix of the will of the said Solomon and the said Mathew and Jane his wife, executrix as aforesaid, then and there by the order aforesaid according to the custom of merchants aforesaid were requested to accept and pay the said £5 sterling to the order of the said Philip. The said Mathew and Jane his wife, executrix as aforesaid, before that time having had thirty days sight thereof at Green Town aforesaid in the Kingdom of Great Britain, to wit, at Frederick County aforesaid the first, second,

---

[3] The term "trespass" is used to cover many very different actions.

26

nor fourth of the same bills not being accepted nor paid the said Mathew and Jane his wife executrix as aforesaid the same third bill of exchange to accept or pay then and there and always hitherto have altogether refused and have not accepted the same nor paid the contents thereof to the said Philip or order according to the use of merchants from the whole time abovesaid and aforesaid used and approved but afterwards and, to wit, the aforesaid twenty-fifth day of August 1748 the aforesaid third bill of exchange according to the aforesaid use and custom of merchants was protested by reason of the non-acceptance and non-payment thereof...."

After all the verbiage, hearings and consideration the Court finally ordered that, because of certain damages that had been incurred and sustained, the plaintiff should have £6/4/3 sterling. He was also to have 206¾ pounds of tobacco for his costs, assessed against the defendant.

One George Parker, Jr., sues Colonel Thomas Cresap for assault. He is represented by his attorney William Cumming, and his complaint is as follows: "That Thomas Cresap, Gentleman, one of his Lordship's Justices of the Peace for the County of Frederick, here present in Court in his proper person, for that the aforesaid Thomas Cresap on the 30th day of April 1749 with force and arms, to wit, swords, cudgels, scythes and knives, upon the same George Parker in Frederick County aforesaid an assault he did make and him did beat, wound and evilly treat so that of his life it was despaired and other harms to him then and there did do to the great damage of the said George Parker and against the peace of the right honorable Lord Proprietary."

After an appearance in a prior Court not indicated, through his attorneys Stephen Bordley, Daniel Dulany, Jr., and Edward Dorsey, Cresap denies the allegations. The Court decides that the suit is without basis and orders that Thomas Cresap recover 196 pounds of tobacco for his costs.

The same George Parker, Jr., sues Hugh Parker on a debt. His complaint is that Hugh Parker, merchant, "on the 10th day of July 1748 was indebted to the aforesaid George Parker in the sum of £54/17/2/1f Pennsylvania current money of the value of £68/11/5/3f Maryland current money and £8/14/- Maryland current money, in the whole amounting to £77/5/5/3f. In support of his claim, he submits a list of debts for material which he claims he had supplied to Hugh Parker. This list is of interest because of the variety of merchandise it contains:

Two horses at £11 per horse, Pa. money	£22/ -/-
One horse, ditto currency	7/ -/-
Cash paid to Van Swearingen, Jr., on defendant's account, Maryland currency	1/10/-
Cash paid ditto to ditto	2/ 6/6
Cash paid to Peter Burrell, Md. currency	2/ 5/6
Assignment of Jonathan Coborns for Pa. cur.	5/ 7/-
54 weight of summer skins	4/ 3/-
54 fall skins	7/ 3/7¾
5 ox skins	8/3
2 fishers skins	10/-
1 otter skin	4/6
1 wolf skin	1/8
2 elk skins	1/ -/-
2 cub skins	6/6
2 half bear skins	6/-
7 whole bear skins	2/ 5/6
Carriage of 80 weight of skins	6/8
2 elk fawn skins	4/-
3 pints of bear oil and bottle	3/-
A fat steer	3/ 7/6
4 days of reaping at 3sh./day Md. cur.	12/-

Col. Cresap appears in Court and "here becomes pledge and manucaptor" for Hugh Parker, should the said Parker be convicted.

The Court appointed Joseph Chapline and Thomas Prather as referees. They found for the defendant and the Court ordered that the defendant recover his costs.

Col. Cresap in his suit previously noted against Evan Shelby is here granted by the Court a writ of attachment against Shelby's property in satisfaction of his debt.

Thomas Owen, obviously a merchant, sues Thomas Cattrall, planter, who Owen claims is indebted to him for 1,588 pounds of tobacco, "being for sundry articles properly chargeable in amount as by a particular account thereof herewith." This suit is of interest because of the merchandise involved. The list is long and only a part of it is reproduced here:

10 yards of droughada linnen	7/6
7 yards cotton check	14/-
$2\frac{1}{2}$ yards sheeting linnen	5/-
5 yards calliminco	7/8
$3\frac{1}{2}$ yards frize	6/1
8 yards narrow broads	2/ 4/-
3 yards shalloon	5/-
1 hank silk	-/8
3 sticks mohair	1/-
$\frac{1}{4}$-lb. brown thread	-/9
4 dozen coat buttons	2/8
1 man's caster hatt	12/6
$4\frac{3}{4}$ ells of oznabriggs[4]	$4/7\frac{1}{2}$
4 gallons rum	1/ -/-
6 lbs. brown sugar	4/-
1 bushel salt	2/-
2 pairs shoes buckels	2/8
7 yards cotton holland	16/-
1 broad axe	3/6
1 lb. shoe thread	2/6
1 clasp knife	-/5
1 quire paper and half-pins	1/6
3 yards Irish linnen	13/6
2M 10d nails	1/ 4/-
half lb. gunpowder	1/6

---

[4] Osnaburg, a type of linen or cloth used by slaves.

3 lbs. shott	2/-
5¼ lbs. lead	3/6
Cash paid William Cullum for	
rolling 1 h[ogs]head of tobacco	10/-

Both the plaintiff and defendant through their attorneys "move the Justices of the Court here that the whole matter in the premises between them.... may be referred according to the approved custom of the Court here to some person indifferently to be appointed by the same Justices to adjust the same." The Court appointed Col. Edward Sprigg to be the referee, who decided in favor of the plaintiff in a slightly reduced amount.

The same Thomas Owen brings suit against Hendery Allison on a debt for merchandise which is of interest only because the items listed contain several not found on the previous list. These are as follows:

1	ivory comb	2/6
1	ready-made coat	1/16/-
¼	lb. of pepper	-/10
3	sett knitting needles	1/-
1	man's caster hatt	1/ 1/-
1	tobacco box	2/6
2	dozen west buttons	2/-
4	yards broadcloth	3/ 4/-

The remaining time of the November Court session was taken up with a large number of suits for debt in widely varying amounts.

MARCH COURT OF 1749[/50]

"....at a County Court of the Right Honorable Charles, Absolute Lord and Proprietary of the Province of Maryland and Avalon, Lord Baron of Baltimore &c., held at Frederick Town in and for said County on the third Tuesday and 20th day of March in the 35th year of His said Lordship's dominion. Present the Worshipful Daniel Dulany, Esq., Chief Justice, Na-

30

thaniel Wickham, Jr., Thomas Prather, John Rawlins and William Griffith, Gentlemen, Justices by his said Lordship's Commission in and for the County aforesaid lawfully authorized and assigned." George Gordon, Gentleman, was Sheriff and John Darnall Clerk.

"George Gordon, Gentleman, Sheriff, returns to the Court here the ensuing pannell of the Grand Jurors ....being good and lawful men summoned out of the several Hundreds of the County who, being sworn and charged as well to enquire and true presentment make of all crimes, offenses, contempts and misdemeanors whatsoever...."

The Jurors were as follows: Joseph Wood, foreman, Arthur Charlton, Andrew Cottrell, Samuel Duvall, David Linn, Stephen Julian, Henry Gaither, John Adamson, Nathaniel Magruder son of Ninian, William Wilburn, William Dyall, Nathaniel Tomlinson, Jonathan Hagar, John DeLashmutt, Michael Hodgkiss, Thomas Manyard [Maynard], Samuel Read, Edward Owen and Joseph Perry

The first presentment by the Jury was of Hance Waggoner, "overseer of Conogocheague Hundred, for neglecting his road." The usual number of women was presented for bastardy: "We present Mary Parry of Catoctin Hundred for having a baseborn child, Lucy Mackaboy of Rock Creek Hundred for having a baseborn child, Ann, the servant woman of Joseph Flint, late of Anteatum Hundred, for having a base-born child."

There may be confusion concerning the same or another Mary Parry because a second presentment further on in the record is that of Mary Parry of Newfoundland Hundred in which it is stated that "she lives at Mr. William Gray's in ye aforesaid Hundred."

Eleanor Gary, "a servant to Dr. James Dowel," was convicted of bastardy by confession.

William Emitt petitions the Court that he is "very

31

much afflicted with sickness and is not in a capacity to serve in the office of Constable" and states that upon recovery he will offer himself for service if desired.

Bigger Head prefers to the Court here the following petition: He "humbly sheweth that your petitioner has a Negro wench rendered incapable of labour through age and infirmity. Your petitioner therefore humbly prays Your Worships to set her levy-free for the future and he as in duty bound will pray."

Mary Parry (noted above) prefers to the Court here the following petition: "Mary Parry, living at William Gray's, being in distress, begs that Your Honorable Bench will consider her poor capacity and allow her as she has been formerly allowed, and your petitioner will be ever bound to pray."

"Upon reading which petition and consideration thereof had, it is ordered by the Court here that the same be referred till the petitioner makes it appear to the same Court that she served her time in this County."

A petition was presented to the Court on behalf of Isaac Eltinge as follows: "Whereas your petitioners are informed that Isaac Eltinge was presented to the Grand Jury for selling of drink last November Court held for Frederick County, we have thought proper to draw this our petition to Your Worships. As a consequence of the presentment perhaps might otherwise greatly attand not only to your petitioners' hurt, but to many others by being debarred of those necessaries whereof we are in need when we are obliged to travel along by said Eltinge's door through heat and cold causes and obliges us to call in his house to get some refreshments against those calamityes the more because there is no house of entertainment along that road for the space of thirty or forty miles. Your petitioners therefore begg you will take in consideration the unreasonableness of the presentment and take no regard to it, but rather encourage the said Eltinge so that he may be the more enabled to be a useful instrument to serve the public. Signed by sundry of the inhabitants of this County." [Names are not included in the Record.]

"Upon reading this petition and consideration thereof had, it is ordered by the Court here that the same be rejected."

There is a suit by the Lord Proprietary against William Roberts, farmer, who was presented by the Grand Jury. "On the twenty-first day of November, 1749 with force and arms at Frederick County aforesaid one hog of the price of 100 pounds of tobacco, the goods and chattels of a certain Richard King Stevenson, then and there being found then and there feloniously took, stole, and carried away against the peace of the said Lord Proprietary, his good rule and government and contrary to the form of the Act of Assembly in such cases late made and provided." Roberts pleads not guilty to the charge and "puts himself upon the County."

"It is therefore commanded the Sheriff aforesaid that he cause to come here immediately twelve &c. [i.e., good men and true] and the jurors of the jury aforesaid by the aforesaid Sheriff to this in due manner impannelled being called, namely Robert Debutts, Joseph Doddridge, Moses Chapline, Harbert Wallace, Peter Stull, John Johnson of Kittocton, Shadrick Hyatt, Patrick Matthews, Elias DeLashmutt, John Purdom, James Spurgeon and John Jones, who to say the truth in the premises to the said William Roberts in the indictment above specified in form aforesaid imposed being elected, tryed and sworn, do say upon their oath that the said William Roberts is not guilty of the felony and theft in the indictment above specified in form aforesaid imposed."

The counsel for the prisoner then requested a "copy of the indictment aforesaid which was granted them."

The following two cases are of interest not only because a member of the Beatty family is involved, but also as one of the few instances in which a man was accused of bastardy, or in this case fornication. The first case involves George Beatty and Alice Dorsey. The charge against Beatty is "that he was guilty of fornication with a certain Alice Dorsey....Beatty in his proper person in Court here comes and says that he cannot gainsay but that he is guilty of the premises above to him in form aforesaid imposed and thereof submits himself to the Grace of the Court here."

"Whereupon the premises being seen and by the Court here fully understood, it is considered by the same Court that the said George Beatty be fined 30 shillings current money for his offense aforesaid and give sufficient security to keep Alice Dorsey's bastard child off the County and hereupon the said George Beatty in Court here pays to George Gordon, Esquire, 30 shillings current money for the fine aforesaid."

"At the same time, to wit, the third Tuesday in March aforesaid, the said George Beatty and also Thomas Beatty of Frederick County, Gentleman, and John Kimbol of the same County, farmer, in their proper persons in Court here acknowledge themselves to owe and stand justly indebted unto His Lordship the Lord Proprietor in the full and just sum of £40 current money which they and every of them yielded and granted should be made and levied of their respective goods and chattels, lands and tenaments into whosoever hands they shall come to the use of His said Lordship, his heirs and successors, on condition that the inhabitants of Frederick County aforesaid from time to time and at all times hereafter be well and truly saved harmless and indemnified from any charge, cost or expense in the maintenance of the bastard child of the aforesaid Alice Dorsey and which was sworn to him and the said George Beatty is dismissed."

Alice Dorsey was accused as follows: "That a certain Alice Dorsey was guilty of having a bastard

34

child....The said Alice Dorsey by Daniel Dulany, Jr., her attorney, comes and says that she cannot gainsay but that she is guilty of the premises....and submits herself to the Grace of the Court here,"

"It is considered by the Court here that the said Alice Dorsey be fined 30 shillings current money for her offense aforesaid according to Act of Assembly." She paid her fine through her attorney and was dismissed.

"Ordered that Thomas Morris be allowed in the next County levy 30 shillings current money for burying Ann Mugg, a poor woman, and at the rate of 12 shillings and 6 pence per month from the thirteenth day of December last to next November Court for taking care of and maintaining the orphan child."

"John Stull in his proper person in Court here makes choice of Jonathan Hagar of Frederick County, farmer, for his guardian of which trust he in Court accepts of."

Teter Laney was presented and charged with stealing two hogs valued at 200 pounds of tobacco from Abraham Miller. Laney pled not guilty and was tried by the following jury: Robert Debutts, Darby Ryan, Thomas Johnson, James Brown, William Beatty, James Smith of Rock Creek, John Jones, John Purdom, Alexander Perry, Samuel Plummer, William Gray and John Howard son of Gideon. The Jury found him not guilty.

"John Carmack is by the Court here approved of to be a deputy ranger of this County."

"Daniel McCay prefers to the Court here the following certificate and prays allowances for the same, towit, Whereas Thomas Barns late of Prince George's County came to the dwelling house of Daniel McCay of Frederick County, Maryland and was taken sick and died at the said McCay's house, said McCay had the trouble of his lying-in, his sickness till death and said McCay buried ye said Barns very desently and all he has for his trouble has been appraised by James Walling and Mathew Clark. May it please Your Worships ....to take it into Your Worships' consideration what you think proper to allow ye said McCay for his trouble for all ye effects of ye deceased is valued to 3 shillings by the above-named....

"Mathew Clarke deposeth that Thomas Barns within named was about two months at Daniel McCay's and about three weeks of that time in a sick and helpless condition. Sworn in open Court.

"It is therefore ordered by the Court here that the said Daniel McCay be allowed in the next County levy £3 current money for his trouble as aforesaid."

"Orlando Griffith prefers to the Court here the following petition, to wit, To the Worshipful Justices of Frederick County now sitting the petition of Orlando Griffith sheweth that about five years ago he took into his house an old woman named Mary Francis with three children, namely Henry, now about 16 years old, Will about 14, and Samuel about 9. Your petitioner, having been at expenses in maintaining the several children humbly hopes you will take it into your consideration and bind them to him for such a term of years as you will judge necessary and will be sufficient to make him satisfaction for the trouble and charges he has been at. And more especially as their mother who is now dead always desired it which your petitioner is ready to make appear.

"Upon reading which petition and consideration thereof had, the Justices of the Court here bind to the said Orlando Griffith the above named William aged about 12 years and Samuel aged about seven years til they severally arrive to the age of 21 years, and the said Orlando Griffith promises and obliges himself to teach the said William and Samuel or cause them to be taught to read and write and to learn them the three first rules in arithmetic. At the expiration of their time of servitude to give each of them a coat, waistcoat and breeches, a hat, pair of shoes and stockings and two shirts. And ordered that Henry stay with the petitioner til next Court which time is allowed him to produce witnesses to prove his age."

"Richard Wells is by the Court here appointed Constable of Pipe Creek Hundred in the room of Maunce Justice and ordered that warrant issue to the said Richard Wells for that purpose."

"The Justices of the Court here appoint Thomas Beatty and Nathaniel Wickham, Jr., Gentlemen, to view the land of John VanMeter an orphan and to make report thereon to the next County Court."

"Samuel Hobbs in Court here prays to have license to keep an ordinary or public house of entertainment at his dwelling house in this County, which is granted him on giving security according to law."

The suit of Lydia Dent against Charles Wood was for breach of promise. "Charles Wood, late of Frederick County, planter, was attached to answer unto Lydia Dent of a plea of trespass upon the case and whereupon the said Lydia by Henry Darnall, her attorney, complains that whereas the said Charles while sole [i.e., unmarried], to wit: On the twenty-fifth day of February 1747 at Frederick County aforesaid within the jurisdiction of this Court in consideration that the said Lydia then and there being sole and unmarried at the special instance and request of the said Charles then and there undertook and faithfully promised the said Charles to marry him, the said Charles. He, the said Charles, undertook and faithfully promised the said Lydia that he, the said Charles, would be joined to the said Lydia in lawful matrimony and although she, the said Lydia, was always ready and willing from the time of making her said promise and

37

undertaking to be joined to the said Charles in lawful matrimony, that is to say, at Frederick County aforesaid with the jurisdiction aforesaid. Nevertheless, the said Charles his promise and assumption aforesaid not regarding but minding and fraudulently intending the same Lydia in this part craftily and subtilly to deceive and defraud the said Lydia to be his wife to take did altogether refuse and still doth refuse and after the promise and assumption aforesaid, to wit, on the 10th day of May 1748 at Frederick County aforesaid within the jurisdiction aforesaid did take to his wife another woman, to wit, Sarah Brightwell, now his wife contrary to his promise and assumption aforesaid to the damage of the said Lydia Dent £100 current money of Maryland and therefore she brings suit &c. [5]

And the aforesaid Charles Wood by Edward Dorsey, his attorney, comes and defends the force and injury when &c., and prays license thereof to imparle here until the next County Court."

Charles Wood by his attorney appeared in several Courts and in each case asked for permission to imparle, which means of course that he wanted a continuance. It finally came down to this particular Court, and a jury was impaneled as follows: "Edward Beatty, Moses Chapline, Harbert Wallace, Peter Stull, Joseph Dodridge, John Johnson of Kittocton, Shadrick Hyatt, Elias DeLashmutt, James Spurgeon, George Bond, Thomas Stoddert and Patrick Mathews." The Jury decided for the plaintiff, Lydia Dent.

The Court ordered that Lydia Dent recover from Wood damages assessed at £30 current money and also 1,443 pounds of tobacco for her costs and charges.

In a suit by Elizabeth Hall, executrix of Clement Hall, against John DeLashmutt for debt, it is shown

---

[5] The Clerk did not always spell out or complete familiar terms or phrases, but placed "&c." [etc.] in lieu thereof.

that Clement Hall had removed to Maryland from Salem, New Jersey.

In a case of Gilbert Ireland versus William Jenkins a notation at the end states, "Case after two imparlances struck off."

The following case of John Hepburn, Esquire, versus Nathaniel Wickham, Jr., is of striking interest because it contains a reference to an early law whose exact effect is not entirely clear. This is a suit for debt and the formal complaint is in part as follows: "To the Worshipful, the Justices of Frederick County Court now in Court sitting, John Hepburn by Henry Darnall, his attorney, complains of Nathaniel Wickham, Jr., one of the Justices of this Court present here in Court in his proper person so that whereas the aforesaid Nathaniel after the first day of May 1705, to wit, on the 26th day of August 1748 at Frederick County aforesaid made his first note in writing called a promisary note with his proper hand thereto subscribed bearing date the day and year last aforesaid and the said Note to him the said John then and there delivered by which said note the aforesaid Nathaniel promised to pay unto him the said John by the name of John Hepburn or order 2,600 pounds of inspected tobacco for value received."

The Court awarded Hepburn 2,600 pounds of tobacco for his costs, to be assessed against Nathaniel Wickham, Jr.

In three suits against William Snowden, the plaintiffs being respectively George Maxwell, Philip Wood and Richard Molineux, in each case Snowden admits his debt and the final judgment of the Court is as follows: "It is ordered by the Court here that the said William Snowden be committed to the custody of the Sheriff of the County aforesaid, to wit, George Gordon, Gentleman, there to remain &c." Here is a man being imprisoned for debt.

In a case transferred from Prince George's County wherein Joseph Vollgemote sues Thomas Cresap, Gentleman, the phraseology is as follows for the complaint in the case: "....Complains of Thomas Cresap, Gentleman, one of his Lordship's the right Honorable the Lord Proprietary his Justices of the Peace for the County aforesaid here present in Court in his proper person for that whereas the aforesaid Thomas on the 10th day of February in the Year of our Lord 1747/8 at Prince George's County aforesaid was indebted to aforesaid Joseph in the sum of £22 current money for 110 gallons of liquor commonly called whiskey by him the aforesaid Joseph to the said Thomas and at his special instance and request sold and delivered...." The Court awarded the full amount sued for in a judgment against Cresap.

Much of the time of this March 1749 Court was consumed in hearing cases transferred from the Prince George's County Court.

JUNE COURT OF 1750

Here begins the June Court of 1750, which convened on the third Tuesday and the 19th day of June "in the thirty-sixth year of His said Lordship's Dominion."

The Justices present were as follows: Daniel Dulany, Esq., Chief Justice, Thomas Cresap, Nathaniel Wickham, Jr., Joseph Chapline, William Griffith, Dr. James Dowel, Nathan Magruder, Hugh Parker, Henry Munday, Thomas Beatty, John Rawlins, Thomas Prather, John Clagett, Nathaniel Alexander and John Needham. George Gordon, Gentleman, is Sheriff and John Darnall Clerk.

The Grand Jury consisted of the following: Samuel Magruder 3rd, George Bussey, John Ramsay, Ninian Beall son of Ninian, Charles Hedge, Ignatius Perry, John Phillips, John Swearingen, Richard Touchstone,

Peter Rench, Charles Chaney, Hugh Gilliland, Philip Prather, John Douthit, Robert Constable, William Beatty, Thomas Osborn, Benjamin Perry and William Williams.

The Grand Jurors made the following presentments:

Ann Cramphin for a baseborn child.

John Cotterel and William Hinton for breach of the peace.

Mary Hall for a baseborn child.

Richard Smith for keeping a disorderly house.

Thomas Maneyeard "for an assault on ye highway on William Slade by ye information of ye aforesaid Slade."

John Nelson "for swearing five oaths."

Daniel Ryan "for getting a baseborn child by Mary Pery."

Margaret White for a baseborn child.

Mary Jackson for a baseborn child.

Sarah Neel for a baseborn child "by the information of John Nelson, Monocacy Hundred, Lower Part."

Elenor David for a baseborn child.

Rebecca Wray for a baseborn child, "living in ye Lower Part of Potomac Hundred."

Phyllis Wilson for a baseborn child "by ye information of Charles Hedges."

The Grand Jury also returned an indictment against Samuel Brown, laborer, marked "felony ignoramus."[6]

"Constables of the several Hundreds are called over to appear."

---

[6] "We ignore" the felony. Formerly Grand Juries used this term on bills of indictment when, after hearing the evidence, they thought the accusation against the prisoner was groundless, intimating that, although the facts might possibly be true, the truth did not appear to them. The modern term is "not found" or "not a true bill."

"Col. Thomas Cresap in Court here qualifies as a Justice of the Peace for this County by taking the several oaths to the Government required by law and also the oath of Judge or Justice appointed by Act of Assembly."

William Dent is sworn as bailiff to the Grand Jury.

The following provides a comment on the relationship between Master and Slave: Edward Owen petitions the Court as follows: "....Sheweth that your petitioner hath a certain Negro girl named Bess who is a deformed cripple and hath been so from her birth, incapable of any service but is a certain charge during her life for her maintenance. Your petitioner therefore most humbly prays that Your Worships and this Honorable Court will grant and cause the said Negro girl to be made levy-free." The Court grants the petition.

Matthew Richards petitions the Court as follows: "He humbly sheweth that your petitioner petitioned Your Worships last June Court and was allowed 800 pounds of tobacco which is most gratefully acknowledged and your petitioner has disposed of it to the doctor though have received but small benefit and may very safely say that I am become a poor miserable object. Therefore most humbly prays Your Worships to allow me this year what Your Worships in pitty thinks proper and your petitioner shall forever pray.
"Upon reading this petition and consideration thereof had, it is ordered by the Court here that the petitioner be allowed 1,000 pounds of tobacco in the next County levy for his support."

"Ordered by the Court here that Robert Evans for insulting and abusing Col. Thomas Cresap, one of the Justices of the Court here, give security for his good behavior."
"And hereupon this day, to wit, the third Tuesday

in June ....Robert Evans of Frederick County, farmer, ...acknowledges himself to owe unto his Lordship in the full and just sum of £10 current money, and also Joseph Chapline, of the same County, Gentleman, in like manner acknowledges himself to owe the said Lord Proprietary £5 of a like money, on condition that the same Robert Evans be of good behavior to all people until the next County Court to be held at Frederick Town on the third Tuesday in August next."

The Court appointed John Claggett and George Gordon, Gentleman, "to agree with any person or persons for to erect a pair of stocks at the warehouse at the mouth of Rock Creek and ordered that they bring in the charge thereof at the next November Court."

Mary Perry, who had previously been presented by the Grand Jury for bastardy, was convicted by confession and fined thirty shillings.

The Court ordered that bench warrants issue returnable immediately for Philip and James Coffee to answer the complaints of orphan children living with them.

"Ordered by the Court here that Alexander Barret, one of the petit jurors, for being drunk in Court be fined 5 shillings current money."

"Ordered by the Court here that an allowance be made in the next levy for keeping Court in the Dutch Meeting House."

Mary Macknaul was on trial for theft as follows: "Mary Macknaul on the tenth day of February 1750 with force and arms at Frederick County aforesaid one snuff box of the value of ten pounds of tobacco, the goods and chattels of a certain Nicholas Bundrick.... feloniously took, stole and carried away." She pled not guilty and a jury was impaneled whose verdict was guilty. The Court sentenced her to "be set upon the pillory for and during the space of five minutes and that afterwards she be set to the whipping post and there receive on her bare body five lashes....and that she pay to Nicholas Bundrick 28 pounds of tobacco for fourfold of the value and restore to the same Bundrick the snuff box so stolen as aforesaid." She was remanded to the custody of the Sheriff.

Daniel Ryan who was Mary Perry's partner in bastardy was found guilty by confession, fined an amount not stated and required to give bond in the amount of £40 "to save harmless and indemnify the inhabitants of Frederick County aforesaid for any cost or expense in the maintenance of the bastard child of the aforesaid named Eleanor Perry."

Andrew Ringold was accused of stealing "one axe of the value of 15 pounds of tobacco from a certain Henry Six." Ringold entered a plea of not guilty. A jury was impaneled which found him guilty. Sentence was as follows: "That the said Andrew Ringold by the Sheriff aforesaid be set upon the pillory for the space of one quarter of an hour and that afterwards he be set to the whipping post and there receive on his bare body twenty lashes well laid on."

Richard Williams presents to the Court a petition in which he states that in April 1749 he had killed nine wolves, but had never received any payment therefor. He asks that he now receive some bounty for the wolf-heads. However, the Court deferred the matter for consideration in the next November Court.

Margaret Riddle aged 10 years on the first day of October next is bound by the Court to William Emmit until she reaches the age of sixteen. Emmit promises to "learn her to read and write and at the end of her time of servitude to give her a pair of shoes and stockings, two shifts, two caps, a pair of boddices, a gown and petticoat, a handkerchief and a spinning wheel."

"Ordered by the Court here that a pillory be erected on the Court House lot in Frederick Town and that Nathaniel Wickham, Jr., and Thomas Beatty, Gentlemen, agree for the same and bring in the charge thereof at the next November Court."

Nathaniel Beall, Sr., is brought into Court charged with indecent behavior to Mr. John Rawlins, a Justice in the execution of his office. Beall submits himself to the Grace of the Court and is fined five pounds current money.

Nathaniel Tomlinson, who had been previously presented for failure to return certain taxables in his list, throws himself upon the mercy of the Court and is fined 250 pounds of tobacco "to be applyed to the use of the free schools in the County." This is the first reference to free schools found in the records.

Thomas Boydstone sues Butler Evans for assault "with force and arms, to wit, with fists, clubs, whips, staves, teeth and nails." Boydstone asked damages of £90 for the assault, but the Court allows him only ten shillings, plus, however, $997\frac{3}{4}$ pounds of tobacco for his costs.

A subsequent case is interesting both for its outcome and for the list of personal possessions it contains. It is a suit of George Valentine Matzger against Nicholas Bunderick. The charge against Bunderick is that he owes £11 to Matzger. The warrant for arrest states that it appeared to the Justice issuing it that Bunderick "had removed in a secret manner from the place of his abode." An order of attachment was issued and the goods and chattels apparently left behind by Bunderick were ordered appraised by John Cramphin, Cleborn Simms, Jacob Verdrees and Thomas Sly. Here for their interest are listed some of the items appraised and the value placed upon them:

16	tumbler glasses	16/-
2	flint glass decanters	8/-
2	looking glasses	1/10/-
3	joiner's saws	12/-
7	curry combs	14/-
1	tankard, pocket bottle	2/6
2	sysses [scissors?]	7/-
8	pare spectacles	8/-
1	hammer and a pincher	4/-
6	fire steels	2/-
1	case with two rasers	3/-
2	pewter plates	4/-
1	blank book	4/-
1	breetches buckle	-/6
1	punch bowl	1/-
1	Dutch prayer book	1/3
4	necklaces	2/-
114	sadler tacks	-/9
2	painted sheel [?] boxes	2/-
1	painted sugar box	2/-
1	pare sizers	1/6
1	large washing tub	4/-
3	jacketts	10/-
1	pare of trousers	1/6
1	old feather bed and pillow	15/-
25	pare hinges	16/8
1	parcel of sewing silk	17/6
11	papers of needles	12/-
1	horse whip	1/6
1	brass kettle	4/-
20	painted spice boxes	1/ -/-
1	walking cane	7/6

The outcome of this case was that the attachment was "struck off, it appearing to the Court here that the defendant was not run away and ordered that the plaintiff make restitution to the defendant of the goods and chattels in the inventory aforesaid."

Michael Reisner also sued Bunderick and the outcome of his suit was the same.

AUGUST COURT OF 1750

The August Court of 1750 met on the third Tuesday and 21st day of August "in the thirty-sixth year of His Lordship's Dominion."

The Justices present were Nathaniel Wickham, Jr., Henry Munday, Thomas Prather, John Rawlins, Nathaniel Alexander, John Needham, Thomas Beatty, Joseph Chapline, William Griffith, John Clagett, James Doull and Josiah Beall. George Gordon was Sheriff and John Darnall was Clerk.

The Grand Jury was as follows: Thomas Stoddert, foreman, Joseph Wood (Linganore), Ninian Beall (son of Ninian), John Middagh, Arthur Charlton, Thomas Dowden, Charles Friend, John Adamson, Joshua Bussey, John Banks, Jr., Jonathan Hagar, Nathaniel Tomlinson, Robert Constable, Patrick Matthews, James Crouch, George Jewell and John Rutter.

"The Grand Jurors present Richard Beaman for stealing and branding a black colt, his face and some other parts intermixed with white hairs, belonging to Arthur Parr, on the information of Gabriel Hughes and William Robert Hinton."

The following indictment arose directly out of the preceding one. "The Grand Jurors, being informed by Gabriel Hughes and William Robert Hinton that they were summoned to appear before a Justice of this County to testify against Richard Beaman for stealing a colt belonging to Arthur Parr and that they appeared before Thomas Beatty accordingly and offered to swear that the said colt was the property of the said Arthur Parr, but that the said Thomas Beatty did not swear them but told the said Richard Beaman to compound the affair with Arthur Parr. Other ways if he swore the said Hughes and Hinton, he must bind him over to Court for horse stealing and that the said affair was

47

HEMPSTEAD COUNTY LIBRARY
HOPE, ARKANSAS

accordingly compounded. We therefore present the said Thomas Beatty for advising the said Beaman to compound the said action contrary to the law. Signed by Thomas Stoddert, foreman."

On page 298, Book C. of the same Judgment Record, it is shown that a writ of certiorari was issued as follows: In the name of the Lord Proprietary "to the Justices of Frederick County, greeting: We, being willing for certain causes that the record and proceedings of a certain presentment and indictment depending before you against Thomas Beatty of the same County, Justice of the Peace, should be certified by you to the Justices of our Provincial Court at the city of Annapolis, command ye that the record and proceedings with everything thereto relating as full and entire and in as ample manner and form as they remain before you by whatsoever name and addition the said Thomas Beatty be reputed ye have before the Justices of our Provincial Court to be held at Annapolis the second Tuesday of April next that our said Justices of our Provincial Court may do therein what of right ought to be done. Witness Benjamin Young, Esquire, Chief Justice of our Provincial Court, the 5th day of October in the 36th year of our Dominion &c."

There is nothing further in the record here to indicate the outcome of the indictment of Justice Beatty, but he was present on the bench in the next Court in his capacity as Justice.

Thomas Eades petitioned the Court for relief from levy because "he has been very much afflicted with the country distemper for some years past with violent pains in his joynts and limbs, which continuance of the distemper keeps him from getting his livelihood for his wife and family, he now having four children.... and the distemper is grown almost past cure by some bones falling from his nose and never taking any rest in bed neither day nor night which some of his neighbors very well [k]nows."

The Court not only agreed to make him levy-free

48

for three years but also allowed him ten pounds of to-bacco in the next levy toward his support.

William Luckett is granted a license to keep a public house of entertainment at Mouth of Monocacy.

Thomas Sligh applied for a license to keep a public house which was granted.

The Court issued an order that William Mitchel "for insulting Col. Thomas Cresap, one of the Justices of the Court here, recognize this security for his good behavior" until the next Court to be held in November.

"The Grand Jurors present Micajah Plummer for stealing a colt belonging to Adam Buttner on the information of Joshua Barton, John Carmack, John Martin, Jr., William Beatty, Catherine Buttner, Anna Buttner, James Buttner, Jeremiah Elroade, Benjamin Barton, Leah Buttner, Adam Buttner and Martha Buttner."

"Ordered by the Court here that attachment issue returnable to the next County Court against Samuel Duval (at the complaint of William Davis) to give countersecurity for the estate of John Harding, deceased."

Henry Dalton, a mulatto aged (as 'tis said) six months the 8th day of September next is by the Court here bound to Samuel Pruit and his assigns until he arrives to the age of 31 [sic] years, and the said Samuel Pruit in Court here obliges himself to give the said Henry Dalton at the expiration of his time of servitude freedom dues according to the customs of the country."

In addition to Thomas Sligh who was licensed to keep a tavern in Frederick Town, several others were also licensed, among them Joseph Hardman, Conrad

49

Crosses, Isabella Farrell and John Crampton.

Elizabeth Reynolds petitioned for a license to keep an ordinary "or public house of entertainment at a place called Hussey's Ford on Monocacy" and her petition was granted.

"Ordered by the Court here that the Clerk thereof write to John Nicholls, Constable of Linton Hundred, to take a list of the taxables in the Hundred aforesaid and make return thereof to the next County Court. Otherwise the law in relation thereto will be put in execution against him."

The Justices adjusted rates of liquors and other accommodations for the ensuing year. Apparently again there had been no inflation of prices for those of the original list were left unchanged except that the difference between the cost of a hot dyet for a gentleman in the town and in the country was removed.

Thomas Maneyeard was presented by this Grand Jury for assault on the highway on William Slade "by ye information of the aforesaid Slade." By his attorney Daniel Dulany, Jr., Maneyeard denied that he was guilty but threw himself on the mercy of the Court. The Court found him guilty and fined him 20 shillings. Michael Hodgkiss became surety for the payment of the fine.

Elizabeth Weaver, who had in a previous Court been indicted for felony, had her case "struck off because of the death of the defendant."

Elias DeLashmutt, who had been presented for keeping a tippling house, was after two continuances released, "no witnesses appearing."

A dozen or more cases are listed as "struck off" after a variable number of continuances.

William Richie sues Charles Bowman through a petition as follows: "The petition of William Richie of the County aforesaid, wagonmaker, humbly sheweth that your petitioner came into this Province under indentures in nature of a servant for the term of five years and was sold to a certain Charles Bowman with whom he has faithfully and truly served out his whole term of servitude and has been free for upwards of these two years past, that your petitioner has often in a friendly manner demanded of the said Charles Bowman his freedom dues as directed by Act of Assembly, who has always refused or delayed so to do. Your petitioner therefore humbly beseeches Your Worships that citation may issue against the said Charles to answer the premises upon a full and fair hearing the said Charles may be ordered to pay unto your petitioner his freedom dues with cost of suit."

The Court ordered that Bowman pay Richie his freedom dues together with 156½ pounds of tobacco for his costs.

"Memorandum: The defendant paid the plaintiff his freedom dues in Court here and it seeming to the Court that one of the shirts and a hoe were insufficient, ordered the defendant to pay him others in their room [place]."

"Ordered by the Court here that John Middagh, surviving executor of John Hann, have time until next County Court to give security for the ballance of said Hann's estate."

"Ordered also that Barbara Hufman and John Middagh, executors of Matthias Reesling, have time until next County Court to give security for the ballance of said Reesling's estate."

"Memorandum: ....Mary Sparks, Col. Henry Munday and Thomas Wilson (Toms Creek) of Frederick County entered into....a certain writing obligatory in £153/1/- current money to be paid unto Solomon, Jo - seph, Charles, Jonas, Jonathan, William, George,

51

Merum, Mary, Ann, Rebecca and Sarah Sparks" on condition that Mary Sparks [obviously the executrix] pay to the above-mentioned beneficiaries "their respective parts or portions of Joseph Sparks, deceased, his estate, according to Act of Assembly in such cases made and provided."

"Memorandum: .... Frederick Onselt, George Loy and Michael Ramar.... of Frederick County, farmers, entered into and executed a certain writing obligatory in £182 current money to be paid unto Elizabeth, Mary, Appolonia, Barbara, George Peter, Rosina and Mary Magdalene on condition that the above bounden Frederick Onselt should pay to the above-mentioned persons respective parts of their deceased father John Hufman's estate."

"Memorandum: .... Magdalen Stoner, Peter Barrick, John Barrick of Frederick County, farmers, ... entered into a certain writing obligatory in £305/18/7 current money to be paid unto John Stoner, Ann Stoner, Benjamin Stoner and Henry Stoner on condition that" the above-mentioned persons pay their respective parts of their deceased father Jacob Stonar's estate to the named beneficiaries according to Act of Assembly.

"Memorandum: .... John Justice, George Becraft and Benjamin Becraft of Frederick County, farmers, entered into a certain writing obligatory in £84/1/1 current money to be paid unto Daniel James and Margaret James" on condition that John Justice pay to the named beneficiaries their respective parts of their deceased father John James's estate.

William Cumming, Esq., sues Abraham Miller, administrator of John Hussey, glover, deceased, who died intestate, claiming that Hussey owed Cumming £7/4/1½ current money and 200 pounds of tobacco. After numerous continuances and what appear to be several demurrers, the case was referred to a jury to be composed of the following: Edward Owen, Joseph Beall, William Pritchet, James Odell, William Boyd, Charles Bussey, Elias Alexander, Abraham Alexander, Michael Jones, William Ervin, Samuel Lamar and John Jack. The Jury "retired from the barr of the Court here to communicate among themselves of and upon the verdict in the premises to be rendered and afterwards to the same barr returned their verdict to render and the said William Cumming, although solemnly called (as the manner is), comes not but makes default &c., whereupon on the prayer of the said Abraham Miller by his attorney Edward Dorsey that judgment for him be rendered for default as aforesaid."

The Court awarded Miller $472\frac{1}{2}$ pounds of tobacco for his costs which were to be charged against Cumming.

In a case the details of which are not recorded wherein Thomas Owen sues James Harrison, it is shown that William Cumming is an attorney licensed to practice before the Frederick County Court.

In another suit by Thomas Owen against Archibald Beall several interesting matters appear. The suit is for a debt of £0/15/6 plus $1,187\frac{1}{2}$ pounds of tobacco, "being for sundry articles properly chargeable in account." Among the articles listed, the following are to be noted:

4 yards of druggatt	18/-
1 juce harp	-/6
2 pounds of gunpowder	6/-
1 boy's fine hatt	8/6
1 pair of shoe buckels	1/6
3 dozen coat gilt buttons	12/-

Ninian Beall of Frederick County, planter, "in his proper person here becomes pledge and manucaptor of the said Archibald Beall that in case the said Archibald Beall in the plea aforesaid should be convict, then the said Ninian Beall yielded and granted that as well all damages and costs which to the aforesaid Thomas Owen" would be guaranteed payment by himself. The

Court rendered a verdict on behalf of Owen for £0/15/6 and 1,189½ pounds of tobacco.

Neal Clark, who may have been a doctor, sues Benjamin Perry, planter, on an account of £3, which is dated June 10, 1747 and sworn before Nicholas Gassaway, son of Thomas, on the 5th of June 1748. The account reads as follows, "To means and attendance in curing your Negro woman of ye flox, £3." After several imparlances the Court ruled that "Col. Thomas Cresap, Mr. George Gordon, Dr. James Doull and Mr. John Needham be referees between the parties aforesaid." The referees decided for the plaintiff.

In a suit by the Rev. William Williams against Hugh Gilliland for a debt of £10, it is shown "that the sum of £10 Pennsylvania currency of the value of £10 Maryland currency" is due, the Court having decided in favor of the Reverend Williams.

While in the preceding case Maryland and Pennsylvania currency were shown to be of equal value, a variation is shown in a case immediately following wherein Benjamin Chambers sues Neale O'Donnel, Arthur McKenna and Marke Foy on a note for "the just and full sum of £14/7/5 current money of Pennsylvania of the value of £19/3/2½ current money of Maryland."[7]

NOVEMBER COURT OF 1750

The November Court of 1750 convened on the third Tuesday and 20th day of November in the thirty-sixth year of His Lordship's Dominion.

The Justices present were Nathaniel Wickham, Jr., Thomas Beatty, Thomas Prather, William Griffith,

---

[7] The 33.3% premium indicated here compares with 26.7% calculable from figures shown on p. 28, above.

Nathan Magruder, John Needham, John Clagett, Henry Munday, Joseph Chapline, John Rawlins, James Doull, Nathaniel Alexander, Josias Beall and Alexander Beall.

The Grand Jury was William Coupland, foreman, Joseph Wood (of Israel Creek), Thomas Manyard, Garah Davis, Peter Rench, William Wilburn, Hugh Riley, Patrick Mathews, John Fleming, John Hallum, Samuel West, John DeLashmutt, Joseph Belt, John Johnson, Joseph Tomlinson, William Summers, John Howard (son of Gideon), William Beatty and Isaac Garrison.

The Grand Jury's presentments included:
Michael Risener for beating John Youngblood.
Henry Cane "for swearing ten oaths by information of Nathan Veach, Constable."
John Rench "for assaulting Col. Thomas Cresap."
Joseph Volgemore "for selling of liquor by small measure on the Sabbath and drunkning by information of John Allen."
Leonard Allbright for not cleaning the roads of his district. The informant was Jonathan Hagar.

George Scott, Gentleman, qualifies as an attorney of the Court.

Sarah Neal presents the following petition which "sheweth that whereas your petitioner being presented by Grand Jury for having a baseborn child brings me under an obligation to make my apology to Your Worships not doubting but Your Worships will be so candid in your judgment as to dispence with my punishment. The case is this: Your petitioner, being a widdow, Nacey Jenings in his lifetime makes suit to me and by his strong inpertunities and sly insinuating tones undermines my constancy, but at last the proposal of marriage was made and published according to law in the Church of England, but pleased God to afflict him

with a spell of sickness just after he was out askt that
brought him to the last period of human glory so that
please Your Worships if it pleased God not to took him
away we had both been married which my neighbors
can all certify so that I think its grate hardship upon
me, being a poor woman and grate charge of children
to maintain so beg Your Worships will take it into your
serious consideration and dispence with my punishment and your petitioner will ever pray."

The Court rejected the petition.

"The Vestry of All Saints Parish prefer to the
Court here the following petition, to wit, To the Worshipful, the Justices of Frederick County a petition of
the Vestry and Church Wardens of All Saints Parish
most humbly sheweth, namely that your petitioners
have agreed with a man to finish the parish church and
therefore humbly prays Your Worships to levy so much
this year on the taxables of the aforesaid parish as is
allowed by Act of Assembly and your petitioners shall
forever pray. Signed By order Joseph Woods, Clerk
Register.

"Upon reading this petition, it is ordered by the
Court here that the aforesaid sum of £50 current
money be levied on the taxble inhabitants of the said
Parish according to the directions of the Act of Assembly in that case made and provided."

"William Luckett contracts with the Court here to
keep a ferry at the Mouth of Monocacy upon the same
terms as it was kept by Mr. Osborne Sprigg, deceased."

Richard Snowden, Jr., petitions the Court as follows: "That your petitioner had six taxables taken by
the Constable in 1749 at his quarters on Snowden's
Manor in Frederick County contrary to his overseer's
knowledge for your petitioner had given all his taxables
in Prince George's County and only sent some of his
servants up to said plantation at times to plow and hill-

up corn and as your petitioner has paid in both Counties for the six taxables, he hopes Your Worships will take it into your consideration and make him a suitable allowance at this Court now sitting for said six taxables and your petitioner as in duty bound shall pray.

"Upon reading which petition and consideration thereof had, it is ordered by the Court here that the petitioner be allowed for the said taxables in this year's levy."

Michael Dowden prefers to the Court here the following petition, to wit, ".... Michael Dowden liver in and inhabitant of the said County humbly sheweth that he the said Dowden lives on the publick road that leads to Frederick Town and is well accommodated for entertaining travelers and he humbly prays that Your Worships will grant him a license for to keep a publick house as it will be very oppressive and chargable to him to live on so publick a road where is oppressed almost every night with travelers. Therefore he hopes that Your Worships will take him under your consideration and not refuse so small a favor and your petitioner as in duty bound shall forever pray.

"Upon reading which petition.... it is ordered by the Court here that the petitioner have the effect of his prayer on giving security according to law."

"Edward Bullen is by the Court here (he being 15 years old the 10th day of March next) bound to Joseph Mayhew until he arrives to the age of 21 years and the said Joseph Mayhew obliges himself to give the said Edward Bullen one year's schooling and at the expiration of his time to give him a mare and saddle and a decent suit of apparel."

"Ordered by the Court here that the Sheriff take Silas Enyart into his custody and keep him safe in gaol till the 23rd inst., for his indecent behavior to this Court."

"Ordered by the Court here that the Constables of Middle Part Rock Creek Hundred, Lower Part Potomac Hundred, Upper Part Potomac Hundred and Lower Part Newfoundland Hundred endeavor to suppress the tumultuous meetings of Negroes in their several Hundreds and ordered that they be allowed for the same according to the Act of Assembly in that case made and provided."

"The Vestrey of Prince George's Parish prefer to the Court here the following petition, to wit, 1750 to the Worshipful Bench of Justices of Frederick County the petition of the Vestrey of Prince George's Parish prays that Your Worships please to grant them two pounds of tobacco on the taxables of the said County belonging to the aforesaid Parish toward defraying the Parish's charge and your petitioners will ever pray. Signed per order of the Vestrey, John Flint, Register." The Court ordered that the desired levy be made in the next County levy.

Nathan Peddycoart presents his petition as follows: "Your petitioner has found [i.e., given board and room to] George Bennett (who was a pentioner of this County) with necessary entertainment since last June Court without any consideration for such his trouble and charge. He therefore prays Your Worships would please to allow him as to Your Worships may see meet and your petitioner as in duty bound will pray. Your petitioner is further willing to keep the said George Bennett for the ensuing year, provided he be allowed according to the prospect of the dearness of the provisions."
The Court ordered rejection of the petition.

Nicholas Bundrick petitioned the Court for a license to keep publick house in Frederick Town, which was granted.
Jacob Beany prefers a petition to keep a house of entertainment at Frederick Town, which is also al-

lowed by the Court.

Richard Harry petitions the Court "that your petitioner thro the infirmity of old age and ill health is entirely incapable of labor. He therefore prays Your Worships will allow a pention to him as to Your Worships may see meet.

"It is ordered by the Court here that the petitioner be allowed 800 pounds of tobacco for his support to next November Court and ordered that the same be assigned to Mr. John Needham for the use of the petitioner."

George Bennett petitions the Court that "your petitioner thro old age and the infirmities incident thereto is entirely disabled from labouring for a support. He therefore hopes Your Worships will consider him an object of charity and allow him a pention as to Your Worships may seem meet.

"Ordered by the Court here that the petitioner be allowed in the levy 1,000 pounds of tobacco for his support to next November Court." [cf. above, p. 58.]

Jacob Bruner petitions the Court "that your petitioner was returned by the Constable last year one levy more than what he really had, therefore humbly prays Your Worships will consider the premises."

The Court rejected the petition.

There follow a number of petitions for relief, some of which were granted and some rejected, without reasons given by the Court.

"James Wallace prefers to the Court here the following petition....that whereas your petitioner had a man named William Lawrance who came to his house some time in September last and was taken sick and so continued till his death which was on the 4th of October. Your petitioner then bought plank and made a coffin and buried him Christianlike therefore as it's

59

customary in such cases to apply to the County Court for relief, your petitioner therefore humbly prays that Your Worships will take it into your serious consideration and grant that I be allowed an allowance from the County for the same as in your grave wisdoms shall think fit and your petitioner as in duty bound will ever pray.

"Upon reading which petition....it is ordered by the Court here that the same be rejected."

"Jacob Barton, Constable of Mannor Hundred, returns to the Court here the following persons for swearing, to wit, Robert Debutts for swearing 25 oaths, Silas Enyart for swearing 6 ditto, Michael Reisner for swearing 7 ditto, and Robert Pearl for swearing four ditto, whereupon it is ordered by the Court here that the said Robert Debutts, Silas Enyart, Michael Reisner and Robert Pearl and each of them be fined as the Act of Assembly in that case made requires and ordered the Sheriff collect the same."

"The Justices of the Court here, having viewed the Court House lately erected in Frederick Town, approve of the same and Joseph Hardman, one of the undertakers thereof, obliges himself to point the gavel [gable] end and fill up the scaffold holes."

The Court ordered issuance of a bench warrant for John Nicholls, Constable of Linton Hundred, for failure to return a list of the taxables of his Hundred.

"Ordered by the Court here that George Beall be allowed 20 shillings in the levy for erecting a pair of stocks at Rock Creek warehouse."

"Ordered also that [Sheriff] George Gordon, Esq., be allowed 10 shillings, 6 pence for irons found [for] the said stocks."

"Ordered by the Court here that the overseer of the road from Frederick Town to the Middle Ford on

Monocacy clear the ford in the best manner he can."

"Nathaniel Wickham, Jr., John Rawlins, John Needham, George Gordon and Thomas Stoddert, Gentlemen, or any three of them, are by the Court appointed to contract with any person or persons toward finishing the Court House of this County."

A list of the Constables appointed for the ensuing year in their various Hundreds is as follows:

Hugh Riley	Potomac Hundred, Lower Part
Clement Davis	Potomac Hundred, Upper Part
Lewis Duvall	Newfoundland Hundred
John Davis	Newfoundland Hundred, Lower Part
John Bean	Rock Creek Hundred, Middle Part
George Jewell	Sugarland Hundred
Alexander Perry	Sugar Loaf Hundred
Joseph Beall, son of Ninian	Linganore Hundred
John Barick	Mannor Hundred
Michael Hodgkiss	Pipe Creek Hundred
William Johnson	Kittocton Hundred
William Bonell	Andietum Hundred
Joseph Smith	Marsh Hundred
James Downing	Salisbury Hundred
Owen Davis	Conocochegue Hundred
John Nicholls	Linton Hundred
William Emmitt	Upper Monocacy Hundred
Peter Stilly	Monocacy Hundred, Middle Part
Notley Thomas	Monocacy Hundred, Lower Part

"The Justices of the Court here appoint the several Constables following to execute the law in relation to the suppressing of the tumultuous meetings of Negroes in their Hundreds and order that they be allowed for the same on complying with the requisites of the Act of Assembly in that case made and provided:

Hugh Riley	Potomac Hundred, Lower Part
John Bean	Rock Creek Hundred, Middle Part
Clement Davis	Potomac Hundred, Upper Part
John Davis	Newfoundland Hundred, Lower Part"

"The Justices of the Court here ascertain the following roads to be main roads of the County and appoint the several persons following overseers of the same:"[8]

From Monocacy Ferry to Henry Ballenger's Branch: William Marshall.

From Nolands Ferry to Frederick Town: Elias De-Lashmutt.

From Henry Ballenger's to Hussey's Ford and the New Road to the Middle Ford and from Frederick Town to the top of Kittocton Mountain: Gaspar Mier.

From Linganore Ford to Anne Arundel County and to the extent of the County: George Becraft.

From Monocacy to Linganore and from thence to the extent of the County near Parr's: William Cumming, Jr.

The River Road and Richard Touchstone's Road: Flayl Pain.

From the top of Kittoctin Mountain to the top of Shenandore, the road that leads from the top of Kittoctin to Shenandore by Richard Touchstone's and from the top of Kittoctin Mountain to the top of Shenandore that leads by John George's, from the road that leads out of John George's road that leads by Robert Evans to the top of Shenandore: John George, Jr.

From Monocacy Ford where John Hussey lived that leads to Lancaster and from Monocacy, crossing my Lord's Mannor, crossing Little Pipe Creek to Great Pipe Creek and from Great Pipe Creek to the temporary line of this Province: [Overseer not named.]

Lower part to Henry Smith's Branch and from thence to John Carmack's and then with a straight line to Linganore: Peter Barick.

Middle part from Smith's Branch to Great Pipe Creek and from Diggs's Works [copper mine] to Balti-

---

[8] Because we are primarily concerned with today's Frederick County, I list only those roads which I can identify as being within its present boundaries.

more County: William Carmack.

Upper part from Great Pipe Creek to the temporary line: John Lemon.

From Major Ogle's Ford to John Biggs' Ford on Monocacy and from thence to Frederick Town and from Ogle's Ford to Biggs' Ford: Nathaniel Wickham III.

From the temporary line to William Ambrose's: Joseph Faress.

From Ambrose's Mill to Abraham Miller's Mill: Barnett Waymar.

From Abraham Miller's Mill till it intersects the nearest main road to Frederick Town: Daniel Shawhan.

From Frederick Town to Daniel Dulany, Esquire's Mill: John Charlton.

From Monocacy Ford to Henry Smith's branch: John Harlan.

From Thomas Beatty's to Baltimore Town: Joseph Wood, John Carmack, Mathew Stalkup.

"The Justices of the Court here appoint the following persons pressmasters of the County for the ensuing year, to wit, Joseph Wood of Israel's Creek and John West."

"Ordered that the actions proprietary against Elizabeth Douglas for bastardy, Elizabeth Burk for bastardy, Henrietta Crampton for bastardy, Sarah Bohman for bastardy, Mary Parry for bastardy, Ann South for bastardy, Mary Parry for bastardy [sic], Ann, a servant of Joseph Flint, for bastardy, be struck off the docket."

Several other women accused of bastardy were not as fortunate as those in the preceding list:

Rebecca Arrow, a servant to James Neal, was convicted of bastardy and fine 30 shillings. James Neal paid her fine, for which the Court ordered Rebecca to serve Neal nine additional months.

Margaret White was convicted of bastardy and fined £3. James Gore, planter, paid Margaret's fine and also posted bond of £40 as indemnity that her child would never become a public charge.

Sarah Neal was convicted of bastardy and fined £3. James Neal of Frederick County, planter, paid her fine and gave bond for £40 to the Lord Proprietary that the child should never become a public charge.

Richard Smith, who was indicted for keeping a disorderly house, was discharged after one continuance.

"Ordered that Mary Perry, who petitioned last March Court for a maintenance and which was referred to this Court, be allowed in the levy 640 pounds of tobacco for her support to next November Court."

"Ordered that Richard Williams his petition for an allowance for wolves' heads preferred last June Court and which was referred to this Court be rejected."

In a suit of John Cooke, Esquire, against Nathaniel Curry, farmer, on an account "for sundry articles properly chargeable in account" a list of these items is exhibited and some of those of particular interest are shown as follows:

1 hair sifter	2/8
1 fine hatt	17/6
1 bandanno silk handkerchief	9/-
1 pair shears	1/6
3,000 10d nails at 12/6 per 1,000	3/19/6
4,000 8d nails at 10/6 "	
150 30d nails at 6/- per hundred	9/-
1 woman's furred hatt and band	1/ 5/-
1 ditto laced	2/10/-
$2\frac{3}{4}$ yards beaver coating	1/18/6
1 large ivory comb	3/-
1 horn comb	-/6
1 large clasp knife	1/3

1 linen handkerchief	2/-
6 pewter basons at 3/6 each	1/1/-
1 large pewter bason	5/-
5 ½-lb. barrs lead at 8d per lb.	1/8
1 quire paper	1/6

Caleb Dorsey sues Uncle Uncles on a small debt of 333 pounds of tobacco.

In a suit by Christopher Lowndes and Company against Henry Sayers, heir at law of James Sayers, on an account, there appear some interesting items not previously found in other accounts, as follows:

1 wasteband buckle			-/8
1 hunting horn			4/6
1 lb. soap			1/-
7 lbs., 7 oz. of loaf sugar			8/8
½-lb. Spanish snuff			2/6
½-lb. Scotch snuff			2/6
1 bushel of salt			1/1
3 gallons of rum			18/9½
a flask oil			3/-
3 dozen glass buttons			3/-
11 fish lines	220	lbs. of tobacco
16 smaller ditto	128	lbs. of tobacco
2 bottles flower mustard	16	lbs. of tobacco
3 hhds. of molasses	9,877½	lbs. of tobacco
1 pair men's stockings	72	lbs. of tobacco

"And the Court then adjourned to the third Tuesday in March next. Signed: John Darnall, Clerk."

MARCH COURT OF 1750[/51]

The March Court of 1750 met on the 19th day of March 1750 with the following Justices present: Daniel Dulany, Esquire, Chief Justice, Nathaniel Wickham, Jr., Joseph Chapline, William Griffith, Alexander Beall, Nathaniel Alexander, Thomas Beatty, John Rawlins, Nathan Magruder, Thomas Prather and John

Needham.

Grand Jurors were David Linn, foreman, Archibald Edmonston, Thomas Clayland, Nathaniel Magruder, Elias DeLashmutt, Peter Stull, Charles Hedge, John Johnson, Henry Gaither, Charles Cheney, William Davis son of Garah, James Gore, Handle Henn, John Jones (Conococheague), Jonathan Hagar, Abraham Alexander, Charles Higginbothom, John Norris III and Moses Chapline.

The Grand Jury presented indictments against a number of persons, some of whom were as follows:

Thomas Cresap for an assault committed on the body of John Rench by information of John Keller and John Rench.

Cornelius Elting and James Holman, Sr., for building a mill dam across Rock Creek below tidewater to the annoyance of the fishing in the said Creek.

James Neale for adultery committed on the body of Rebecca Arrow and begetting a baseborn child of the same Rebecca. [See above, p. 63, and below, p. 67.]

Joseph Mayhue for receiving one pistole from Edward Bullen and concealing the same, knowing it to be stolen.

Elizabeth, the daughter of William Ellorburton, for having a baseborn child.

Sary Hall of Potomac Upper Hundred for having a baseborn child.

William Williams, son of Thomas, for "burning the Reverend Richard Hartswel's wigg and hair and for taking him out of bed and afterwards pulling the seat from under him. We likewise present Robert Owen, John Richards and George Wilson for assisting the said William Williams in abusing Reverend Hartswel."

Lawrence Owen, ordinary keeper, for keeping a disorderly house.

George Gordon, Esquire, Sheriff of this County, for extortion by information of Joseph Wilson.

William Lucket for refusing to carry some bags of corn over Monocacy Ferry.

"It appearing to the Court here that the Reverend Mr. Richard Hartswell is lays in a very languishing condition and must inevitably perish without immediate assistance, having nothing to support himself, Dr. Joshua Warfield therefore agrees with the Court to find and provide for the said Richard Hartswell a convenient place to be in and to find medicines for him and give him good attendance for which it is ordered that he be allowed in the next County levy."

It appearing to the Court here that William Slade is a person of a bad fame and reputation, it is therefore ordered that the said Slade recognize himself [give bond] in £20 current money for his good behavior until the next County Court. And the said William Slade is committed to the custody of the Sheriff until he gives the security aforesaid." Similar orders were issued against Robert Ward, Benjamin Hopkins and Thomas Maynard.

"Mathias Malloro, servant to Daniel Dulany, Esquire, came to anchor in Virginia the 4th day of January 1744 as produced by himself."

"Rebecca Arrow prefers the following petition.... that your petitioner has served her time honorably and truly to James Neal, said Neal happening to get said servant with child for which he designs to make her serve a longer time without any satisfaction. May it therefore please Your Worships to take into consideration your petitioner's case.

"Upon reading this petition.... it is ordered by the Court here that the said Rebecca Arrow be discharged from the said Neal's service on giving new security for the fine which she was by the last Court adjudged to pay for having a baseborn child and for the fees occasioned thereby and hereupon Robert Mark of Frederick Town, shoemaker, undertakes for the said Rebecca Arrow that as well the fine aforesaid as all and singular the fees due to the officers of the same Court by occasion of the premises shall well and truly be paid, and the said James Neal, the former security, is discharged of the same."

"Ordered by the Court that George Gordon, Esquire, his bond for the Sheriff's Office of this County be transmitted to the Clerk of the Provincial Court, this Court approving of the same."

A petition "signed by sundry of the inhabitants [unnamed] of the County" is presented to the Court by Jacob Peck as follows: "Your petitioners, the inhabitants on the east side the Mountain on Tuscarora Run, having no road to Frederick Town that we can pass either with waggon or with loads on horseback but with great difficulty for want of a road cleared which might be done with little labor to the great advantage of your petitioners and the other inhabitants further up the Mountain in going to our County Court and to market, we therefore humbly pray Your Worships would grant us an order to have a road lay'd out and cleared from Frederick Town to Jacob Peck's fulling mill on Tuscarora Run."

Upon reading the petition, the Court appointed Nathaniel Wickham, Jr., and Abraham Miller to lay out a road "according to the prayer of the petitioners and that the petitioners clear the roads themselves."

James Smith of Rock Creek presents the following petition: "Your petitioner has had for three months last past a great deal of fatigue and trouble in his family as well as expense occasioned by Mr. Richard Hartswell as will appear by his letter sent to Henry Darnell, Esquire. Your petitioner therefore humbly prays Your Worships to allow him a sufficiency for his trouble and expense and he as in duty bound will pray."

The Court ordered that the petition be referred to the next November Court.

The bastardy suits against Ann Cramphin and

Mary Hall were ordered struck off, "the defendants being married."

"Jacob Meek, John Rench, John Keller, John Rawlins, Edward Bullen, William Patridge, Robert Bowen, Charles Clagett, George Wilson, Jonathan Markland, Joseph Wilson, Robert Debutts, George Beall, John Wilcoxon, Butler Evans, William Plummer, Rebecca Arrow, Thomas Barnet and Nathan Gregg sworn evidences to the Grand Jury."

In a suit by William Cumming, Esquire, against Henry Gaither, the latter is accused of killing "a certain mastiff dogg belonging to the said William Cumming of the price of £20 sterling." The case was referred to a jury composed of Edward Owen, William Williams son of Thomas, Charles Coates, Garah Davis, Robert Debutts, Richard Touchstone, Thomas Dowden, Wadsworth Wilson, Hendery Allison, John Purdom, William Wallace and William Wheat.

The jurors found for the defendant and ordered Cumming to pay him $808\frac{1}{4}$ pounds of tobacco for his costs and charges.

A suit by William Pritchet versus James Queen is of legal interest because it is the first time in the records that the use of habeas corpus is found. The suit charges Queen with finding four young slaves belonging to Pritchet who were apparently lost and with failing to return them. Pritchet claims damages of £100 sterling. Queen through his attorney William Cumming presents the following writ of habeas corpus: "Charles, absolute Lord and Proprietary of the Provinces of Maryland and Avalon, Lord Baron of Baltimore &c to the Justices and Sheriff of Frederick County, greeting. Whereas a certain James Queen, late of Frederick County, planter, is detained in the prison of our said County under the custody of you, our said Sheriff, at the suit of a certain William Pritchet of a plea of trespass upon the case which said plea as it is said still

69

depends before you our said Justices undetermined and we, being willing for divers causes that the plea aforesaid shall be heard and determined before the Justices of our Provincial Court, wherefore command you that you have the body of the said James Queen by whatsoever name he be called in the plea aforesaid together with the day and cause of his caption and detainer and all things thereunto relating before the Justices of our Provincial Court to be held at Annapolis the second Tuesday of April next that our Provincial Court may further proceed therein as to justice appertaining. Hereof fail not at your peril and have you then and there this writ. Witness Benjamin Young, Esquire, Chief Justice of our said Court, the 5th day of October in the 36th year of our Dominion AD 1750. Issued December 3, 1750."

In a suit entered in a previous Court, the Reverend William Williams sued Hugh Gilliland on a promissory note in the amount of £10 current money. In the prior Court, Gilliland first claimed that the signature on the note was not his and then changed his plea and threw himself on the mercy of the Court. Williams was awarded the amount of the note. In the present Court, Williams sues for damages said to have been received by reason of the long failure of Gilliland to pay the note and a writ of enquiry was issued to the Sheriff of the County in the name of the Lord Proprietary ordering him to conduct an inquisition by twelve good men and true to determine what damages the Rev. Williams had sustained.

The report of the Sheriff is as follows: "An inquisition indented and taken this 19th day of March 1750 at the dwelling house of Kennedy Farrell in Frederick County before me, George Gordon, His Lordship's Sheriff for the said County, by virtue of His Lordship's writ to me directed and to this inquisition ....the jurors say upon their oaths that the same William Williams in the said writ mentioned has sustained damages by occasion of the premises (besides his costs and charges)....the sum of one shilling one penny half penny (1/1½d) current money of Maryland. In witness whereof as well, I, the said Sheriff and the Jurors aforesaid have hereunto set our hands and seals the day and year first above written."

Signed by George Gordon, Sheriff, and the following Jurors: James Smith R[ock] Creek, Van Sweringen, David Cox, John Perins, Richard Touchstone who signs by mark, Elias DeLashmutt who signs by mark, Robert Debutts, John Adamson, William Beall, George Jewell, Arthur Nelson, Jr., and Thomas Cleland.

JUNE COURT OF 1751

The June Court of 1751 convened "on the 18th of June of 1751 in the 37th year of His Lordship's Dominion. Justices present were Thomas Beatty, Joseph Chapline, William Griffith, Nathan Magruder, Alexander Beall, Nathaniel Wickham, Jr., Thomas Prather, John Rawlins, John Clagett, John Needham and Josias Beall, Gentlemen."

Joseph Wood of Israel's Creek was foreman of the Grand Jury, which opened its session with the usual presentments for bastardy: Ann Winters of Conococheague Hundred, Mary Ryan of Middle Hundred, Elizabeth Merritt and Mary Clark, both of Sugarland Hundred.

The Jury also presented:

Benjamin Hopkins of Lower [Potomac] Hundred for striking and abusing Hugh Riley, Constable, when Riley was executing the duties of his office.

John Harlan, "overseer of the road called Lower Part that leads from Monocacy Ford to Pennsylvania for not clearing the aforesaid road."

Thomas Thresher for cheating Alexander Beall and John Cleckitt, inspectors, by putting bad tobacco in one end of a hogshead after being pickt out as bad tobacco."

In addition, "We, the Grand Jurors, upon enquiry into the orphans that Elizabeth Maugridge bound to Robert Evans is brought up in cussing and swearing and other ill languages."

The Court ordered that a bench warrant issue against Casper Myre, overseer of the Road "from Frederick Town to Henry Ballengers Branch, for neglect of duty as overseer of the same."

In a bastardy suit against Hannah Busey, the unusual situation arises as follows: "Forasmuch as the said Hannah Busey had already swore before Thomas Beatty, Gentleman, one of His Lordship's Justices, that John Kemp of Frederick County, farmer, is the father of her bastard child," John Kemp is haled into Court and found guilty. Both are fined, and Kemp is required to give bond in the amount of £40 that the child will never become a public charge.

"Ordered by the Court that subpoena issue....for Elizabeth Scaggs, Executrix of Charles Scaggs, to contersecure Stephen Hampton and Joseph Beall, son of Ninian, her suretys who complain that the said estate is likely to be wasted."

Pearce Noland presents a petition to the Court as follows: "That whereas Ann More dyed at my house and I buryed her and she not having wherewith to pay me for my trouble and expense for the same, I humbly pray Your Worships to allow me what Your Worships thinks proper, and your petitioner shall forever pray."
The Court referred the petition to the August Court next.

A suit is brought in the name of the Lord Proprietary against Nathaniel Tomlinson "for neglect of duty when Constable. The charge is "concerning his suppressing a mittimus [9] for a certain George William Lawrance who was committed by Thomas Prather,

72

Gentleman, one of His Lordship's Justices, about 18 months ago for default of security for his good behavior towards a certain William Anderson and delivered the said Tomlinson when he was Constable."

Tomlinson admits his guilt and throws himself on the mercy of the Court. The Court fines him 80 pounds of tobacco.

"William Gyles, an orphan aged as it is said 16 years, is by the Court here bound to Robert Story 'til he arrives to the age of 21 years and the said Robert Story obliges himself to give the said orphan a year's schooling and to learn him the weaver's trade and at the expiration of his time of servitude to give him a young mare and saddle, as also a decent suit of apparel."

"Elizabeth Gyles, an orphan aged as it is said 12 years the 10th day of March last, is by the Court here bound to Joseph Wood of Israel's Creek 'til she arrives to the age of 16 years, and the said Joseph Wood in Court here obliges himself to learn the said Elizabeth to read and at the expiration of her time of servitude to give her a decent suit of apparel."

Sundry inhabitants of Frederick County prefer to the Court here the following petition: "A considerable number of waggons travel the new road that leads to Bladensburg and are very much impeded for want of a bridge over Great Bennet's Creek. Therefore prays Your Worships to take the same into your consideration and allow such a sum of money as you shall think sufficient to build a bridge over said Creek...."

The Court referred this petition to the next County Court.

---

[9] Latin: we send. A Court or Justice's direction to a Sheriff to convey to prison the person named therein until he shall be delivered by due course of law.

Jacob Mire petitions the Court for a license to keep a public house of entertainment in Frederick Town. The Court grants his request.

Michael Stumpff petitions the Court for a license to keep a public house in Frederick Town and the Court also grants his request.

"Ordered by the Court here that Baruch Williams, and Samuel Warner, Prince George's County, witnesses in the cause depending in this Court between Rachel Sprigg, plaintiff, and John Bell, taylor, defendant, and summoned to testify for the defendant, be allowed four days itinerant charges each at the rate of 23 pounds of tobacco per diem and ordered that the defendant pay the same."

"Ordered by the Court here that William Marshall who is overseer of the road from Monocacy Ferry to Ballengers Branch keep in repair all roads that lye between Ballengers Branch and Potomac River that leads to the top of Kittocton Mountain and ordered that the said roads be deemed part of his district and ordered that Elias DeLashmutt who is overseer of the same roads be discharged thereof."

"Ordered that the road from Frederick Town to Ballengers Branch by Peter Apples be deemed as part of Gaspar Myre's district and ordered that he keep the same in good repair."

"Ninian Beall son of Ninian produces to the Court here his servant, namely William Evans, to be adjudged for runaway time and makes oath that he absented himself from his service twenty days and that he was at £11/15/6 current money in regaining him to his service. Whereupon it is ordered by the same Court that the said William Evans serve his said master eighteen months for the runaway time and expenses as aforesaid."

"Richard Hartswell prefers to the Court here the

following petition....that your petitioner has long time laboured under an inposthumation [abscess] in his thigh which altho cured has left such a stiffness in the joint of the knee as rendered your petitioner incapable of doing anything for subsistence and as the person with whom your petitioner boards is unwilling to keep a boarder any longer your petitioner therefore humbly craves that Your Worships will take into consideration the necessity of your said petitioner and allow him something to subsist on and likewise provide a place of abode for him and he as in duty bound shall ever pray, &c.

"Upon reading this petition....it is ordered by the Court here that the same be rejected."

Nehemiah Ogdon petitions the Court as follows: "that your petitioner is 63 years of age and past his labor and desires Your Worships will take it into consideration to set him levy free."

The Court grants his request.

Michael Jesserang petitions the Court that he is "desirous of keeping an ordinary or public house of entertainment in Frederick Town" and asks for a license, which the Court grants.

"Ordered by the Court here that further process do not issue against Eleanor David for bastardy, it appearing to the Court that the said Eleanor David is since married."

"Ordered also that further process do not issue against Alexander Wells for a breach of His Lordship's peace, it appearing that the said Alexander Wells does not live in the County."

"Ordered likewise that further process do not issue against Richard Beaman for felony, it appearing to the Court here that the said Richard Beaman is run away."

Leonard Albright was preferred to the Court charged with "neglect of duty as overseer of the highway." Albright admits his guilt and throws himself on the Grace of the Court. The Court fines him 500 pounds of tobacco for his offense.

William Kelly was brought into Court on a similar offense, neglect of duty, and was fined 500 pounds of tobacco.

John George, Jr., received a similar fine for a similar charge.

A presentment against William Luckett "for refusing to carry some bags of corn over Monocacy Ferry was marked "struck off."

In connection with a suit of the Lord Proprietary against Col. Thomas Cresap, the following memorandum is entered into the record: "That at a County Court of the Right Honorable Charles &c., held at Frederick Town in the County aforesaid on the third Tuesday in November in the 35th year of His said Lordship's dominion, the vestry and church wardens of All Saints Parish in the County aforesaid returned to the Justices of the same Court Col. Thomas Cresap for cohabiting with Elizabeth Lumme [Lummy].

"Having refused or neglected to appear before the aforesaid vestry after being legally summoned thereto and now at this day, to wit, the 3rd Tuesday in June in the 37th year of His Lordship's dominion to which time the information aforesaid was continued, Henry Darnall, Gentleman, Attorney General of the Province of Maryland and prosecutor of His Lordship's pleas in the Court here in his proper person says that he will not further prosecute against the said Thomas Cresap of and upon the premises.

"It is therefore considered by the Court here that the said Thomas Cresap of the premises to him above imposed be acquit and discharged by the Court here adjudged and the said Thomas Cresap is dismissed &c."

William Williams, son of Thomas, who with several accomplices had been accused of burning the Reverend Richard Hartswell's wig and hair and for taking him out of bed and afterwards pulling the seat from under him, throws himself on the Grace of the Court and the Court finds that he is not guilty as charged.

Likewise, his accomplices, Robert Owen, John Richards and George Wilson, are also found not guilty as charged.

AUGUST COURT OF 1751

The August Court of 1751 met on the third Tuesday and 20th day of August. Justices present were Nathaniel Wickham, Jr., Thomas Prather, Joseph Chapline, Thomas Beatty, Nathaniel Alexander, William Griffith, John Rawlins, Josias Beall, Nathan Magruder and John Needham.

Joseph Wood of Israel's Creek was foreman of the Grand Jury which presented:

William Ervine of Conococheague Hundred for beating and abusing William Clemmens.

Joseph Mahue [Mayhew] of Salisbury Hundred for kicking and abusing of Elenor Brown, wife of David Brown.

John Johnston of Conococheague Hundred for beating and abusing Isaac Rees.

Elizabeth Norris of Capt. John Hundred for having a baseborn child.

George Reed and James Wallace, Sr., for failure to clear the roads in Lower Part of Potomac Hundred.

Four other road overseers for failure to give proper care to their roads, namely: Bigger Head of Rock Creek Hundred; Caspar Myer, overseer of the road from Frederick Town; Alexander Barnett, overseer of Potomac Hundred; William Marshal, overseer from Mouth of Monocacy to Ballengers Branch.

John Mobley of Linganore Hundred for beating and abusing Henry Manyard.

The Grand Jury "also returned a bill of inditement against Thomas Cresap, late of Frederick County, Gentleman, for a breach of the peace true bill and one other bill of inditement against John Rench, late of Frederick County, farmer, for a breach of the peace ignoramus[10] to which presentments and on which inditements the above-named Joseph Wood, foreman, subscribed and endorsed his name."

"Ordered by the Court that John Compton who was sometime since committed to the Sheriff's custody on suspicion of his being a runaway servant be discharged thence paying fees."

Petitions to keep ordinaries or public houses, all of them in Frederick Town, were approved by the Court for Michael Jesserang, Joseph Hardman, Conrad Cross, Mary Simms, Daniel Davis, Thomas Sly (signed as Shlye) and Jacob Beney.

Similar petitions to continue keeping public houses were approved for Lawrance Owen "where he now dwells" and Ninian Beall, son of Ninian, "on ye Sugarland Road."

William Luckett likewise petitioned the Court for a license to keep a tavern at the Mouth of Monocacy and the Court granted that petition.

John Roberts, aged 14 years, is bound to Van Swearingen, Jr., until he becomes 21 years of age, and Van Swearingen promises to teach him the blacksmith's trade and give him a year's schooling.

Thomas Anderson appeared in Court in a suit against him by William Norris on a promissory note and at the prayer of the plaintiff was "adjudged to give Special Bail.... for want of which he is committed to the custody of the Sheriff....there to remain until &c."

---

[10] Cf. note above, p. 41.

Benjamin Howard, "aged (as it is said) 5 years next April is by the Court here bound to Joseph Dickerson until he arrives to the age of 21 years and the said Joseph Dickerson in Court here promises to give the said Benjamin Howard one year's schooling and at the expiration of his time to give him freedom dues according to the custom of the country."

When Joseph Mayhew was brought to trial under his presentment, he was found guilty and was ordered by the Court to pay to Thomas Fletchall, Gentleman, one of the Under-sheriffs, one shilling current money for his offense.

James Wells petitions the Court, "that the pention allowed to your petitioner last year is not sufficient to maintain him. Therefore prays Your Worships for such allowance as you shall think meet and he as in duty bound shall ever pray."

The Court allowed him in the next levy 300 pounds of tobacco for his support to the next November Court.

Samuel Gates, aged 10 years, is bound to Samuel Cecil until he becomes 21 years old, and his brother John Gates, aged 8 years, is bound to Thomas Witton.

Robert Gates, said to be 6 years old the 26th day of March next, is bound to Thomas Witton until he becomes 21 years of age "and the same Thomas Witton in Court here promises to learn the said Robert Gates or cause him to be learned to read and write and at the expiration of his time to give him freedom dues according to the custom of the country. The said Thomas Witton being sworn on the Holy Evangels of Almighty God in Court here declares that the father of the above Samuel, John and Robert is quite unable to support and maintain his said children."

"Ordered by the Court here that Damsel Montgomery who was committed to the Sheriff's custody on suspicion of felony, be discharged, nothing appearing against her."

"Ordered by the Court here that Elenor Williams recognize herself [give bond] in the sum of £10 currency and sufficient security in the sum of £5 of a like money for her appearance and good behavior to the next County Court to be held at Frederick Town on the third Tuesday in November next and in default thereof the said Elenor Williams is committed to the custody of the Sheriff of the County."

"The Justices of the Court here appoint Nathaniel Wickham, Jr., Joseph Ogle, Thomas Stoddert and John Middagh or any two of them to treat with any person or persons to build a bridge over Israel's Creek by Mr. Thomas Beatty's and to maintain the same ten years for any sum not exceeding £15 currency and ordered that they bring in an account thereof at the next County Court."

The Rev. Richard Hartswell repeats his petition (cf. p. 74) that "for about five months past he has labored under a grievous inposthume occasioned by some bruised blood settled in his thigh for which he was lame and cut nine times, one of the wounds $7\frac{3}{4}$ inches long, and whereas the sinews over the instep of his foot are so stretched that he cannot bend his knee and the back sinews so contracted that he cannot put his heal to the ground so as to have the use of that legg and consequently is unable at present of providing of for himself which otherwise he might do without being burdensome to any (the thoughts of which adds to his affliction). He the petitioner prays a subsistence from the Court for some time at least till it shall please God to strengthen him so as to be of service to himself when he hopes to be in a capacity of repaying what Your Worships shall think fit to levy for him and personally acknowledge the favor with the great obligation he is already under, and your petitioner as in duty &c."

The Court now orders 400 pounds of tobacco levied in the next levy "and assigned Mr. John Rawlins for the petitioner's support to next November Court."

Further licenses to keep houses of entertainment were granted to Kennedy Farrell and Martin Adams in Frederick Town, Joseph Belt, Jr., at the Mouth of Rock Creek, and Jacob Mire, a tavern in Frederick Town.

At the trial of Robert Evans, who had been presented "for bringing up Elizabeth Maugridge, an orphan in cursing and swearing and other ill language," Evans was found guilty by the Court and fined 1 pence current money.

Dennis McLamar who was tried for bastardizing was found guilty and fined 30 shillings.

"Ordered by the Court here that Mary Robinson's petition against Henry Maroney for freedom dues be struck off the docket, it being by consent of the parties."

James Macklochland enters suit against John Champian on the basis of a petition to an earlier Court wherein he "humbly sheweth that your petitioner is now in a state of freedom, notwithstanding which he is detained as a servant by a certain John Champian who your petitioner conceives has no right to keep him" and asks that the Court grant him such relief as it shall think proper.

The present Court orders Macklochland to stay with his master until the next term of Court, but declares him to be entitled to his freedom and awards him $614\frac{1}{2}$ pounds of tobacco for his costs, to be paid by Champian.

Dr. Richard Cooke, "physician and chirurgean," sues Robert Debutts on an account in the amount of

£11/8/- current money. The basis for the suit is that Debutts failed to "render unto him (Dr. Cooke) his reasonable account during the time that he was bailiff to the said Richard Cooke in Frederick County." It is further claimed by William Cumming, attorney for Dr. Cooke that "whereas the said Robert Debutts had been receiver to the said Richard Cooke from the first day of April 1746 until the 10th day of June 1749 and during all that time had the care and management of divers and sundry medicines as by the account annexed may appear to the value of £11/8/- current money of and belonging to the said Richard Cooke to merchandize and make a profit thereof for and to render a reasonable amount to the said Richard Cooke when he should be thereunto requested."

The account is listed, but many of the items are undecipherable. Those which are readable are of considerable interest:

mercurial oyntment	£1/ -/-
20 vomits hipocociuana[11] at 2 sh. ea.	2/ -/-
24 vomits of tarter	1/ 4/-
20 purges at 2/6 ea.	2/10/-
4 oz. of volatiles (ammonia)	10/-
4 oz. of Spanish flys[12] at 2 sh. ea.	8/-
1 mollilot plaister	4/-
4 oz. elix. ditriols	8/-
4 oz. eye water	4/-

The two parties agreed to appointment of John Darnall and Joseph Ogle as referees. They reported to the August Court, but their verdict is not recorded.

In a suit of Elizabeth Donaldson against Robert Debutts, the latter is indicated as being a merchant, perhaps explaining the relationship between himself and Dr. Cooke.

---

[11] Ipecacuanha: roots of this South American plant were used pharmaceutically as an emetic or purgative.
[12] For raising blisters.

Dr. Joshua Griffith sues Daniel Shawhan on a debt. Richard Smith sues John Jones, also on a debt.

The Court again set prices for liquors and accommodations. Only one item was changed, the price of Maryland spirits, distilled from grain, which was reduced to 8 shillings per gallon from the former 9 sh., 8 pence. Three items were added, however:

Vidonia wine, quart, sealed	3/-
Good lemons, a piece	-/6
Good limes, a piece	-/1

At this point the Court adjourned to the 18th day of November next. However, the record is carried on under the heading "August Court of 1751," as follows: "At a County Court continued and held at Frederick Town in Frederick County on Monday, the 18th day of November in the first year of the Dominion of the Right Honorable Frederick, Absolute Lord and Proprietary of the Provinces of Maryland and Avalon, Lord Baron of Baltimore, &c., and in the year of our Lord 1752...."[13]

There was a general recommissioning of Justices by a rereading of the original commission and a qualifying of Justices and other officers through the taking of new oaths.

A number of suits were heard, in one of which, that of the Rev. William Williams against James Fowler, a debt was described as "five pounds Virginia currency of the value of £7/10 Maryland currency, the price of a silver watch by the said Williams to the aforesaid Fowler." A Jury was impaneled which found for Williams in the amount of £6/8 current money of

---

[13] Charles Calvert, Fifth Lord Baltimore (1699-1751), had died and the Court is here being reestablished under the Dominion of his successor. Reference to the year 1752, however, is confusing.

HEMPSTEAD COUNTY LIBRARY
HOPE, ARKANSAS

Maryland plus 764¼ pounds of tobacco for his costs.

The records of this Court are cluttered with suits by Rachel Sprigg, executrix of Osborn Sprigg.

Again the Court adjourned, this time to the third Tuesday in November next, presumably the next day.

NOVEMBER COURT OF 1751

The November Court of 1751 was held on the third Tuesday and 19th day of November in the first year of the new Lord Frederick's Dominion. Justices present were: Daniel Dulany, Chief Justice, Nathaniel Wickham, Thomas Prather, William Griffith, John Rawlins, Josias Beall, John Clagett, Alexander Beall, Nathan Alexander, Nathan Magruder and Henry Wright Crabb.

The Grand Jury made a number of presentments:
Susanna King for having a baseborn child.
Jane Lindsay, a servant woman of Jonathan Markland for having a baseborn child.
Mathew Mallerce for "beating, binding and abusing Mary Sanwilla and for attempting a rape upon ye body of the said Mary."
Leonard Rumel "for an assault and battery committed on Mary Adams."

"Michael Coker, 12 years of age next March, is by the Court here bound to Leonard Moser until he arrive to the age of 21 years and the said Leonard Moser in Court here promises to learn the said Michael Coker to read and write and weaver's trade and at the expiration of his time to give him a decent suit of cloathes."
Michael's sister Elizabeth, age 13 years, is likewise bound to Leonard Moser until she becomes 16 years of age.

John Sweet, who states that he lives on the road between Frederick Town and Monocacy, petitions for a license to keep a house of entertainment.

William Luckett contracts again with the Court to keep a ferry over the Monocacy River at its Mouth until the last day of next November Court in consideration of 7,200 pounds of tobacco.

He binds himself "to give good attendance at the said ferry at all times, nights and days (Sundays not excepted) and also to supply a cart or waggon to carry tobacco or other things over said ferry when the boat or schow can't pass."

Richard Beall agrees to repair the bridge over Rock Creek by Caleb Litton's and to keep it in good repair for two years. The Court orders that he be allowed £15/10 in the next levy and requires him to give bond of £31 current money for the faithful performance of his contract.

"Clementius Davis agrees with the Court to repair the bridge over Senecar and to make it ninety feet long and to keep it in good repair during the term of ten years." The Court orders that he be allowed £30 current money for the work and requires him to give bond in the amount of £60 current money for the faithful performance of his contract.

"Thomas Johnson, one of the sureties for the estate of Thomas Linch, deceased, who's widow married Thomas Compton, which Thomas Compton and wife he makes oath are removed out of the Province and that the estate is wasting. It is thereupon ordered that the [said] Thomas Johnson take possession of all the goods of the deceased that can be found."

"Ordered by the Court that attachment of contempt issue against Samuel Duvall, son of John, for not obeying an order of March Court, last."

85

"Ordered by the Court that Elenor Williams who was committed last Court to the custody of the Sheriff for defect of security for her good behavior to this time be discharged thence, nothing appearing against her."

John Medley petitions the Court for relief from future levies on the ground of his age and crippled condition.

In the trial of Matthew Mallerce, presented above, he pled no contest, and the Court fined him £2/10, requiring him to give security bond in the amount of £20 "for his good behavior for a year."

"Clementus Davis, Constable of Upper Part Potomac Hundred, in Court here swears that he visited the Negro quarters in his Hundred according to Act of Assembly."

James Smith was brought before this Court, charged with "indecent behavior to the Justices of the said Court." He was found guilty and was ordered to be confined by the Sheriff "to close gaol for the space of 48 hours and give security for his good behavior for six months in the sume of £30 currency."

"The Court purchases of Mr. Isaias Beall a drum for the use of the County and ordered that he be allowed 40 shillings for the same in the next County levy."

Edward Dunfield states that he lives on a public road at the Mouth of Conococheague and is desirous to keep a public house of entertainment there. The Court grants him license.

"Mary Sligh prefers to the Court here the following petition in which she humbly sheweth that your petitioner desired that you give her any allowing to pay the debts about the 26 weeks sickness [of] Jacob Sly.

"Upon reading which petition, it is ordered by the Court that the same be rejected."

Christina Lans prefers a petition to the Court, "being a poor widow woman which is not able to git her owen bread, begging of the Honorable Bench to consider her state and condition, your petitioner shall ever pray.
"Upon reading which petition, it is ordered by the Court here that the same be rejected."

Esther Matew and Esther Leach in a petition to the Court state that they "continue quite unable to support themselves and pray the same allowance as last year." The Court allows them 1,600 pounds of tobacco in the next County levy for their support to the next November Court.

Charles Higdon in a petition to the Court states that he "is going in the one and twentieth year of his age and never walked any....He begeth that Your Worships would be pleased to allow some small matter more, he being very helpless and not having any to support him."
The Court ordered that he be allowed 500 pounds of tobacco in the next levy for his support to the next November Court.

Mary Perry petitions the Court "to continue my former allowance...."
The Court ordered that she be allowed 640 pounds of tobacco in the next levy.

The Vestry of Prince George's Parish petitioned the Court "to allow them 5 pounds of tobacco per pole [poll] on the taxbles that are in the said Parish toward defraying the charges of the Parish." It was ordered that the requested levy be made.
The Vestry of All Saints Parish petitions the Court to levy 6 pounds of tobacco per pole to defray

87

the parochial charges of the Parish. The Court orders the levy made.

The Vestry of All Saints Parish also petitions the Court as follows, "Your petitioners humbly pray Your Worships to assess this year the remainder part of what money is allowed by Act of Assembly to finish the Parish Church." Signed per order of Joseph Wood, Clerk Register. The Court ordered the levy made.

Sundry inhabitants of Frederick County petition the Court as follows, "Your petitioners having no road convenient to go to Frederick Town therefore pray Your Worships to order a road to be laid out from Touchstone's Road by Alexander Jones' to cross the Mountain by George Mathew's and from there the nearest and best way to Frederick Town as Notley Thomas, John Hooke and James Hooke shall think most convenient."
"The Court appointed Notley Thomas, James Hooke and Capt. William Griffith or any two of them to lay out the road prayed for and to make report thereof to the next Court."

"Ordered that the Sheriff of this County pay to the Clerk thereof 25½ pounds of tobacco and three pence sterling out of the money ordered to be levied by Act of Assembly for purchasing lots to build a Court House and prison, &c., it being for recording the deed for the same and alienation fine thereon."

"Alexander Jones agrees with the Court to beat the drum from next March Court to the end of November Court and to clean the Court House for which he's to be allowed 30 shillings current money in the next year's levy."

Joseph Wood of Linganore is appointed overseer of the Middle Part of the Road from Thomas Beatty's to Baltimore.

"Ordered that James Smith who petitioned last March Court to be allowed for keeping Richard Hartswell in his sickness which was referred to this time be allowed 1,920 pounds of tobacco for the same in the next levy."

A suit of William House against Henry Touchstone, the charge being that of debt, was settled amicably.

In a suit of James Burgess and his wife Alice against Joseph Hill "in a plea wherefore with force and arms he the said Joseph Hill upon her the said Alice at the County aforesaid an assault did make and her the said Alice did beat, wound and evilly treat so that of her life it was despaired and other harms to her did to the great damage of them the said James and Alice and against our peace, &c.," after numerous imparlances a jury was impaneled who found for the plaintiffs, awarding them a judgment against Hill for 10 shillings current money and 1,293 pounds of tobacco for their costs.

A suit by Dr. Philip Lynham against Martin Whetsel was, after two imparlances, settled by the defendant's agreeing to pay all costs.

The suit of William Marshall and Robert Perle against William Snowden is primarily of interest because of the valuation placed upon certain of Snowden's chattels. The suit alleges that Snowden "had removed in a secret manner from the place of his abode" and that he left behind him an unpaid debt to the plaintiffs in the amount of 6,800 pounds of tobacco. At the request of the plaintiffs, the Court issued an attachment in their behalf and ordered the estate inventoried.

Some of the items with their valuations follow:

1 feather bed, bolster, pillow, 2 sheets, one blanket and 1 old quilt	500 lbs. tobacco
1 feather bed and old blanket	200 lbs. tobacco

1 iron pott, 2 pair potthooks, 2 frying panns, a pair tongs, 2 hoes, 1 pail, 15 pewter spoons, 1 noggin, 2 hammers, 1 iron pestle, 1 old mettle kittle, 1 old funnel, 1 old skimmer	175 lbs. tobacco
2 leggons, 1 horse bell and collar, 1 handsaw, 2 iron wedges, 2 old pillow cases, 1 box of iron, 1 looking glass, 1 mettle spice morter, 5 caseknives and 6 forks, 1 small spoon, 1 pair snuffers, 80 lbs. of bakin	316 lbs. tobacco
4 pewter basons	43 lbs. tobacco
1 pair of steelyards	50 lbs. tobacco
1 cow and calf	300 lbs. tobacco
1 cow	200 lbs. tobacco
1 bull	250 lbs. tobacco

Dr. Gustavus Brown sues Ignatius Tennison on a debt, but the parties agree before the case comes to trial.

Robert Debutts sues Joseph and Charles Hedges, farmers, on a debt of £12/19/8 which he states they owe him as administrator of the estate of Isaac Bloomfield. The Court found for the plaintiff.

Proceedings of a Court of Election:

MEMORANDUM that on the fourth day of November in the year of the Dominion of the Right Honorable Frederick, Absolute Lord and Proprietary of the Provinces of Maryland and Avalon, Lord Baron of Baltimore, &c., in the year of our Lord 1751 by virtue of His Lordship's writ out of His High Court of Chancery issued to George Gordon, Gentleman, Sheriff of the County aforesaid, requiring him on receipt thereof to call together three or more Justices of his County

Court (one whereof being of the Quorum) and the Clerk of the said County Court who were required thereby to sit as a Court and during their sitting by virtue of his said office to give notice by public proclamation to all freeholders within his said County that they appear at the Court House of the said County at a certain time not less than 10 days after such proclamation in order to elect and choose four deputies or delegates to serve for said County at a General Assembly of the said Province of Maryland to be held at the City of Annapolis on the 6th day of December then next."

Monday, November 25th, was set as the day for the election to be held. The record then reads as follows: "The election was proceeded to by the freemen of the County aforesaid who being examined according to the force, form and effect of divers laws thereof made and provided chose, elected and deputed Daniel Dulany, Jr., Nathan Magruder, Henry Wright Crabb and Joseph Chapline, Gentlemen, four good and sufficient freemen of the County aforesaid being residents therein."

MARCH COURT OF 1751[/52]

The March Court of 1751 O.S. met on the third Tuesday and 17th day of March in the second year of His Lordship's Dominion. The Justices present were Nathaniel Wickham, Thomas Cresap, John Rawlins, Josias Beall, Nathan Magruder, Thomas Prather, Alexander Beall, John Needham, Nathaniel Alexander and Henry Wright Crabb, Gentlemen.

The Grand Jury was comprised of the following: Joseph Wood, foreman, Thomas Davis, Nathaniel Tomlinson, Henry Gaither, Solomon Turner, Charles Hedge, William Williams, Stephen Julian, John Johnson (Kittocton), Alexander Weddle, John Perrin, John Henthorn, John Swearingen, Samuel Lamar and Elias DeLashmutt.

The presentments of the Grand Jury included:

James Wallace "for philloniasly [feloniously] taking and remarking [rebranding] a hogg, the property of Nathaniel Magruder.

Richard Touchstone for "passing a Spanish old piece of eight to James Burgess for 7 sh. 6d."

Luke Carroll "for seling of licker on the Sabbath Day."

Paul Noland "for being drunk and abusefull on the Sabbath Day."

Jane Nailes of Upper Part of Newfoundland Hundred for having a baseborn child.

Mary Nowles of Linganore Hundred for having a baseborn child. "Lives with O'Patrick Burk."

Edward Dunfield "for extortioning and taking from William Langford one silver watch, one piece of eight and one shilling bill pretended to be damages for an abuce his horse had received which horse said Dunfield had hired to James Dickson."

Elizabeth Hill of Lower Part of Monocacy Hundred for having a baseborn child.

Isaac Baker for "taking and rebranding a colt the property of Nathaniel Curry."

John Mobley "for beating and abusing Thomas Manyard on the Main Road."

The Court appoints Richard Watts Constable of Sugar Loaf Hundred "in the room of William Cecil."

Thomas Conn petitions the Court and reminds them that at the last November Court they appointed him an overseer of the highways. Then he goes on to say, "And it is well known to many of the neighbors that I have laid under a consuming and wasting disease of a long time and has rendered me incapable of doing my own business and am dayly growing worse. Your petitioner humbly prays therefore that Your Worships will take my condition under consideration and discharge your petitioner from that office that I am not capable of performing."

The Court ordered that the petition be rejected.

Robert Debutts petitions the Court as follows, "That Rebecca Depanny came to his house in a deplorable condition upon which he employed Dr. Lynham who salivated her and has since furnished your petitioner with an account of £5 as then yr. petitioner's house and family has been greatly discomoded on her account and she is very old and decrepped, prays Yr. Honors will remove her or allow him where with to support her...."
The Court allows him 640 pounds of tobacco for support of Rebecca to next November Court.

"Ordered that summons issue returnable to next County Court for Edward Dunfield to show cause why his license to keep tavern should not be suspended.

"Ordered that Richard Smith keep tavern no longer, it appearing to the Court here that he is a person of bad character."

"Grand Jury discharged from this present service and allowed 400 pounds of tobacco in the next County levy."

"Ordered that habeas corpus issue to the Sheriff of the County for Nathaniel Beall (who is detained in the prison of this County in execution) to appear at the next County Court to testify for Charles Ridgely against Francis Culver."

"Ordered by the Court here that the overseers of the road from Frederick Town to Ballenger's Branch make a causeway by the bridge in Frederick Town."

William Downin, aged 11 years, is bound to John Hallum until he reaches the age of 21 years. Hallum obliges himself to give the said William two years' schooling and at the expiration of time of servitude to give him "working and decent" suits of apparel.

"Ordered by the Court here that the Sheriff take William Welsh, a servant to Charles Higginbothem, to the whipping post and give him 25 stripes on his bare body well laid on for his insolent behavior to his said master."

"Francis Pennygrue, a runaway servant having been in the custody of the Sheriff of this County six months and the master not applying for him, the Court orders the said Sheriff to sell the said servant to discharge his imprisonment fees."

John Larkin petitions the Court "that your petitioner having a child aged about 17 thro most grievous afflictions is rendered incapable of any support of the necessarys of life and that your petitioner being not able to assist her therein through his poverty most humbly implores Your Worships' consideration therein and your petitioner as in duty bound shall ever pray....
"Upon reading which petition.... it is ordered that the same be rejected."

Thomas Dobbs in his petition to the Court states "that your petitioner was servant to John Cramphin (deceased) for the space of seven years before the expiration of which time the said John Cramphin died. Your petitioner served the remainder of his time to Jane, the wife of the said John Cramphin. As she did not administer her husband's estate, she refuses to give your petitioner any freedom dues. Your petitioner therefore humbly prays Your Worships as he conceives there is freedom dues due him to order who is to give them, the administrators or wife, and he in duty bound will pray, &c."
The Court ordered the petition referred to the next County Court.

"Ordered by the Court that process do not issue against John Nicholls of neglect of duty as Constable. Robert Ward to give security for his good behavior."

Leonard Rummel, accused of assault and battery on Mary Adams, throws himself on the mercy of the Court and is fined 7 sh., 6d for his offense.

A suit by the Lord Proprietary against John Rench for assaulting Col. Cresap was, after four continuances, struck off.

An action is entered against George Gordon by the Lord Proprietary for extortion. No details are given, but the outcome is as follows: "Henry Darnall, Gentleman, Clerk of the Indictment and Prosecutor of His Lordship's Pleas.... says that he will not further prosecute against the said George Gordon, Sheriff, of and upon the premises." Whereupon the said Sheriff "is acquitted and discharged."

A suit of the Lord Proprietary against Joseph Mayhew wherein Mayhew is charged with "receiving a pistole from Edward Bullen and concealing it, knowing the same to be stolen," is after three continuances struck off.

John Harlan, overseer of the road called Lower Part that leads from Monocacy Ford to Pennsylvania was before the Court charged with not clearing the aforesaid road. Harlan threw himself on the Grace of the Court and was fined 500 pounds of tobacco for his offense, to be applied as the Act of Assembly in that case directs.

The case against Thomas Thresher "for cheating the inspectors of Rock Creek warehouse" was struck off after two continuances.

"Ordered by the Court that Charles Miller his petition against Thomas Radford for freedom be struck off the docket."

"Ordered that the petition of sundrys near Tuscarora Run by Kittocton for a road to Frederick Town preferred last March Court and which was referred from Court to Court until this time be further referred until the next County Court."

Memorandum: William Carmack, John Kimbol and Robert Debutts entered into a writing obligatory in £156/1/11½ "to be paid unto Mary, John and Catherine Carmack on condition that the above bounden John Carmack [sic] or some person on his behalf shall and do well and truly satisfy and pay unto the above named Mary, John and Catherine Carmack, their executors, administrators, assigns or lawful guardian or guardians, their respective parts or portions of their deceased father Cornelius Carmack his estate according to the Act of Assembly."

"Ordered that attachment of contempt issue returnable to the next County Court for Samuel Duvall."

William Newell petitions the Court that "whereas Mary Bradout came to my house in September last with three children and craved houseroom which I granted, she being destitute of a dwelling place, upon condition she would find corn for her family but she being taken sick of a deep consumption and laboring under it till the tenth of January and died so that all the burthen and costs lay on your petitioner, as likewise the said Mary Bradout was buried at the costs and charges of your petitioner and as Mary Bradout left nothing to defray the charges of her funeral, your petitioner humbly prays Your Worships to make him some allowance for same."

The Court referred this petition to the next November Court.

Elias DeLashmutt enters suit against Ninian Beall, garnee of Thomas Dulany, for a debt due from Dulany in the amount of £2 current money and 600 pounds of tobacco. In the suit it is alleged that Dulany has left

his abode in a secret manner and DeLashmutt undertakes to attach property in the hands of Beall. After
many continuances, referees are appointed and they
make an award as follows: "The defendant in the above
cause did pass his note to Dulany seven or eight years
ago for the sume of £3/10/- current money and as yet
has not discharged the same; therefore, as the statute
of limitations is in his, the defendant's, favor against
the said note, we do award that the said defendant pay
unto the plaintiff the said sum of £3/10/- current
money."

In a suit of Thomas Chittam against Hilleary Williams on a debt due by Williams on account, the items
listed are of some interest both as to what they are and
as to their prices. Some of those more easily deci-
phered are listed:

Your order to John Smith Prather for	
4 bottles of white wine at 6 sh. ea.	£1/4/-
1 year's rent of a house in Bell Town	20/-/-
3 games at the billiard table at 3d ea.	-/9
A bowl of punch at 1/6 and 1 gill of	
rum with bitters at 1/-	2/6
2 gills of rum with mint, &c.	2/-
Club in punch	3/6
1 gill of brandy and sugar	1/-
3 gal. of rum	30/-
Shaving	1/-

Messrs. Armour & Stuart, merchants, sue Alexander Lamar on an account with judgment rendered in
favor of the plaintiffs.

George Gump sues Peter Smith on a note executed
by Smith. Michael Jesserang, innholder, becomes
manucaptor for Peter Smith and judgment is rendered
in favor of Gump.

Dr. David Ross sues John Howard, merchant, on
a debt, and verdict is rendered in favor of Ross.

Messrs. William Trent and George Croghan sue John Johnson on a note and the verdict is rendered in their favor.

A suit of John House against Barnet Waymour is marked "abated by death of plaintiff."

Thomas Cresap, administrator of William Griffith who is identified as a merchant, deceased, sues Patrick Mathews on a debt due Griffith's estate. The outcome is marked "cepi mortuus est."[14]

The values placed upon certain chattels of one Andrew Cotterell in a condemnation proceeding are of interest as follows:

1 servant man	£6/-/-
4 hoggs	4/7/7
1 grindstone, 2 iron potts and pothooks, 1 frian pann	115# tobacco
1 plow, 1 hoe, 1 old box	50# tobacco

JUNE COURT OF 1752

The June Court of 1752 met on the third Tuesday and 16th day of June. The Justices present were: Nathaniel Wickham, Jr., Thomas Prather, William Griffith, Alexander Beall, Thomas Cresap, John Rawlins, John Needham, Josias Beall, Henry Wright Crabb and John Clagett.

The Grand Jurors were: Robert Debutts, foreman, Moses Chapline, Alexander Lamar, Benjamin Harris, Benjamin Biggs, Robert Lamar, Jr., David Jones, William Carmack, Jeremiah Hays, Charles Chaney, John Hopkins, Stephen Ransberg, Samuel Cecill, John Radford, Alexander Magruder, Thomas Hogg and Ninian Magruder.

---

[14] Latin: I have served [warrant]; he is dead.

The Grand Jury made the following presentments:
Leucey Mackbee "for having a baseborn child.

Elizabeth Greenwood and Susanah King for having baseborn children, "by information of Robert Walles, Constable."

Philip Mackquier "for concealing and swap[p]ing a horse belonging to Robert Buckell."

George Mercraft "for beating and assaulting Richard Smith."

Jacob Miller "for using a mare of John Darling's, contrary to law."

George Bond and Joseph Johnston "for a breach of the Sabbath."

Moses Shelby "for assault and battery against Joseph Alexander."

Eleanor Ryan [probably daughter of Mary Ryan], aged three years last March, is bound by the Court to Michael Dowden.

"The Court appoint Alexander Beall, John Needham and Josiah Beall, Gentlemen, or any two of them to direct the overseers of the roads to Georgetown to lay out the roads to the said town and ordered when the roads are layd out that several overseers clear the same and the streets in the said town."

"Jane Mathews, daughter of Patrick Mathews, deceased, aged eleven years last February, is by the Court bound to John Charleton til she arrives to the age of 16 years."

"Ordered that summons issue returnable to the next County Court for Joseph Hedge, executor of Andrew Hedge, deceased, to answer the complaint of Mary Mathews in behalf of Andrew Hedge, a minor, the son of the deceased."

"Thomas Wales, Jr., (son of Thomas Wales who is run away), aged 13 years the tenth day of August next, is bound to Richard Beall til he arrives at the age of 21 years." Beall agrees to give him two years schooling and teach him the carpenter trade.

In a suit by the Lord Proprietary against Lawrence Wilson "for insulting Mr. Thomas Prather, a magistrate in the execution of his office," Wilson admitted his guilt and was sentenced to 48 hours in the "close gaol."

"Ordered that the petition of several of the inhabitants of this County for a road from Touchstones to Frederick Town be referred to the August Court next."

In a suit by Elizabeth Scaggs, executrix of Charles Scaggs, versus Robert Hasse, Mrs. Scaggs submits a transcript of the account on which she sues. Some of the items are:

2 pare of leather briches	£1/5/-
3 pare of men's shoes	1/1/-
1 lb. of wool yearn	3/-
1 felt hatt	5/9
weaving	1/9
spinning	1/9
lead and powder	1/2
1 shirt	5/9

AUGUST COURT OF 1752

The August Court of 1752 convened on the third Tuesday and the 18th day of August in the second year of the Dominion of His Lordship Frederick.

The Justices present were Nathaniel Wickham, Chief Justice, Thomas Cresap, Thomas Prather, Josiah Beall, John Rawlins, William Griffith, John Needham, John Clagett and Henry Wright Crabb.

The Grand Jurors were William Webb, foreman, George Jewell, Thomas Osborn, Charles Hedges,

William Chambers, Nathan Veach, Stephen Julian, Hugh Riley, William Wallace, Jr., Ninian Magruder, John Hooke, John Veach, Elias Harding, John Hopkins, John Radford, William Bowers and Nathaniel Beall.

The Grand Jury presented the following:

Zachariah Davis, Mary Fryer, William Cotterell and Grace Cotterell "for stealing about four bushels of engen [Indian] corn from James Lemar."

Thomas Dobbs "for stealing of a paper of necklaces and sundry other goods from Charles Conner."

Henry Lewis and Frederick Long "for forcing into the house [of] Conrad Hogmire and misbehaving, by information of Magdalin Hogmire, and striking Catherine Lewis."

Henry Goesler "for stealing of a horse from Peter Rench."

Elizabeth Beech for having a baseborn child.

Jacob Beney "for allowing gaiming on ye Sabbath and likewise Henry Lazarus, Philip Coonce for gaiming in the said Beney's house."

Isaac Eltinge, "administrator of John Thomas' estate, for suffering and allowing the caplins [saplings] land to be cut down and destroyed."

Stephen Nuton Chizsell [Chiswell] for turning the road through Thomas Fletchall's plantation, by information of the said Fletchall."

More than a dozen innkeepers applied for new or renewal licenses to keep taverns or public houses. Those seeking renewals in Frederick Town were: Michael Stumpf, Joseph Hardman, Michael Jesserong, Conrad Cross and Jacob Beany.

Others requesting renewal licenses were: Charles Higginbothem who does not indicate in his petition the location of his tavern, John Sweet who states that his tavern is "on the road that leads from Frederick Town to the Mouth of Monocacy," William Luckett whose tavern is at the Mouth of Monocacy, Michael Dowden

101

whose tavern is situated "on the road that leads from Frederick Town to Lawrence Owen's, Lawrence Owen who does not locate his tavern in his application and Joseph Belt and Ninian Beall who also do not locate their taverns in their applications.

Two applicants for original licenses were: Joseph Williams who states "that your petitioner lives at the Mouth of Conococheague, it being a very public place, he is desirous of keeping tavern there" and George Frouck who declares "your petitioner is desirous to keep a tavern at Pipe Creek in this County."

All the petitioners were granted licenses.

In a trial of Col. Thomas Cresap for an assault on John Rench notation is made "then and there in the peace of God and of our said Lord Proprietary being and then and there beat, wounded, evilly treated him the said John Rench, so that his life was dispaired of and then and there under the other injuries to him did to the great damage of him the said John Rench and against the peace of our said Lord the Proprietor, His good rule and government."

Cresap comes into Court represented by his attorney Daniel Dulany, Jr., denies his guilt, but puts himself "upon the County." A Jury was impaneled consisting of David Linn, William Pritchet, Uncle Uncles, Joseph Beall son of Ninian, Isaac Baker, Richard Beall, Zachariah Magruder, Nathaniel Magruder, Alexander Magruder, James Jack, William Norris and Matthew Markland. The Jury found him guilty as charged and he was fined one shilling.

Ordered by the Court that attachment of contempt issue against Nathaniel Curry "for not obeying the process of this Court heretofore served on him."

"Ordered by the Court that James Montgomery, who was committed last March for want of security for his appearance be discharged, nothing being objected against him."

Stephen Julian and John Beard, farmers, "special bail for a certain Thomas Douthit, ...bring into Court here the said Thomas and deliver him up. It is therefore ordered that the said Douthit be committed to the custody of the Sheriff there to remain until &c."

John Shroiner petitions the Court for a license to keep a house of entertainment. It is granted.

James Manson presents a petition to the Court as follows: "That a certain James Carson, who is an idiot now living with him [Manson], has some estate in Cecil County left him and being uncapable to act in the affair, your petitioner desires you to appoint him the Guardian to the said Carson." The Court does so.

The Court ordered the Clerk to write to Mr. Charles Ridgley "the presiding Justice of Baltimore County, to issue his warrant against John Metcaffe of that County for stealing a wigg said to be the property of Mr. Edward Dorsey and send him to Col. Wickham, one of the Justices of this Court, for examination."

Thomas Dobbs, who had been presented earlier, is brought to trial for stealing "with force and arms ....20 pares of women's necklaus of the value of 100 pounds of tobacco, 1,500 needles of the value of 100 pounds of tobacco, the goods and chattels of a certain Charles Conner." A Jury was impaneled, consisting of David Linn, William Pritchett, Uncle Uncles, Joseph Beall son of Ninian, Isaac Baker, Richard Beall, Zachariah Magruder, Nathaniel Magruder, Alexander Magruder, James Jack, Henry Beall and John Hallum — with two exceptions the same Jury as in the Cresap case above, p. 102. The Jury found Dobbs guilty.

The Court then sentenced Dobbs "to be set upon the pillory for the space of half an hour and afterward to be set to the whipping post and there receive on his bare body ten stripes well laid on and pay to Conner the value of the goods stolen."

John Hallum testified that Joseph Volgemot had "kept an ordinary and house of entertainment and in the same house publicly and commonly did sell and utter and did cause to be sold and uttered rum and other liquors unto divers of the good people of this Province and to the said John Hallum unknown."

Apparently Hallum, acting as an informer, expected to receive a reward for his services. This part of the charge reads as follows: "Whereas the said John Hallum prays remedy according to the form of the Act of Assembly in such cases and the said Joseph Volgemot forfeit and pay £10 current money, the one-half to His said Lordship, the other half to the said Hallum." Volgemot denies his guilt and pleads for a jury trial.

The same Jury as in the preceding case, except for John Radford's replacing Hallum, is impaneled and it finds Volgemot not guilty.

One Conrad Hickman sues Peter Smith for his freedom dues. The Court ordered Smith to pay Hickman his dues "(except the coat) and also give the said Hickman a set of smith's tools, sufficient to shew [shoe] a horse." They also awarded him his costs in the amount of 154 pounds of tobacco.

Thomas Sly asks for a renewal of his license for twelve months "for selling liquor," and the Court grants him a license.

"John Radford agrees with the Court to erect a pair of stocks in Frederick Town in consideration of 40 shillings to be levied in the next County levy."

"The Justices of the Court appoint Col. Thomas Cresap to agree with some merchant to send to England for the following weights and measures for the use of this County, to wit, a half bushel, a peck, a half-peck, a gallon pot, a half-gallon, quart, pint, half-pint, gill and half-gill pots of pewter, also the following weights, to wit, seven-pound, four-pound, two-pound, one-pound, half-pound, quarter-pound, two ounces, one-ounce, half-ounce, also an ell and one yard."

Thomas Richardson, accused of stealing "with force and arms 300 foot of walnut plank of the value of 300 pounds of tobacco from Ninian Beall, son of Ninian," was found not guilty and was dismissed.

Notley Thomas and James Hook, who had been appointed by the Court to lay out a road "from Touchstone Road by Alexander Jones's and to cross the Mountain by George Matthews and from thence to Frederick Town," report that they have laid out the road as ordered. They say that they have come over past George Matthews and from there into the Conococheague Road near Mr. Kimboll's and then on to Frederick.

"Ordered that mulatto Isaac his petition against John Barnard for his freedom be rejected."

"Ruled by the Court that no security be necessary for the estate of Thomas Lamar, deceased, it appearing to the Court that the orphans are all paid off."

In a suit by Mary Simms against John Charlton on a debt, several items in the account show prices at the time:
   $23\frac{1}{2}$ bu. of barley from Michael Risener at 3/6 ea.
   28 bu. of barley from John Beard at 3/- ea.
   31 bu. of barley from Frederick Unsell at 3/- ea.
   $3\frac{3}{4}$ bu. of malt from Thomas Palmore at 4/- ea.

Contemporary wage rates appear in a suit of William Flintham against John Beresford on a debt:
   1 day's work   2 sh.
   2 days' work of my horse   4 sh.
   2 days' threshing of barley 4 sh.

Further price comparisons may be found in the suit of Mark Kuhl against Jacob Beck on an account:

3 doz. pen knifes at 5 sh. per doz.	15 sh.
1 doz. pen knifes inlaid	8 sh.
1 doz. sissers	5 sh.
1 doz. rasors	8 sh.
1 dubble gross mettle buttons	18 sh.
1 gross of gartering	18 sh.
1 doz. worsted stockings at 50 sh. per doz.	£2/10/ -
1 doz. ink pots	4 sh.

The account sued on originated in Philadelphia. Kuhl made affidavit as to its accuracy before one Thomas Lawrence, a Philadelphia Justice of the Peace, whose official authority was in turn attested by one James Reed, Notary and Tabellion.

Thomas Cresap, administrator of William Griffith, sues Charles Higginbotham.

The Court set prices for liquors and accommodations for the ensuing year. The price of services remained approximately unchanged, but there were reductions in a number of liquor prices, including, for example, Maryland spirits distilled from grain, which had been 9 sh., 8d per gallon in 1748 and 8 sh. in 1751, now set at 6 sh. Peach brandy per gallon was reduced from the 1748 price of 13 sh., 4d to 10 sh. One item not previously listed was English strong beer now set at 1 sh., 6d per quart.

NOVEMBER COURT OF 1752

The November 1752 Court met on the third Tuesday and the 21st day of November. [15] The Justices present were: Nathaniel Wickham, Thomas Prather,

---

[15] The New Style calendar was instituted during the previous September. See above, pp. ix-x.

John Rawlins, William Griffith, Josiah Beall, Nathan Magruder, Alexander Beall, John Clagett, Henry Wright Crabb and John Needham.

The Grand Jurors were as follows: Basil Beckwith, foreman, William Wallace, Sr., Mathew Markland, James Lamar, Edward Crone, Thomas Logsdon, Samuel White, William Manson, Enock Enockson, Samuel Ellis, Edmund Rutter, Charles Bussey, Joseph Smith, Nathaniel Magruder, Jr., William Wheat, Sr., Thomas Hogg and William Davis.

Among the Jury's presentments were:
Michael Jones for selling liquor without a license "and suffering bad orders in his house."
John Jones for stealing a mare, the property of Josiah Hules.
Richard Watts "for an asalt on the Sabbath Day on Chr. Groom."
Martin Adams for "suffering and encouraging an asalt on Joseph Wilson, George Bussey, William Davis, John Sweat, Alexander Magruder and John Nelson at his house, being public housekeeper in Frederick Town."

Mary Perry petitions the Court to consider her helpless condition, "being so sickly as not able to help herself" and asks that the Court grant her "a little more toward her subsistence." They allow her 640 pounds of tobacco for her support to the next November Court.

The Justices appoint Captain John Middagh and Mr. Peter Butler "to agree with any person or persons for building a bridge over Linganore by Thomas Beatty's and order that they do not exceed the sum of £16 current money for the same."

William Luckett renews his contract with the Court to keep a ferry at Mouth of Monocacy.

"Ordered that the Sheriff take Benjamin Norris into custody for half an hour for misbehaving to the Court."

Sarah Garrison is tried before the Court for bastardy. She admits her guilt "and in open Court makes oath that a certain John Howard, son of Gideon, is the father of the bastard child aforesaid." Sarah is fined 30 shillings, which John Howard pays. The Court thereupon issues a bench warrant for Howard returnable immediately.

Howard appears in Court in answer to the bench warrant, pleads guilty and is fined thirty shillings.

John Jones of Elkridge, planter, gives bond for his later appearance in Court.

George Fee petitions the Court "that whereas he having had a sick man in his house a month and then died, I have buried same man in a Christian manner and begg Your Worships will allow me for this trouble." Fee presents a bill as follows:

For making a coffin	10/-
A sheet	12/-
33 days trouble I had with him in his sickness	£2/ -/-
Offset against this total	£3/ 2/-
By his wearing apparel	10/2
Balance due	£2/12/- [sic]

The Court orders that he be allowed that amount in the next County levy.

Dr. Charles Carroll presents a petition to the Court in which he emphasizes on his own behalf and behalf of others the importance of good roads. He asks that "a road be cleared and made a public road from the waggon road under the South Mountain about half a mile to the southward of the Meeting house[16] and to the northeast side of the plantation of Michael Risener and from thence to Mr. Ogle's sawmill and thence to Owens Creek about two miles below Mr. Ogle's house, and a little below the Mouth of Beaver Dam Branch, thence to Monocacy below the plantation of David Baily, thence through Mr. Munday's land to Great Pipe Creek about 20 perches to the northwest of the Mouth of Little Pipe Creek and crosses the said Great Pipe Creek unto the Fork between both and up the said fork to the main waggon road that leads to William Farquers as the same has been lately marked by Matthew Sparks at the instance and charge of your petitioner."

The Court rejected the petition.

"Robert Brightwell petitions the Court for a license to keep a tavern "within about five or six miles of Licking Creek."

The Court rejects his application.

Thomas Yates petitions the Court that he "is now 85 years of age and having no land of his own, his wife sixty-odd, and all the subsistence he has is from a son-in-law." He asks to be tax free.

The Court rejects his application.

Owen Humphrey appears before the Court and states that sometime past he had the misfortune to

---

16 This would appear to be a hitherto unknown fourth geographical reference to the old "Monocacy" Lutheran Church, in addition to and confirming the three references documented in my book, New Facts and Old Families, From the Records of Frederick County, Maryland (Redwood City, Calif., 1976), pp. 175 et seq. This part of Carroll's proposed road would have approximated today's Kelly's Store Road, which runs midway between (or approximately a half mile from both) Michael Reisner's GREEN SPRING plantation and SMITH'S LOT on which the church was undoubtedly located, as described and platted in my earlier book.

have "what few household goods he had consumed by fire.... and your petitioner being upwards of 60 years of age and not able to do any hard labor for the support of his family consisting of a wife and four small children and my wife's mother, a very old woman," therefore prays to be levy free in the future, which the Court grants.

William Norris states to the Court that for the past two years he has been overseer of the highways in the lower part of Marsh Hundred between the Marsh and Andietam. He then prays the Court to relieve him from the same. "The persons returned by me are Joseph Robinett, John McFaddin, William Norris and Joseph Tomlinson." Nothing further was done in the premises.

"Jacob Fry, a prisoner in the County goal [sic: gaol] now in Court, complains that Peter Butler, one of the Undersheriffs, beat and abused him in the said goal without any reasonable cause, whereupon at the request of the said Jacob Fry a summons is ordered issued returnable immediately for Mary Simms, Christopher Edelen, John Cary and Thomas Douthit to testify on behalf of the complainant which said evidences being sworn and having declared to the Court [what] they knew concerning the premises the Court are of the opinion [the complaint] is frivolous and idle."

"Ordered that Esther Matew and Esther Leach have the same allowance this year for their support that they had last year."

Sundry inhabitants petition the Court "that a bridge over Seneca Creek at the Middle Foard on the new road near Charles Trail would contribute much to the ease and happiness of the people who live above the said Creek, the said road being found by experience to be much nearer for rolling tobacco [cf. above, p. 20] than the other for those who live at the lower end of the County....we therefore pray that you will order a bridge to be built there at the County charge and that the same may be completed by June Court next which thereby renders it of great use and benefit to such of your petitioners as made tobacco above the said Creek, which are now for want of it obliged to be at the expense of cartage."

The Court rejected the petition.

Lucy Macbee was found guilty by confession and fined £3.

"Ordered by the Court that process do not issue against Susannah King for bastardy, Moses Shelby for a breach of the peace and Philip McGuire for concealing and swapping a horse belonging to Robert Buckle [they] not being to be found in the County."

George Bond who had been presented for breach of the Sabbath was dismissed but with no reason shown.

Jacob Beney who was presented for allowing gambling in his house on the Sabbath Day was not as fortunate. He was found guilty and was fined 200 pounds of tobacco for the breach of the Sabbath.

Henry Lazarus and Philip Coonce, both of whom had been charged with breach of the Sabbath, were each fined 200 pounds of tobacco.

Stephen Newton Chiswell was presented for neglect of duty as overseer of the highway for failure to clear "the new road." He was fined 500 pounds of tobacco for this failure to perform his duty.

Frederick Long who had been presented "for forcing into the house of Conrad Hogmire and misbehaving" and who was represented by Daniel Dulany, Jr., his attorney, "comes and it appearing to the Court that the presentment aforesaid is erronious it is thereupon

considered by the Court that the presentment aforesaid be quashed and the said Frederick Long discharged."

The charge against James Wallace, Jr., for
stealing a pig, the property of Nathaniel Magruder
was after three continuances, "struck off, the defendant being run away."

Zachariah Magruder had given bond for the appearance of James Wallace, Jr. He was brought into
Court and required to pay £20 as a forfeit for his failure to produce Wallace.

The case of Isaac Baker for stealing a colt of the
value of £5 "with force and arms" from Nathaniel Curry
was removed to the Provincial Court in Annapolis.

Charges against Zachariah Davis and Grace Cotterel who were charged with stealing corn from James
Lamar were, after one continuance, ordered struck
off, "the defendants being run away."

Thomas Dobb's petition for freedom dues which
had been referred to this Court is rejected.

George Becraft sues William Slade for slander.
Becraft, by his attorney Edward Dorsey, complains
"that whereas the aforesaid George is a good, true,
honest and faithful subject of our said Lord the King
that now is, and from the time of his natitivity as such
hitherto has behaved and governed himself and of good
name, fame, gesture, condition and honest conversa-
tion amongst good and brave men as of his own neighbors as other faithful subjects of the same Lord the
now King with whom the said George was known and
with whom the said George has acquaintance through
all the time aforesaid was known, had and reputed and
without any spot of falsity, theft, deceit or of any
other the like of or of any suspicion of the same hitherto untouched and unspotted hath remained and continues

112

by pretext of which said good name the said George great love, favour and good will of his neighbors and other subjects of our said Lord the King that now is, to himself not undeservedly procured and obtained. Nevertheless the said William not being ignorant of the premises, but minding and fraudulently intending the same George not only into scandal, reproach, vexation and infamy with his neighbors and other faithful subjects of our said Lord the King that now is to induce and bring the said George in Manifest danger of the punishment of paying fourfold the value of stolen and palling [paling] in the pillory and whipping so many stripes as the Court before whom the matters would be tried should adjudge. On the first day of June in the year of our Lord 1751 at Frederick County aforesaid in the presence and hearing of many of the liege and faithful subjects of our said Lord the King that now is, of and concerning the same George openly and publicly said and reported, made manifest and published in these English words following, to wit, 'George Becraft, the said George meaning, stole my beehive the beehive of him (the said William meaning) and I the said William will prove it' by pretext of same and publishing of which said false, scandalous and opprobrious English words he the said George not only in his good name, fame and estimation is grievously hurt and wronged, but also many of the liege subjects of our said Lord the King that now is by reason thereof from the company of the said George hath withdrawn, and daily more and more do withdraw to the damage of the said George in the sum of £50 current money and therefore he brings suit, &c."

In order to adjudge this heinous slander, a Jury of the following was impaneled: William Williams, John Middagh, John Hopkins, George Bussey, Benjamin Harris, Zachariah Magruder, Richard Beall, William Norris, James Gow, Nathaniel Magruder, James Jack and Daniel Thomas. The Jury found for the plaintiff and awarded him damages of £2/10 sh. current money. The Court also awarded Becraft $873\frac{3}{4}$

pounds of tobacco for his costs.

In a later suit in the November Court wherein Sarah Garrison sues George Becraft on a debt of £3/2/- for a cow he purchased from her in 1750/51, the Court found for the plaintiff and awarded her the amount sued for, together with $319\frac{1}{4}$ pounds of tobacco for her costs.

Robert Wilson, who is obviously a merchant of some sort, sues Mathew Markland on an account. The only interesting thing in the account rendered is the notation "for your wife's account formerly Ann Cramphin."

John Row, who is designated as a merchant, sues John Bell, Dutchman, on an account for goods sold. There is a notation on the account which states, "Then came Kennedy Farrell who sold the goods mentioned in the above account for John Row."

By way of interest, it is noted that John Row, merchant, enters suit against a number of his debtors, including Stephen Julian, Robert Mark and Michael Reisner.

Richard Smith sues Philip Kiefalper [Kefauver]. The case is struck off after four continuances.

A suit in this November Court shows the death of Evan Shelby, Sr., shortly before the convening of this Court. Apparently Shelby was a pioneer in the Hancock area.

In another suit against the administrators of Evan Shelby, Sr., there is exhibited an account for 6 stoavs [stoves?], £24.

Thomas Cresap, executor of Hugh Parker, sues George Croghan, merchant, for a debt of £15/14/10, which he is ordered by the Court to recover.

In a suit by William Cumming, Jr., who apparently was a merchant, against Robert Mark on an account there are several items of interest because of their prices:

1 padlock	3/6
1 pint of rum	1/3
1 snuff box	3/6
12 lbs. of sugar at 1/1d	13/-
1 double cap	3/-
7 yards damask at 6 sh.	£2/ 2/-
1 4-bladed knife	3/-

Joseph Belt, Jr., and Company sue Edward Burgess on an open account of £2/6/2.

William House and Andrew House, executors of John House, sue Adam Linn. The outcome is an agreement out of Court.

MARCH COURT OF 1753

The March Court of 1753 convened on the third Tuesday and the 20th day of March in the Second Year of His Lordship's Dominion.

The Justices present were Nathaniel Wickham, Gentleman, Chief Justice, Thomas Prather, John Rawlins, Henry Wright Crabb, Alexander Beall, Thomas Cresap, William Griffith, Joseph Wood, James Smith and William Webb, Gentlemen.

The Grand Jurors were Richard Beall, foreman, John West, John Jacobs, Charles Wood, Stephen Ransberg, Josiah Emmit, John Banks, Basil Williams, Samuel Cicell, John Banks, Jr., James Henthorn, James Taylor, Peter Rench, John Dowden, Peter Barrick, Elias DeLashmutt and Edmund Rutter.

The Grand Jury presented the following:
Thomas Carter "for taking away two guns by vilance

from Ninian Veach."

Joseph Mayhew "for a sault and battery of Andrew Baninger."

Mary Hartling, "the wife of John Hartling, for feloniously intermarrying with a certain Thomas Johnson, her first husband being then living in Frederick County."

Michael Miller petitions the Court for a license "to keep tavern on the wagon road which leads to York Town near the upper end of this County." The license is granted.

William Tenelly petitions the Court for a license "to keep public house of entertainment at Senicar Bridge at the house where Andrew Tanyhill lately lived." The Court grants him the license.

Basil Beall petitions for a license "to keep a house of entertainment at George Town," and it is also granted.

"Ordered by the Court here that Stephen Hampton for his trouble in keeping of Michael Hipsley from last November to this time and on his delivering the said Hipsley to the Justices of Prince George's County.... be allowed the sum of £3 current money in the next County levy."

"Ordered by the Court here that William Cooke for his indecent behavior to this Court be put in the stocks for half an hour."

In obedience to the directions of the Act of Assembly, the Rev. Mr. Barnet Michael Howsen brought into Court here Dorothy Margaret Hinen, a servant transported in this Province without indentures within six month last past and the said servant being so brought as aforesaid upon view being had of the said servant it is considered by the Court and they determine and adjudge that the said servant is of the age of 14 years."

"Ordered by the Court here that Col. Nathaniel Wickham and Honest Cooper, overseers of the roads from Hussey Foard to Smith's Branch and from Major Ogle's Foard to John Biggs' Foard on Monocacy, assist (with their male taxables) Daniel Pippinger, overseer of the road from Smith's Branch to Great Pipe Creek, in repairing the said road."

"Ordered by the Court here that Mary Hartline [Hartling] give security, that is, two securities, in the sum of £40 each, for her appearance at the next Provincial Court to be held at Annapolis on the second Tuesday of September next to answer the presentment by the Grand Jurors of this County for polygamy for want of which she is committed to the custody of the Sheriff, there to remain until, &c., who being present took charge of her accordingly."

"Alexander Beall, one of the Justices of the Court here, returns to the Court the following conviction and recognizance by him taken, to wit, I hereby certify that Christian Dickson was brought before me for having a baseborn child and on examination was found convicted of fornication and fined agreeable to Act of Assembly."

"John Rawlins, Gentleman, one of the Justices of the Court here, returns to the Court the following convictions and recognizances, to wit, Sarah Hivion[?] swore a child to John Jacobs the 31st day of January in 1753. John Jacobs bound to the Lord Proprietary for adultery, £5. Robert Lamar, son of Thomas, security for the said fine to keep the child of[f] the County."

"Mary Dunkin swore a child to John Jacobs the 1st day of February, 1753. John Jacobs bound to the Lord

117

HEMPSTEAD COUNTY LIBRARY
HOPE, ARKANSAS

Proprietary for adultery, £5. Ninian Beall and Michael Jones became sureties for the fine "to keep the child of[f] the County."

"Mary Conerly bound to the Lord Proprietary for having a baseborn child and not discovering the father, £3."

"Mary Robinson bound to the Lord Proprietary for having a bastard child and not discovering the father, £3."

"Ann Dickson Bound to the Lord Proprietary for having a bastard child, £1/10." William Tracy, Jr., is bound for the amount of the fine to keep the child off the County.

Dr. Richard Brooke sues George Beall on a debt, the outcome of which is not indicated.

In a suit by John Howard, son of Gideon, against David Forbes on an account, some of the items of interest were:

½-bushel of salt	3/-
½-bushel of flower	1/6
50 lbs. of pork	12/6
3 bushels of corn at 3 sh. ea.	9/-
7½ lbs. of bacon at 8d	5/-
1 grubbing hoe	7/6
6 quarts of wheate flower	-/9
For the milk of one cow, one summer	10/-
1000 pins	2/2
1 pair men's shoes	10/-
2 pairs of women's shoes at 8/6 each	17/-

John Rice sues Martin Wetsel on a note in the amount of £46 current money. Wetsel is required to give special bond, and the bondsmen are Jacob Bonet and Melker Wise. The Court awards Rice his £46 and 297 pounds of tobacco for his costs.

Dr. Charles Carroll sues Jacob Fry "for the use of Frederick Onsell and George Loy, executors of Francis Wise."

JUNE COURT OF 1753

The June Court of 1753 met on the third Tuesday and the 19th day of June in the third year of His Lordship's Dominion.

The Justices were: Nathaniel Wickham, Chief Justice, Thomas Prather, John Rawlins, John Claget, William Webb, William Griffith, Henry Wright Crabb, Joseph Wood and Joseph Smith.

Josiah Beall, Gentleman, was Sheriff. He brought together the following Grand Jurymen: Thomas Fletchall, Samuel Cicel, Alexander Magruder, William Wilson, James Holmeard, Jr., Michael Jones, Alexander Pearee, Jacob Kellor, John Johnson, Nicholas Johnson, William Chambers, Lancelot Wilson, James Walling, James Gilliland, Enoch Enochs, John Dowden and Stephen Hickman.

The Grand Jury presented the following:
John Avey and Adam Hufman for assaulting Edward Dunfield and his wife, by information of Elizabeth Dunfield.
John Elliott for feloniously stealing a sheep from John Dowden.
Edward Dunfield for "selling of beare at the rate of 6d per quart by information of John Avey."

Edward Dunfield petitions the Court stating that since he is "living on a public road, he is desirous of keeping tavern." The Court granted him a license.

Mary Edwards petitions the Court "that her husband James Crumton Edwards grossly abuses her in such manner as can be made apeir [appear] and has turned her out a dores [out of doors] and say she shall not live with him.... if Your Worships would take into consideration to alowe your petitioner maintenance of the said James Edwards' estate...."

The Court rejects the petition.

Certain unnamed inhabitants petition the Court to erect bridges over Seneca Creek and Bennet's Creek at points which they designate. The decision of the Court is "that the Clerk send directions to the several over-seers of the roads contiguous to the fords above-mentioned to meet at the said fords with all their male taxables and make bridges over the Creeks aforesaid."

Charles Neale presents a petition in which he "sheweth that your petitioner has been claimed by Mathew Edwards as a servant under pretence of an indenture which your petitioner humbly insists is void, that your petitioner is still detained in the service of the said Edwards although your petitioner is entitled to his freedom." The Court issued a summons returnable immediately for Edwards and upon hearing both sides of the case ordered that "the aforesaid Neale be absolutely free and discharged from the service ot the said Edwards and that he recover against Edwards his costs and charges."

John Hufman brings in a servant woman "to be adjudged for runaway time and brings in an account of £6/15/- current money, which he swears in open Court he was at in regaining her to his service and for the charge of a midwife," whereupon the Court decided that "the time the said servant has served from April to May is a sufficient recompense for the runaway time" and rejects the charges.

In a criminal suit of the Lord Proprietary against Abraham Trotter, charged with stealing "with force and arms one hand gun of the value of 500 pounds of tobacco," the property of Charles Carroll, Trotter claims his innocence and a jury is impaneled as follows: Samuel Beall, Sr., Conrad Hogmire, Solomon Turner, William Wheat, Robert Brightwell, Jonathan Hagar, John Hopkins, Thomas Harris, Richard Beall, David Foutz, James Jack and Nathaniel Beall. The jury found Trotter guilty and the Court ordered that "he be set upon the pillory for the space of one hour and that afterwards he be set to the whipping post and there receive on his bare body 30 lashes well laid on.... according to the Act of Assembly in such cases late made and provided." The Court also ordered him to pay to Charles Carroll 1,600 pounds of tobacco and give him back the gun.

"Samuel Beall in Court here swears that Daniel Carroll told him that he would remit Abraham Trotter's fourfold [fine] provided the said Abraham Trotter was sold out of the said Carroll's neighborhood."

"Mary Price aged (as it is said) one year and 8 months is here bound unto Richard Smith until she arrives at the age of 16 years. The said Richard Smith promises to cause the said Mary to be learned to read distinctly in the Bible and at the expiration of her time of servitude to give her freedom dues agreeable to Act of Assembly."

"Ordered by the Court that Mr. George Gordon, late Sheriff of this County, pay unto Mr. Josiah Beall, the present Sheriff, the sum of £56/18/4 current money, it being the balance due from him to the inhabitants of this County."

"Ordered by the Court here that Mr. Josiah Beall, Sheriff, pay unto Capt. Henry Wright Crabb the sum of 30 shillings, it being due to him for erecting a pair of stocks at Lawrence Owen's."

"Ordered that Richard Richardson, who is overseer of the main road from Frederick Town to Ballinger's Branch, clear the streets of the said town and keep them in good order."

John Avey and Adam Hufman, who were indicted for assault on Edward Dunfield and his wife, were required to give bond for good behavior for six months.

Justice John Clagett, apparently sitting alone, convicts Susannah King "for having one bastard child begotten in fornication." Thomas Clagett gives bond of £30 for "keeping Ann King, bastard child of Susannah King from being chargeable to the County."

Memorandum made the 22nd day of June in 1753: Susannah Apple, Peter Stilly and George Matthews of Frederick County executed "a writing obligatory in the sum of £31/0/6 to be paid unto Margaret Shelman, Susannah Fout, Baltus Fought, Jacob Fought and Catharine Fought" on condition that Susannah Apple pay to the above-named "their respective parts of their deceased father Baltus Fought's estate."

George Gordon, George Reed and John Clagett entered into an obligation of £133/1/5 to be paid to Robert and Bennett Wood, Charity Wood, Juda Wood, Jennet Wood and Stephen Wood on condition that George Reed pay to the above-named their respective parts of the estate of their deceased father Jacob Wood.

AUGUST COURT OF 1753

The August Court of 1753 met on the third Tuesday and the 21st day of August in the third year of His Lordship's Dominion. The Justices were Nathaniel Wickham, Jr., Joseph Wood, William Webb, Nathan Magruder, Henry Wright Crabb, William Griffith, Joseph Smith, John Rawlins and Thomas Cresap.

The Grand Jurors were William Williams, foreman, Thomas Fletchall, Mathew Markland, Charles

122

Jones, Benjamin Perry, Robert Beall son of Ninian, Christian Barrick, Samuel Cissell, William Erwin, Moses Chapline, Mesach Hyatt, Michael Jones, Edwin Rutter, James Downey, Benjamin Biggs, Charles Hedges and John Dowden.

The Grand Jury made several presentments:
Richard Watts "as Constable for assaulting and beating James Worfford, Jr., with a club."
William Luckett "for denying set[t]ing John West, Jr., over Monockesey Ferry without pay and likewise stopped his horse for the pay."

The petition of Mary Newkirk "sheweth that your petitioner sometime ago left a child in the care of one Christian Miller which was sometime after bound to John Huffman without the consent or knowledge of your petitioner. She therefore humbly prays Your Worships to order her said child to be returned to her. Upon reading this petition, nothing further was done in the premises."

"Sundry inhabitants of Potomac Hundred, Upper Part, petition the Court as follows....The petition of the new settlers on the draft of Senica humbly sheweth that from want of an highway from Monockesey new road to that leading to Capt. Henry Crabb's several of Your Honors' petitioners and others are obliged to roll their tobacco out of the County to the prejudice of the same. We therefore humbly crave that Your Honors will grant an order for the laying out of one to begin at the head of the Back Branch unto ditto Capt. Crabb's Road in distance about three miles."
The Court rejects the petition.

Daniel Davis, John Shroiner, Michael Stump, Mary Simms, Jacob Baney and Kennedy Farrell were all granted renewals of their licenses to operate taverns in Frederick Town. So also was Michael Jesserong, presumably also in Frederick Town.

"James Smith, Gentleman, in Court here qualifies as an attorney of the Court by taking the several oaths prescribed by Act of Assembly to be taken by the Government as also the oath of office subscribing the oath of abjuration and repeating and signing the test."

Samuel Thomas was fined one shilling "for abusing the Court."

William Luckett was acquitted of the charge preferred by John West, above.

"Martin Kern, a German aged 7 years (as it is said) is by the Court here bound to John Brunner till he arrives to the age of 21 years, and the said John Bruner obliges himself to learn him to read and write Dutch."

"Cathrine Hartline, aged one year the 25th of July last (daughter of Mary Hartline who is run away), is by the Court here bound to John Burton till she becomes 16 years of age."

In a suit of the Lord Proprietary against Negro Toby, the slave of Elias DeLashmutt who was brought into Court on a bench warrant for striking George Baxter, the following notation closes the case: "Whereupon the premises being seen.... it is considered by the Court that the said Negro be discharged and that the fees arising hereon be charged to the County."

"Adam Huffman is required to give bond for £20 as proof that he will keep the peace and be of good behavior to all His Majesty's subjects for the space of six months from the date hereof."

Casper Meyer sues Bartholemew Jesserang on a debt. After numerous imparlances, the case came to trial at this Court. "But the said Casper Meyer, although solemnly called, comes not but makes default nor does he further prosecute his writ.... Therefore it is considered that the said Casper Meyer take nothing by his writ but be in mercy for his false clamour and the said Bartholemew go thereof without day &c."

In a suit dated July 30, 1751 at Lancaster [Pennsylvania] of Francis Fortnee against Michael Jesserang on a debt, sundry items in an account are listed:

6 brass kettles
3 brass panns
2 brass watter bolls [bowls?]
12 panns (ironware)
6 fryan panns
50 witt [whet]stones at 1 sh.
6 hand saws at 6 sh.
3 lampes at 2 sh.
50 glasses at 9d each

The account is notarized in Lancaster County. Referees were appointed who found for the plaintiff.

Jacob Belt, Jr., & Company enter suit against Joseph Gray on an open account, which contains these items:

3 snuff boxes	4/6
3 large silk handkerchiefs	£1/2/6
2 pair shoe buckels	3/-
3 yards plain ribbon at 3/9	11/3
1 pair women's white kid gloves	4/2
1 silk bandanna handkerchief	8/4

Ninean Beall son of Ninian sues Daniel James, blacksmith, on a debt of £10/3/8½.

NOVEMBER COURT OF 1753

The November Court of 1753 met on the third Tuesday and the 20th day of November in the third year of His Lordship's Dominion. The Justices present were: Nathaniel Wickham, Jr., William Griffith, Alexander Beall, William Webb, Thomas Prather, John

Rawlins, John Claggett, Joseph Wood, Henry Wright Crabb and Joseph Smith.

Josiah Beall, Gentleman, was Sheriff and John Darnell was still Clerk. The Grand Jury included Thomas Fletchall, foreman, Enoch Enochs, William Offutt, John Jacobs, Robert Downey, Thomas Johnson (Kittock [= Catoctin]), Robert Lee, William Boyd, John Dowden, Peter Barrick, James Lamar, William Norris, Jr., John Perrin, James Smith, Elias DeLashmutt, John Hook and Benjamin Kelly.

Among the Grand Jury's presentments:
Jeremiah Prather, Jonathan Browning and Benjamin Browning "for forcing into the plantation of John Davis and likewise assaulting the said Davis son of Charles."
Samuel Emmitt and Agness Emmitt for assaulting John Emmitt, Constable.
Joseph Earls for "philonesly [feloniously] picking and stealing of appels from John Tyson."
John Barrisford for assaulting John Brown.
John Brown for assaulting John Barrisford.
Jacob Sturm, Sr., "for driving a loaded wagon into Frederick Town on the Sabbath Day."
Robert Strawbridge "for philonesly stealing of a pig, the property of Elias DeLashmutt, on information of the said DeLashmutt and Moses Harding."[17]
John Brook McCain "for philonesly stealing a snuff box, the property of Archibald Henderson."

George Bennett petitions the Court to the effect that for the past three years it had allowed him 1,000 pounds of tobacco for his support and he now asks that they make him a small additional allowance. They do

---

[17] Robert Strawbridge, founder of Methodism in Maryland, allegedly did not preach at Sam's Creek, then in Frederick County, until 1766 or in Frederick Town until 1772.

so by allowing him 1,200 pounds of tobacco in the next levy.

Mary Perry petitions the Court that she is so helpless that she asks the Court to continue its last year's grant of £6 currency. However, the Court cut this to £4.

The Vestry of Prince George's Parish petitions the Court as follows: "....that Your Worships please to allow them two pounds of tobacco per pole [poll] on the taxables that are in the County aforesaid belonging to the said Parish, towards defraying the charges of the aforesaid Parish." The Court orders that the same be granted.

Samuel Selby petitions the Court to the effect that he was appointed Constable in the year 1752 and attended the Quarters in his Hundred once a month in order to prevent the tumultuous meetings of Negroes. As he did not make oath of his attendance, he has not any allowance for so doing and he prays such an allowance now. The Court rejects his prayer.

"The Vestry of All Saints Parish petition the Court "that Your Worships would levy on the taxables of this Parish the quantity of 5 pounds of tobacco per tax [able poll] in order to defray the prorocal [parochial] charge of said Parish." The Court orders the levy to be made.

Daniel Davis petitions the Court "that some time in October there came a poor woman to his house and was taken ill and after a long spell of sickness she died. Your petitioner prays that he may be allowed his amount on the levy." The bill which he presents is for Mrs. Barbara Forricor and the items are for 36 days attendance during sickness at 2 shillings per day and for making a coffin and finding a sheet at £1.
The Court grants him a total of £4/12 sh.

Michael Dowden petitions the Court "that your petitioner petitioned Your Worships for an allowance for keeping a poor woman in her sickness. Your Worships rejected the petition. He prays You'l consider his case anew."

The Court allows him £3 current money in the next levy.

Joseph Linn, overseer of the roads of Kinnoloway [Tonoloway] Hundred, states that "he has about twenty miles of very bad road to open and to make and can't raise but about ten hands for to finish it, which is impossible for him to do or to accomplish with such few hands. Therefore I hope that Your Worships will take it into consideration."

They reject his petition.

Dr. Philip Lynham petitions the Court that "by the late honorable November Court your petitioner was adjudged £5 for the salivating of a certain Rebecca Deparmi and received no satisfaction. Therefore begs relief and will always pray."

The Court rejected the petition.

Richard Cooke petitions the Court as follows: "Your petitioner having rented a plantation formerly in the possession of one Stephen Julian that Your Worships about two years ago gave orders for the clearing of a new road through the above plantation at the request of Stephen Julian which was never cleared till last July. Your petitioner prays that Your Worships will order the old road to be cleared again, that being farr the best which all my neighbors are willing to attest not only the new road being a great damage to me by destroying one whole field and as not having the liberty of clearing any more ground. The old road is a leavel piece of ground and not twenty yards farther. The new road is one entire hill and so full of grubbs [stumps] that it is dangerous to travel. I hope Your Worships will take it into your serious consideration

128

and give orders for the old road again."

The Court decides to grant the petition.

Thomas Shlaye [Schley] petitions the Court for a license to sell liquor for six months, and it is granted.

"The Grand Jury discharged from this present service and allowed 400 pounds of tobacco in the next County levy."

"Capt. Thomas Prather in behalf of Mrs. Mary Simms agrees with the Court [for her] to beat the drum and clean the Court House from this time to the end of next November Court in consideration of 35 shillings current money to be allowed in that year's levy."

John Elliot is presented in Court charged with stealing a ewe of the value of 100 pounds of tobacco. Elliot denies his guilt and demands a jury trial. A jury is impaneled as follows: David Linn, Hugh Riley, Stephen Newton Chizwell, Charles Coates, William Brashears, Benjamin Harris, John Hopkins, Solomon Turner, William Offutt son of William, James Offutt, Alexander Waddle and Robert Lazenby. The jury finds Elliot guilty and the Court orders that he be taken by the Sheriff "to the whipping post and given ten lashes on his bare body well laid on and sat him for the space of one half hour in the pillory and that execution thereof be done immediately."

Richard Watts, charged with two cases of breach of peace, is found guilty by submission [he pleads guilty] and in each case is fined one shilling.

Joseph Chapline sues Thomas Gilliland on a debt "for going to [Upper] Marlborough and bearing my own expense £5/8 sh." The Court appoints a referee who awards the amount sued for to Chapline.

James Walker sues Mathew Howard on an open

account, and the items I find interesting include:

½-lb. of all spice	1/6
1 hour glass	2/-
1 candle stick	1/6
1 funnel	1/6
1 pair of knee buckles	1/6
1 pair strong boots	£3/-/-
1 stick seal wax	1/-
1 home chamber pot	2/6
1 sauce pan	1/8
1 yard white flannel	4/6
Large vial menill epitham[18] for your wife	4/6
Red precipitet [19]	2/6
6 doses Jesuits bark[20] powder	6/-
Digest tincture	3/6

In a suit by John Worthington vs. Mathew Howard on an account which originated in Baltimore County in 1751, the price of Indian corn is shown as 3 shillings per bushel.

In a suit on behalf of John Philpot and Edward Lee of London against Bigger Head the account or debt is listed as follows: "To Mr. Bigger Head of Maryland for his draft on me dated June 30, 1737 payable to Henry Boteler for £5/18/6." Referees were appointed but there is no record of the outcome.

William and Andrew House, executors of John House, sue Michael Reisner on a debt due House's estate.

---

[18] Epithem: any external topical application to the body other than ointments and plasters; a poultrice.
[19] Red precipitate or mercuric oxide, used in ointments for diseases of the skin and affections of the eyelids.
[20] Cinchona or Peruvian bark: a source of quinine.

Andrew Hoover[21] sues Alexander Waddal on a promissory note in the amount of £1/19/6.

A new list of appointments of Constables for the various Hundreds includes:

William Wallace, Jr.	Potomac Hundred, Lower Part
Daniel Kennedy	Potomac Hundred, Upper Part
George Darby	Newfoundland Hundred
Archibald Beall	Ibid., Lower Part
Joseph Wheat	Rock Creek Hundred Middle Part
Henry Hickman	Sugarland Hundred
John Riley	Sugar Loaf Hundred
John Prather	Linganore Hundred
William Carmack	Manor Hundred
William MacCubbin	Burnt House Woods Hundred
George Soope	Pipe Creek Hundred
William House	Kittocton Hundred
John Vandever	Andietum Hundred
John Swan	Marsh Hundred
Joseph Volgamot	Salisbury Hundred
John Jack	Conococheague Hundred
James Crabtree	Linton Hundred
Thomas Wilson	Monocacy Hundred, Upper Part
John Rightsman	Monocacy Hundred, Middle Part
John Jacobs	Monocacy Hundred, Lower Part
Thomas Price	Frederick Town Hundred

The following roads and overseers were designated by the Court:

From Captain John's Bridge to Lawrence Owen's and from thence down to Rock Creek Bridge beyond Caleb Litton's and from thence to Rock Creek Bridge near James Smith's and from Lawrence Owen's to a bridge over Rock Creek by Peter Butler's plantation: William Oneall.

From Monocacy Ferry to Ballingers Branch and from the Main Road that leads to Mouth of Monocacy to

---

[21] Ancestor of President Herbert C. Hoover.

131

the ford commonly called Powel's Ford and all the roads that lye between Ballingers Branch and the Potomac River that leads to the top of Kittocton Mountain and the new road that leads from the top of the Gap of Kittawkin by George Matthews to Ballingers Branch: George Gump.

The road called the River Road, Touchstone Road and the road that leads from Alexander Jones to the top of Kittocton that leads to Frederick Town: Abraham Lakin.

From the top of Kittocton Mountain to the top of Shanandore and the road that leads from the top of Kittocton to Shanandore by Richard Touchstone's and from the top of Kittocton to the top of Shanandore that leads by John George's from the road that leads out of John George's road that leads by Robert Evans' to the top of Shanandore: Richard Smith.

From Hussey's Ford to Smith's Branch: William Barrack.

From Smith's Branch to Great Pipe Creek and then to John Digges' Works: Paul Woolf.

From Major Ogle's Ford to John Biggs' Ford on Monocacy: Samuel Swearingen.

From Great Pipe Creek to the temporary [Pennsylvania] line: Andrew Hull.

From the temporary line to William Ambrose's: Samuel Emmit.

From Ambrose's Mill to Abraham Miller's Mill: Felty Vantrees.

From Abraham Miller's Mill till it intersects the nearest main road to Frederick Town: Peter Balsel.

From Frederick Town to Richardson's and to the new ford and from Town to Peter Apple's and from Town to Dulany's Mill: Patrick Doran.

From Frederick Town to the top of Kittocton and from Town to Reynold's Ford and from Town to Abraham Miller's Mill and from Town to Jacob Peck's Fulling Mill and the new road from Ballinger's Branch into the road that leads from Frederick to Conococheague near John Kimbol's: Christian Thomas.

MARCH COURT OF 1754

The March Court of 1754 met on the third Tuesday and the 19th day of March in the third year of Frederick, Lord Baltimore's Dominion.

The Justices were the Worshipful Nathaniel Wickham, Jr., Alexander Beall, John Rawlins, William Webb, Thomas Prather, Henry Wright Crabb, Joseph Wood, William Griffith and Thomas Beatty. Samuel Beall was Sheriff and John Darnall was Clerk.

The Grand Jury included Thomas Stoddart, foreman, Charles Jones, Thomas Fletchall, James Gilliland, Samuel Cissell, David Jones, Matthias Stalcup, John Hooke, Thomas Clagett, Archibald Edmonston, James Edwards, Ignatius Perry, Mark Whitacre, Thomas Odell, James Henthorn, Nicholas Johnson, Jonathan Hagar, Thomas Hogg and Henry Keene.

Presentments of the Grand Jury included:
Henry Meroney for keeping an "unlawful measure at his mill."
Arthur Charlton for "selling peach brandy at 4d per gill."
Samuel Swearingen for "going into the house of John Beard and taking from thence one hone."
Isaac Eltinge for "selling liquor on the Sabbath Day."
William Summers for "striking Benjamin Price on the Sabbath Day."
Louisa Martin, "the wife of John Martin, Jr., for murdering Ester Winright, servant to John Martin."

"The Justices appoint Samuel Farmer, Jr., overseer of the roads in the Forks of Haling's and Snowden's River in the room of John Purdum, who is run away."

The Court appoints "Messrs. John Rawlins and William Griffith to view the place where the bridge was

133

built at Eltinge's Mill and carried away and to appoint a place where the same may now be rebuilt."

The Court appoints Mrs. Elizabeth Donaldson guardian of John Donaldson DeButts, a minor, on giving security according to law. "The Court approves Dr. Richard Cooke and Robert Perle as security for the filial part or portion of John Donaldson DeButts, son of Robert DeButts, deceased, for Elizabeth Donaldson, his guardian."

Ann Stonar makes choice of Benedict Esleman for her guardian "which he accepts of and the Court appoints him guardian to Benedict and Henry Stoner, sons of Jacob Stonar, deceased."

"Ordered that unless Richard Beall repair the bridge over Rock Creek by Caleb Litton's by the last day of April next that his bond be put in suit."

The Court appoints Messrs. John Rawlins and William Griffith to view the scales and weights at Rock Creek warehouse.

John Pearce petitions the Court as follows: "Whereas your petitioner at divers times past lost the use of his limbs being thereby not able to subsist without being the object of charity beggs Your Worships to have the same regard for him You have for others in the like distress, desire You will order some skillful physician and subsistence to make a cure so that he is able to get his living.
"Upon reading which petition, the Court agrees with Dr. George Jacob Troutwine, present here in Court, that he the said Troutwine shall accomodate the said John Pearce and cure him of his disorder for and in consideration of the sum of £3 for his accomodation and £5 for the cure and in case he does not cure him then he agrees to be paid only the £3 for his accomodation."

John Trundle petitions the Court "that he has lost the sight of his eyes for a long time past and has been with Dr. Hamilton and sundry others for help and with great fatigue and expense finds no benefit, has a wife and three small children and has no way to support them so prays Your Worships will take his case in consideration in letting him be levy free and making him some allowance from the County as Your Worships shall seem meet.

The Court ordered that Trundle be levy-free for the future and "that he be allowed one shilling in the next County levy as a pension."

Joseph Williams of Conocogeague, "living at a very public place and has all convenience for keeping a house of entertainment," requests a license therefor, which is granted.

Robert Whitwall is charged in Court as follows: "That on the 26th day of December, 1752....with force and arms in and upon a certain Anne Parker, spinster, an assault did make and her the said Anne did then and there carnally know, the said Robert then and there being a single man and unmarryed and with her the said Anne then and there the crime of fornication did commit by means whereof the said Anne was afterwards, to wit, on the 26th day of September 1753 delivered of a bastard male child at Frederick County against the peace of the said Lord Proprietary, His good rule and government, and contrary to the form of the Act of Assembly in such cases late made and provided."

Whitwall pleads not guilty and a jury is impaneled as follows: Alexander Magruder, Alexander Perry, Hugh Riley, James Rimmer, Nathaniel Magruder, William Fee, Samuel Wade Magruder, Thomas Whitten, George Beall, Jr., Samuel Plummer, John Plummer and Ezekiel Gosling. The jury finds him guilty as charged. He is fined 30 shillings and is obliged to give bond to the amount of £40 with sureties that the child shall never become a public charge.

George Mason and [the Ohio] Company sue Catherine and Evan Shelby, administrators of Evan Shelby, on a debt which is indicated as to George Mason and the Ohio Company. The item is dated July 3, 1750 "to one peice of Tandem Holland No. 50" and the price is £4/15 sh. The verdict was "judgment when assets" [come to the now depleted estate]. Thomas Cresap certified as follows, "That I have examined and compared the above account with the books belonging to George Mason and the Ohio Company and find it to be a true copy."

In a suit of John Buchanan and John Graham against Benjamin Harris on an account, Harris is given credit for hogsheads of tobacco delivered to the plaintiffs and numbered as follows:

No. 217 1,080 lbs.
         - 62 "
       1,018 lbs.⎤
No. 218 1,106 lbs.⎬ 2,062 lbs. at 14 sh.   £14/ 8/8
         - 62 " ⎥
       1,044 lbs.⎦
No. 219 1,108 lbs. second tobacco at 9 sh.   4/14/2
         - 62 "
       1,046 lbs.
(Prices are per 100 lbs.)

Dr. Philip Lynham sues Robert Davis on an account for services rendered, including as the principal item "for curing your son of the yaws as per agreement, £5."

Christopher Lowndes and Company sue Thomas Stoddert on an open account in which certain items are stated in current money and others in sterling. The totals of the two columns are shown as £2/19/9 current money and £15/17/0½ sterling, respectively. The sterling total is then restated as 3,804½ pounds of tobacco at the rate of 8 sh. 4d per 100 pounds of tobacco.

Henry Feer [Fehr, Fuhr] is sued by Zacharias Shugart on a promissory note. The Sheriff is instructed by the Court to "take Henry Fuhr, late of Frederick County, carpenter, otherwise called Henry Fehr of York Town in the County of Lancaster in the Province of Pennsylvania, carpenter, "and deliver him into Court." Feer, by his attorney Edward Dorsey, pleads that he cannot be held on the note because at the time he executed it he was under 21 years of age. The Court agrees and the suit is dropped.

In a suit by Patrick Creagh vs. John Radford on an open account an item credited to the account is:
4 pistoles [coins] at 26 sh. ea.   £5/ 4/-

Andrew Reid and John Stewart, trading as Reid and Stewart, sue Thomas Thompson, Jr., on a debt of 5,000 pounds of inspected tobacco.

Peter Butler sues Henry Cameron, blacksmith, on a debt of £5/18/9 and secures from the Court an order of attachment. Kennedy Farrell, John Kimbol, John Charlton and Christopher Edelen appraise the assets of Cameron as follows:

1 black and 1 red cow	£4/10/-
1 grindstone and axle tree of iron	2-/-
1 pair of steelyards	10/-
6 smith's hammers	17/-
7 pair smith's tongs	9/-
Sundry shoeing tools	13/-
1 vice and screwplate	15/-
1 small pot and bell	7/6

In succeeding appraisals the following items are added:

1 pair smith's bellows	4/ -/-
1 smith's anvil weighing 138#	6/18/-
A servant lad named Jacob Doup, aged 18 years, having three	

years and 6 months from the
25th day of December 1753 to
serve   8/ 1/-
1 iron stove with 5 plates   2/15/-

JUNE COURT OF 1754

The June Court of 1754 met on the third Tuesday
and the 18th day of June in the 4th year of Frederick,
His Lordship's Dominion.

The Worshipful Justices present were Nathaniel
Wickham, Thomas Prather, John Rawlins, Joseph
Wood, William Griffith, Thomas Beatty, William
Webb, Joseph Smith, Thomas Cresap and Alexander
Beall.

The Grand Jurors included Thomas Stoddert, fore-
man, Charles Jones, Elias DeLashmutt, Samuel Cis-
sell, Michael Legatt, John Baker, Frail Pain, Aaron
Prather, Michael Jones, Hugh Thomas, James Coffee,
John Swearingen, Jr., William Campbell, Richard
Wells and John Carmack.

Their indictments included:
James Hook "for striking Samuel Jacobs."
Anne Russell for bastardy.
Maudlin Friscus "for striking Mary Hance Steel-
man."
Jacob Mason "for keeping faulse, measures at his
mill."

Thomas Hinton, declaring to the Court that he
lives "on the Main Road between Frederick Town and
Lawrence Owen's," applies for a license to keep a
public house, but the Court rejects his application.

Mary Smith petitions the Court that "her son H.
Keene is bound to Joseph Williams who uses him very
ill" and prays a summons for the said Williams to an-

swer her charge. The Court rejects her petition.

"The Court appoints James Dickson, Peter Butler, John Charlton and Christopher Edelin or any two or three of them to lay out a road from Frederick Town to the late plantation of Abraham Miller."

Elias DeLashmutt and Arthur Nelson, who were bail for Alexander Barrett, deliver him up "in discharge of themselves." The Court orders that Barrett "be committed to the custody of the Sheriff until &c."

When the case against Robert Strawbridge, who was charged with stealing a pig, was called up after one continuance, it was ordered struck off, "defendant being run away." [Cf. above, page 126.]

Likewise in the suit against Jacob Storum, Sr., for driving a wagon on the Sabbath Day, after one continuance the presentment was quashed and Storum was discharged after paying a fee.

William Summers, who was tried for striking Benjamin Price on the Sabbath Day, was fined one shilling for his offense.

John Smith Prather, on trial for striking Benjamin Price on the Sabbath Day, was fined one shilling for his offence.

John Smith Prather on trial for assaulting Samuel Thomas on the highway denies his guilt but throws himself on the mercy of the Court and is fined £5 current money.

Thomas Aubrey on behalf of the Lord Proprietary sues John Wilcoxen, Jr., claiming that Wilcoxen had appropriated a servant of Aubrey's by the name of Elizabeth Magess and he sues for 28,000 pounds of tobacco. After several continuances, referees are appointed who decide that the servant is the property of Wilcoxen and "that the plaintiff has no right or title to her," ordering Aubrey to pay 1,715½ pounds of tobacco to Wilcoxen for his costs.

Several suits by Dr. Philip Lynham for medical services rendered have resulted from his failure to collect his bills. Here now is a suit by Henry Maroney against Dr. Lynham for 18 months board at £20 per annum, or £30 total. The suit, however, allows credit for certain medical attention and cash paid. Obviously Dr. Lynham was not in very good financial circumstances, probably because of his inability to collect for his services.

Dr. Lynham sues Henry Maroney and wife Rachel executrix of Samuel Duvall, deceased. The suit, for £2/5/6, is struck off without collection.

In several suits against Dr. Lynham, the opposing attorneys come into Court to enter a plea, always granted, that Dr. Lynham be required to give bond so that in the event he loses the case there would be no question about their ability to collect. Since Dr. Lynham was evidently unable to raise those bonds, he was forced to drop the suits and pay something to the other side for costs. This is an interesting counterploy.

In a suit of Benjamin Levy against Alexander Lamar on an account there is an item for "1 lb. of coffee delivered to Eleanor Ross by your order, 3 shillings." The total debt is £3/3/5 which is converted into 600 pounds of tobacco "at 10 sh. per 100 lbs."

A suit by Peter Barrick against Christian Barrick is marked "after two continuances abated by the death of the plaintiff."

Michael Jesserong in a suit against Daniel Jesserong for a debt of £18/19/4 secures an attachment on goods appraised at £24/2/11. Some of the items belonging to Daniel Jesserong were appraised as follows:

4 small looking glasses	9/-
Parcel of coloured thread	7/-
3 small combs	2/6
Parcel of curtain rings	2/-
4 doz. finger rings	3/-
14 Dutch pipe stems	3/-
5 pairs stockings	15/-
$5\frac{1}{2}$ yards of coarse diaper	11/-
One-quart decanter	3/-
$9\frac{3}{4}$ lbs. of pewter	20/-
A cow and calf	60/-

The Court turned over this confiscated property to Michael Jesserong and he binds himself to the Court, if the debt is ever paid, to return it to Daniel Jesserong, who had supposedly "removed in a secret manner from the place of his abode." The specific wording reads: "If the said Daniel Jesserang at any time within a year and a day to be computed from the time of obtaining the above attachment shall come and discount the demand of him the said Michael Jesserong in the attachment above contained by the Court adjudged according to Act of Assembly above mentioned...."

Hans Zimmerman through his attorney James Smith sues William Baker on two notes whose wording is of interest. One reads, in part, "....I promise him the aforesaid sum to pay from this day two years hence with the interest for every pound one shilling per a year and if the said Hans Zimmerman desire an English bond, then I will give him one according to law that I acknowledge, witness my hand and seal."

AUGUST COURT OF 1754

The August Court of 1754 met on the third Tuesday and the 20th day of August in the 4th year of His Lordship Frederick's Dominion.

141

Justices were Nathaniel Wickham, Jr., Gentleman, Chief Justice, Thomas Beatty, John Rawlins, William Webb, Thomas Prather, William Griffith, Joseph Smith, Alexander Beall, David Linn, John Smith Prather and Joseph Wood.

The Grand Jury consisted of Thomas Stoddart, foreman, Samuel Cissell, John Chambers, Charles Hedges, James Holmeard, Weaver Barnes, Elias De-Lashmutt, Benjamin Becraft, William Bowers, John Phillips, John Ogle, Samuel Rogers, James Coffee, John Rutter, Edward Burgiss, Van Swearingen, Jr., Benjamin Biggs, Nathaniel Tomlinson and John Hallom. Samuel Beall, Gentleman, was Sheriff and John Darnall Clerk.

The presentments of the Grand Jury included:
Henry Braddock for striking James Beall.
Henry Braddock for stealing a bell, the property of James Beall.
Dr. Richard Cooke and Christian Smith "for concealing each of them a taxable."

Some of the applications to operate taverns included the following:
Lucy Beall and Joseph Belt, a petition for renewal of licenses for their taverns in George Town.
Thomas Shly, place [Frederick] unstated.
John Shroiner, for renewal of his license in Frederick Town.
Mary Simms, Michael Jesserang and Michael Stump, licenses in Frederick Town.
Benjamin Tomlinson in Frederick Town, a new application, which is granted.

Nathaniel Tomlinson petitions the Court "to grant the liberty of turning the road that leads to the Mouth of Conocogheague by his mill door which will be but a small distance if any 'round and much the best road."
The Court rejects his petition.

142

George William Lawrence petitions as follows: "Being 63 years of age and unable to get his living, having a wife and seven small children," to be levy-free in the future. The Court grants him freedom from levy and allows him one penny in the next County levy.

Although the purpose is not clear (see above, page 83), Samuel Beall, Sheriff, now "produces here in Court His Lordship's new commission of the peace for Frederick County, whereupon Nathaniel Wickham, Jr., David Linn, John Smith Prather, Thomas Prather, Thomas Beatty, John Rawlins and William Griffith, Gentlemen, qualify as Justices of this County by taking the several oaths to the Government required by law and the usual oath of a Judge or Justice and also repeated the test and subscribed the same and oath of abjuration."

"William Webb, Joseph Smith and Joseph Wood, Gentlemen, in Court here likewise qualify as Justices of this County by taking the several oaths."

"Dorothy Bold, wife of Daniel Bold, in her proper person in Court here makes oath that a certain John Emmit, Jr., farmer, did ravish and carnally know her ....against the will and without the consent of her. It is thereupon ordered that bench warrant issue returnable to the next assizes for John Emmit, Jr., to answer the premises."

John Shelman and Thomas Sligh agree "with the major part of the Justices of this County in Court sitting to build a prison in Frederick Town agreeable to the specifications laid down and lodged in this Court for and in consideration of the sum of £400 current money and give bond with sufficient security next November Court for the performance of the work by that time twelve month. The Court approves of Thomas Beatty and Conrad Grosch as security for the said Shelman and Sligh."

A list of prices for accommodations, liquors, etc., was again approved by the Justices, but there were no noticeable price changes from the previous list.

Justice William Griffith presents Jacob Sinn as convicted "for begetting a baseborn child on the body of Elizabeth Rorestripe; Henry Lazarus and Casper Schaff, security to secure the fine and fees paid."

Dr. Richard Pile sues Henry Keene on a note for £4 and is awarded a judgment for that amount.

In a suit against John Wilcoxen, Jr., on a debt the principal item in the account is
   1 riffle gun   £4/10/-

In a suit by Andrew and William House against Martin Adam and Jacob Beney, Adam is shown as a shoemaker and Beney as an innholder.

Thomas Stoddert, foreman of the Grand Jury, was himself sued on a debt for £4 by William Wallace and was ordered by the Court to pay the same.

In an earlier suit against Dr. Philip Lynham by Henry Maroney, the latter had been awarded damages of £15/6/3, which Lynham had not paid. He is now brought into Court, admits non-payment and "is committed to the custody of the Sheriff, there to remain until &c."

NOVEMBER COURT OF 1754

The November Court of 1754 met on the third Tuesday and the 19th day of November in the fourth year of Frederick's Dominion.

The Justices were listed as follows: Nathaniel Wickham, Jr., Gentleman, Chief Justice, Thomas

144

Beatty, Thomas Prather, William Griffith, John Rawlins, William Webb, Joseph Wood, Joseph Smith, David Linn, John Smith Prather and Charles Jones.

The Grand Jury consisted of Thomas Stoddert, foreman, Jacob Holland, Joseph Robinett, John Carmack, Jacob Barton, Robert Lamar, Westall Ridgley, William Campbell, Stephen Ransberg, Jonathan Hagar, Charles Springer, William Wilson, Matthew Markland, Peter Stilly, William Hays, John Hooke and Joseph Wilson.

The Jury's presentments included:
Joseph Johnson, John Winford and William Flinton for stealing three beehives from John White.
John Vandever, William Allison and Charles Chaney, Jr., "for letting Joseph Johnson make an escape from them, he being legally committed for felony."
Jacob Storum, Jr., farmer, John Turnbull, sadler, and Henry Bradwick, planter, all indicted for felony ignoramus.

Elizabeth Broadaway petitions the Court "that your petitioner is an ancient, helpless person and almost past her labour, having also the charge of a poor decrepid orphan and wants the use of his reason." She asks for some help from the Court and is granted 600 pounds of tobacco in the next levy.

Thomas Cresap, Jr., petitions the Court "that at last November Court your petitioner had by assignment four wolves heads from sundry persons for which your petitioner was not allowed." He asks for payment of bounty by this Court, but his petition is rejected.

Ann Brunton petitions the Court "that your petitioner had something bred upon her arm sometime last spring which turned to a very bad ulcer that rendered her unfit for work most of the last summer, that your petitioner was obliged to apply to a doctor of whom she

145

had several medicines and has undergone a salivation in October last, that she was also obliged to hire a nurse who found provision for and took care of her all the time she was in the salivation." She asks for help from the Court "to enable her to pay the Doctor and nurse" but her petition is rejected.

George Bennett who had previously petitioned the Court now states that "being still alive but more uncapable of helping himself than he usually use to be prays Your Worships continue his allowance."
The Court allows him 1,200 pounds of tobacco until the next November Court.

John Trundle petitions the Court that "he was taken blind of one eye three years since and one year with the other, that he has a wife and four small children and was with Dr. Hamilton and sundry others for help with great fatigue and expense and could get none, that he stayed three months and his wife seven weeks which prevented him from making corn, that he got some help there but not capable of doing his business." He asks to be levy free and for some additional help.
The Court grants his petition and allows him 600 pounds of tobacco till next November Court.

Hugh Campbell and Charles Watts present the following petition to the Court: "Having served our time well and truly, and some months over, which our master made a promise before witnesses with a proviso we serve him enduring six years lawfully and truly and never to make any breach in the said term at the end of six years he would be to his promise which now has flown from it. Hoping that Your Worships will be pleased to see us righted before our master himself has told the neighbors that he never would desire two better servants than what we are which have no complaint against us but has proved very honest and thought we did to the uttermost. Your Worships to take the humble petitioners into consideration to see us both righted according to promises."

The Court rejects the petition.

Jacob Gripe petitions the Court as follows: "He being appointed overseer of Conococheague roads and the one being twenty miles in length and the other seven that it is too much for me to comply with and the inhabitants also think very hard of being compelled so farr when said roads would give work enough for three overseers with such roads as is wanting and useful in said limits which are these following, viz: A road from Isaac Baker's to another from William Thompson's and from there another to Conolloway [Tonoloway], all of which said roads are here mentioned is needful and we the subscribers most humbly pray relief to us and overseer and commissions granted for other two overseers and such roads as here exprest order of Court for clearing the same and we your petitioners do pray. N.B. There also ought to be a road from Joseph Volgemore's to said Conococheague."

The Court rejects this petition.

John Trammell, Jr., petitions the Court that your petitioner is conveniently situated for keeping a ferry over Potowmack River at or near a place called Conoy Island within six miles of the Mouth of Monocacy where numbers of inhabitants of this County and others frequently ferry over. Your petitioner therefore humbly prays Your Worships to permit him to keep a ferry over the said place.

"And nothing further was done in the premises."

"The Vestry of Prince George's Parish prefer to the Court the following petition: "....prays that Your Worships please to grant them 8 pounds of tobacco per pole on the taxable inhabitants within said Parish towards defraying the charges of the said Parish."

The Court ordered the requested levy made.

James Gilliland and "sundry of the inhabitants of

Frederick County" [not named] present the following petition: "Several of your petitioners labour under great hardships for want of a road being laid out to said Gilliland's mill and therefore humbly pray Your Worships to be pleased to grant them a road to be laid out at the west line at a place called the Flaggy Meadow and at a road already cleared by the inhabitants of Pensilvania for to come to said mill, their mill being generally frozen up in the winter." In response to the petition, the Court appointed Isaac Baker, Allen Killogle and Evan Shelby to view and lay out the above road as prayed for and make report to the next Court.

"Ordered by the Court here that Priscilla Baker be allowed in the next levy 25 shillings for attending John Beall, a poor man, and finding him necessaries in his sickness."

"The petition of sundry of the back inhabitants residing in Frederick County humbly represent that there is great necessity of building a bridge over a creek called by the name of Sideling Hill Creek, which is very dangerous at present for people to pass over, several having already narrowly escaped drowning.... They humbly crave that an order may be granted for the building of the aforesaid bridge."

The Court appointed "Messrs. Col. Thomas Cresap, William Webb and Joseph Flint to agree with any person to build a bridge over the Creek mentioned for any sum not exceeding £20 and to keep the same in repair 10 years."

Robert Harper petitions the Court as follows: "Your Worships did by petition of the freeholders of Antieatum Hundred last November Court issue an order for the clearing of a road from Alexander Jones's to the Mouth of Shanadore, part of which is cleared and part is not, which renders the part that is done of no service to the public." The petition asks that the overseers of said Hundred be ordered to complete the

148

road. The Court ordered that the overseers clear the road prayed for.

John Smith petitions the Court "that on the west side of Antieatum Ford on the main road that goes from Frederick Town to Capt. Swearingham's Ferry on Potomack, the road being washed into such deep ruts and uneven places by the continual course of water in wet seasons descending from the hills on each side that it hath made it very difficult for travelers to go with waggons. With the approbation of the Court, I will amend the road by turning it after it passeth through the Ford about 20 perches down the Creek to a much better place for ascending the hill and will also make the way some small matter shorter and would render it better for the use of all travelers and to me a much better way to and from my house."

The Court orders "that the petitioner have leave to alter the road aforesaid agreeable to the prayer of the petition."

Peter Bergh and John Bergh petition the Court "that your petitioners were security for Ann Stoner for the balance of Jacob Stoner's estate who intermarried with one Christian Smith and is since dead. Your petitioners are apprehensive that the estate is wasting and your petitioners likely to suffer and further sheweth that the said Christian Smith has great part of the said estate in his possession. They therefore pray that the said Christian Smith may give your petitioners counter-security or else that an order may be made for him to deliver up the said estate to your petiioners."

The Court ordered "that summons issue returnable this session for the above-named Christian Smith to counter-secure the petitioners."

"Mr. Samuel Beall, Sheriff of this County, acknowledges to have received of Capt. William Griffith the sum of £3 in discharge of a certain John Burgesse's fine for begetting a baseborn child on the body of Elizabeth Ann Maccabbee. The Sheriff also acknowledges receipt from John Rawlins, Gentleman, one of the said Justices, the sum of £5 in discharge of a certain John Jacobs' fine for adultery."

"William Luckett agrees with the Court here to keep the ferry at the Mouth of Monocacy upon the same terms as he did last year."

Joseph Wheat, Constable of Middle Part of Rock Creek Hundred, and William Wallace, Jr., Constable of Lower Part of Patowmack Hundred, swear that they visited "the Negro quarters in their respective Hundreds agreeable to Act of Assembly."

John Smith Prather, Gentleman, certifies that John Gatherall, Constable of Lower Part of Newfoundland Hundred, made oath before him that he visited the Negro quarters in his Hundred.

"The Justices of the Court here draw on the Commissioners of the Loan Office for the sum of £400 bill of credit payable to Thomas Sligh and John Shelman for erecting and building a prison in Frederick Town."

"The Justices of the Court order that the Sheriff take Frederick Hawkelberger, a servant to Evan Shelby, to the whipping post and give him ten lashes on his bare body well laid on for making a complaint against his master without foundation."

"Summons ordered and issued, returnable to next Court for William Wofford, Jr., to answer the complaint of John Pain, his apprentice, for ill-usage."

The Court appoints John Ferguson overseer of the road "from the Inspection House in George Town down to the common landing on Potomac River and from the Inspection House to Nathan Peddicort's late plantation and from Rock Creek Ford that leads to the Church and from Rock Creek New Bridge into the main road that leads to the warehouse and thence down to Rock Creek Bridge upon Potomac."

The Court designated many roads in the County as Main Roads and appointed overseers for them. Some of those which are identified as being within the present boundaries of Frederick County are the following:

"From Monocacy Ferry to Ballinger's Branch and from the main road that leads to the Mouth of Monocacy to the ford commonly called Powell's Ford: William Marshall, overseer.

"All the main roads that lye between Ballinger's Branch and Potomac River that lead to the top of Kittocton Mountain: Philip Henry Thomas.

"The new road that leads from top of Kittocton Mountain by George Mathews to Ballinger's Branch: Thomas Taylor.

"The road called the River Road and Touchstone's Road and the road that leads from Alexander Jones's to the top of Kittocton that leads to Frederick Town: Michael Creager.

"From the top of Kittocton Mountain to the top of Shanandore and the road that leads from the top of Kittocton to Shanandore by Richard Touchstone's and from the top of Kittocton to the top of Shanandore that leads by John George's, from the road that leads out of John George's road that leads by Robert Evans to the top of Shanandore: Frederick Garrison.

"From Frederick Town to Richardson's and to the New Ford on Monocacy and from Town to Peter Apple's and from Town to Dulany's Mill: Gaspar Sheep.

"From Frederick Town to Reynold's Ford and from Town to John Biggs's Ford: Jacob Storm.

"From Frederick Town to the top of Kittocton and the new road from Ballinger's Branch into the road that leads to Conococheague near John Kimbol's: Francis Pierpoint.

"From Town to Jacob Peck's fulling mill: Jacob Staley."

151

"Complaint being made to the Court here that Robert Story is a man of bad character and no visible way of his getting a livelihood, it is thereupon ordered that bench warrant issue returnable to next Court against the said Robert Story of Linganore to answer such things as shall be objected against him on behalf of the Lord Proprietary."

"The Justices of the Court here appoint Nathaniel Wickham, Jr., and Joseph Wood, Gentlemen, to agree with any person or persons for keeping a ferry over the Monocacy by Reynolds for a sum not exceeding £20 from this time to the end of next November and so in proportion from the time they shall have a boat or schow to carry persons, horses and wagons over the said ferry."

"The Court also appoint Thomas Beatty and William Griffith, Gentlemen, to agree for keeping a ferry at the Middle Ford on Monocacy on the same foregoing terms."

"The Court appoint Messrs. Nathaniel Wickham, Jr., Joseph Wood, Peter Butler and Reverdy Ghiselin or any three of them to establish the place on the Court House lots for building a prison in Frederick Town."

At the trial of Jacob Storm, Jr., presented for stealing a plowshare, Storm protests his innocence and throws himself on the mercy of the Court. He is released upon payment of costs.

Jacob Storm, Sr., farmer, makes himself liable for payment of the fees assessed against his son.

Henry Braddock had been presented by the Grand Jury for felony ignoramus. When his presentment comes to trial, he is accused of two things, breach of the peace and stealing a bell. In the former, the case is marked "writ returned non est inventus."[22] In the latter, the case is marked merely "discharged."

Mary Stubs, servant to Thomas Kelly, was fined £3 for bastardy for which fine Kelly becomes security. Mary is ordered by the Court to serve "her said master 19 months in consideration of the trouble she has given his house, and for his becoming security for her fine and fee."

"Ordered that the petition of sundry inhabitants of this County for a review of the River Road, commonly called Touchstone's Road, preferred in March Court 1754 and referred to this Court, be further referred until the next Court."

In a suit against Thomas Edmonston on a delinquent account there are two items in the account of interest:

4 lbs. Castle [Castille] soap	10 sh.
62¾ gal. of rum at 5/6 per gallon	£17/ 5/1½

Joseph Belt sues Philip Tracey on an account, some of whose items are:

2 gills of rum	1/-
1 gill of sweetened rum	-/8
3 gills of cherry rum	1/6
Hot diet	1/-
3 pts. of cyder at 3d ea.	-/9

John Gibson sues David Wood on an open account, including:

Your part of 5 gal. of rum and breaking of jugg	10/-
To cr[edit] you in Mr. Clark's store for a saddle (security)	35/-
1 silk cap (security)	10/-

James Brook sues Nathanial Tomlinson, blacksmith, James Henthorne, farmer, and John Charlton,

---

22 Latin: He is not found.

brewer, on a debt. They confess judgment in his favor.

George Beall, Jr., sues William Herbert on an account which reads, "To building a tobacco house 50 x 22 feet, 1,000 lbs. of tobacco."

Proceedings of a Court of Election

A Court of Election was held on November 11, 1754 by virtue of a writ from His Lordship's High Court of Chancery to Samuel Beall, Gentleman, Sheriff, requiring him to call together three or more Justices of the County Court "(one whereof being of the quorum) together with the Clerk of the said County Court who are to sit as a Court and by virtue of their office with public notice to all freeholders to appear at the Court House not less than 10 days after the proclamation to elect four deputies or delegates to serve for the County at a General Assembly of Maryland to be held at Annapolis on the 10th day of December next." Present were Samuel Beall, Gentleman, Sheriff, Nathaniel Wickham, Jr., David Linn and Joseph Wood, Gentlemen, Justices, John Darnall, Clerk.

This Court of Election set Tuesday the third day of December next (1754) as the date of the election and "to the end that all freemen within the County having therein fifty acres of land or resident there and having a visible estate of £40 sterling at least might have due notice for attendance.... it was then and there resolved by the Court that the Sheriff make proclamation in the most public places of his Sheriffwick of the day as aforesaid" and the Court adjourned until the day set for the election.

It met on that day at the Court House with Samuel Beall, Gentleman, Sheriff, Nathaniel Wickham, Jr., David Linn and Joseph Wood present. "When and where after proclamation and publication again of the aforementioned writ, the election was proceeded to by the freemen of the County who, being examined according to the force, form and effect of divers laws, chose, elected and deputed Henry Wright Crabb, Josiah Beall, Edward Sprigg and Joseph Chapline, Gentlemen, four good and sufficient freemen of the County aforesaid being residents therein and indentures between the Sheriff aforesaid and the electors pursuant of the same writ of election were executed."

MARCH COURT OF 1755

The March Court of 1755 met on the 18th day of March in the fourth year of Frederick's Dominion. Present were the Worshipful Nathaniel Wickham, Jr., Gentleman, Chief Justice, Thomas Beatty, Thomas Prather, William Griffith, John Rawlins, Joseph Wood, William Webb, Charles Jones and David Linn. Nathaniel Beall, Jr., was Sheriff and John Darnall was Clerk.

The Sheriff had summoned the following Grand Jurors: Thomas Fletchall, foreman, Peter Rench, Joseph Flint, Jacob Holland, Henry Gaither, Elias DeLashmutt, Peter Stilly, Michael Hodgkiss, Owen David, Charles Wood, Alexander Perry, Jonathan Hagar, Arthur Nelson, Thomas Hogg and Edmund Riggs.

Some of their presentments included:
Edward White "for wilfully and molishesly cutting off part of William Windfield's hand."
Michael Reasonar for "forceable taking out of the possestion of Richard Cook a horse without proving the same."
Honagle Morningstar for "assaulting of Robert Baker."

Esther Matew petitions the Court "that whereas your petitioner has for several years past been allowed by Your Worships a pension of 800 pounds of tobacco for herself and also the like quantity for her grand-

daughter Esther Leach which said allowance may be
made appear to Your Worships to be no imposition on
the Court by a sufficient number of reputable people
who are acquainted with their circumstances but it has
been represented to Your Worships that the aforesaid
Esther Leach is in a capacity of getting her living by
her labor and in consequence of which Your Worships
have left her out of the list of pensioners and have not
made her her usual allowance as heretofore. This is
therefore to certify Your Worships that the aforesaid
Esther Leach is actually a lunatick and not capable of
supporting herself by her labor as was insinuated and
albeit she may have some intervals wherein she may
now and then possibly do some little or light thing, yet
it is only accidental and cannot be depended upon for
support of life." She asks that the Court restore the
pension to her granddaughter. "Signed by sundry [un-
named] inhabitants of Frederick County."

The Court restores to Esther Leach the 800 pounds
of tobacco given her in the past.

William Beall presents an application for a license
to keep a public house of entertainment at Frederick
Town, which the Court grants.

Philip Jackson petitions the Court that since he
"intends to keep ordinary at the dwelling house where
now Col. Thomas Cresap lives" he prays for such a
license and the Court grants it.

Maurice Turner in a petition states that "living on
the waggon road from the Old Town to Wills Creek
[present Allegany County] and there being no ordinaries on the same road by which means your petitioner
is very much troubled with travelers." He requests a
license to keep an ordinary, and it is granted.

Doctor Adam Erlivine petitions the Court to the
effect that "he attended and supplied with medicines
Elizabeth Roreshibin of Frederick Town, spinster now

deceased, from the 30th of August 1754 to the 28th of February 1755." He states that he considers his services worth £4/3/- and he asks that he be paid that amount for those services.
The Court rejects his petition.

Thomas Nicholls petitions the Court to the effect that there is a road through his plantation and that during the growing season when he has corn planted in his field, travelers leave the gates open and many times he has driven horses, hoggs and cattle out of his corn field. He states that in order to remedy this he has laid out a new road which is just as good as the old one and he begs the Court to permit him to close the old road.
The Court rejects his petition. See below, p. 161.

Elizabeth Burlington petitions the Court that she is very infirm and unable to provide the necessities of life for herself and therefore prays "that Your Worships will take her case under consideration and represent her case unto the Justices of Prince George's County where she served her time in order to allow her a small pension from that County."
The Court rejects her petition.

John Chambers petitions the Court "whereas a certain Isabel Grant late deceased did happen to be taken sick at my house in February last and dyed in about seven days after taking sick," he asks that he be given an allowance for burying Isabel Grant.
The Court rejects the petition.

John Keller petitions the Court that "he is at the age of 67 years last December and very unable to work. Therefore he prays Your Good Worships out of your accustomed goodness will exempt your humble and aged petitioner from paying any levy for the future. And your aged petitioner will for your eternal happiness ever pray." Petition rejected.

157

Josiah Gosling petitions the Court that "he had one Elizabeth Hare hired to live along with me for one year, she having a young child about 14 months old. Now she has absconded her service since the 8th of February last and your petitioner desires of Your Worships to know what might be done with the child.
"Upon reading which petition, nothing further was done in the premises."

Thomas Waller petitions the Court that a certain Jane Jeniss, servant to your petitioner, had some time past a baseborn child for which your petitioner paid all costs and charges on the same and the said Jeniss is now almost free and your petitioner prays that Your Worships would please to have the baseborn child bound to your petitioner till it comes to age in lieu of the aforesaid costs and charges paid and also the maintenance of the said child hitherto.
"Upon reading which petition, nothing further was done in the premises."

Michael Jesserong petitions the Court as follows: "I, Michael Jesserong of Frederick Town, tavern-keeper, have had the trouble of keeping and attending a certain woman belonging to the County and Town abovesaid, named Elizabeth Rockiberen, who was in a most deplorable condition with running sores which rendered her nauseous so that no person would take any care of her and probably she would [have] perished for want of care and sustenance had I not brought her into my house the 18th day of July 1754 and provided for and dressed her sores til the 25th of February 1755 at which time she departed this life. Then at my own expense I buryed her in a decent and customary manner, and, Gentlemen, it is too much for one person to undergo the trouble and expense totally thereof and whereas all the inhabitants of Frederick Town knew she was an object of charity as great as could be, being quite uncapable of helping herself in any manner, I hope therefore you will allow me as you will see

158

proper for my trouble and expense which, Gentlemen, is the petition of your humble petitioner as in duty bound will ever pray."

"Upon reading which petition, nothing further was done in the premises."

Loyd Buchanan, Gentleman, qualifies himself as an attorney of the Frederick County Court.

"John Claget, one of the inspectors at Rock Creek Warehouse, in Court here takes the oath appointed by the Inspection Law for preventing the clandestine exportation of tobacco."

"Ordered by the Court that Negroe Jack, the slave of Dr. Richard Cooke, be levy free for the future."

"Summons ordered and issued returnable immediately for Joseph Holmes, his appearance to answer the complaint of Simon Harden, an orphan."

"Ordered by the Court here that Joseph Williams bring before the Justices at the next County Court Elkanah Smith, an orphan whose mother complains to the Court here is very much abused by the said Joseph Williams, the master."

"Rebecca Plummer fined £1/10 sh. for bastardy, swore the child to Alexander Perry. Samuel Plummer security to see the fine paid by the 25th of January 1756 and Alexander Perry and Robert Patrick bound in £20 to the Lord Proprietary to keep the child from becoming a charge to the County.

"Alexander Perry fine 240 pounds of tobacco for begetting a baseborn child on the body of Rebecca Plummer and bound to the Lord Proprietary for the payment of the same on or before the first day of February 1756.

"These convictions and recognizances taken before John Rawlins January 28, 1755."

In a suit of John Casteel, Jr., against Thomas Johnson, Jr., for slander, the suit was struck off after four continuances.

JUNE COURT OF 1755

The June Court of 1755 was held on the third Tuesday and the 17th day of June in the 5th year of His Lordship's Dominion. The worshipful Justices were Nathaniel Wickham, Jr., Gentleman, Chief Justice, John Rawlins, William Griffith, Thomas Beatty, Thomas Prather, Joseph Smith, Joseph Wood, David Lynn, John Smith Prather and Charles Jones.

The Grand Jury consisted of Richard Beall, foreman, Henry Boteler III, Michael Jones, Thomas Case, Samuel Rogers, William Biggs, Allen Killough, Thomas Dowden, George Winters, George Divelbess, Jonathan Hagar, Conrad Hogmire, Robert Lamar Jr., James Reed, Samuel Beall, Sr., John Radford and Peter Stilly.

Presentments by the Grand Jury included:
John Plummer "for traveling and seling goods without a license as pedlar."
Elizabeth Buttman "for a breach of peace on Martha Nicholson."
John Plummer, laborer, on a true bill for the above offense.
Benjamin Browning, Gentleman, "for a breach of the peace ignoramus."
Jeremiah Prather, Gentleman, "for a breach of the peace ignoramus."
Jonathan Browning, Gentleman, "for a breach of the peace ignoramus."

John Smoot petitions the Court "that Thomas Fletchall has the estate of Edward and Barton Smoot in his hands and is now going to move to Carolina. Therefore your petitioner prays Your Worships would make some order in behalf of said Edward and Barton Smoot."

The Court ordered that a bench warrant issue returnable immediately for Fletchall and that the "Sheriff go immediately to execute the same."

Thomas Nicholls petitions again (cf. p. 157) that he "has a main road that goes thro' his plantation and the travelling people going back and forth in the night oftentimes leave the gates propt wide open so that your petitioner has oftentimes turned out hoggs, horses and cattle....that have been destroying his crops....But your petitioner has cleared another new road that in the opinion of all the neighbors and other gentlemen that ride the road that the new road that your petitioner has cleared is as full out as good and as nigh a road as the road is that goes through his plantation." He begs the Court to grant him an order to turn the road.

The Court now decides that "he shall have the effect of his prayer."

Robert Hardee petitions the Court "that whereas your petitioner being confined in gaol, aged 64 years and having five small children destitute of cloathing as well as himself and depending upon charity for bread even to support life, therefore humbly hopes Your Worships will in compassion to his poor children grant him such reasonable support to obviate the aforesaid oppression as to you shall seem meet....

"Upon reading this petition it is ordered by the Court here that the petitioner be allowed 200 pounds of tobacco for his and his family's support until next November Court and that the petitioner shall be levy-free for the future."

"Isabell Brown petitions the Court that "your petioner's husband did enlist himself into His Majesty's service with Captain Polson and was discharged in Frederick Town where he left your poor petitioner in the utmost distress, not being able either to return to

161

Carlisle Town in Pensilvania where she could hope for a maintenance or work for one in this place she being grievously afflicted with palsy and must have perished in this town were it not for the humanity of the inhabitants thereof. Therefore humbly prays Your Worships to have so much compassion on your petitioner's miserable circumstance as to order some method for her being returned to the place from whence she came or grant her some subsistence in this place and she as in duty bound will pray.

"Upon reading which petition and consideration thereof had, it is ordered by the Court here that Thomas Dobbs be allowed 24 shillings in the next County levy for carrying the petitioner to Justice Allison's in Pensilvania and finding her provisions in her journey."

Thomas Shlay and John Shelman present the Court the following petition, "that the great number of waggons and waggon horses that have been impressed into His Majesty's service have rendered it impossible for your petitioners to get either the stone, lime or timber brought into town for the building of the County prison, that those persons who had their waggons and teams [of horses] at home will not be prevailed on for any reasonable consideration to hire them in Town for fear of being likewise impressed into said service so that your petitioners apprehend it will be out of their power to compleat the said prison according to agreement. Therefore humbly pray Your Worships to grant your petitioners such further time to finish the said work as you shall think reasonable....

"Upon reading this petition, it is ordered by the Court here that the same be rejected."

Jacob Lowestaber, George Spangler and Henry Six present separate petitions to the Court for relief, all stating that they are sixty years or, in one case, sixty-odd years old and unable to work.

In each case the petition is rejected.

"Ordered by the Court here that Negro Peter, the slave of Samuel Magruder III, be set levy-free for the future, it appearing to the Court that the Negro aforesaid is lame and subject to fitts."

"William Haymond, aged 15 years, in Court here makes choice of Nicholas Haymond for his guardian, which trust the said Nicholas Haymond in Court here accepts of."

Thomas Dobbs petitions the Court that "your humble petitioner hath served John Cramphton, deceased, the full term of seven years as a servant and never hath received nor had any freedom dues. Therefore hopes it will please Your Good Worships out of your accustomed goodness to look into it and rectify your petitioner who is bound to pray for Your Worships' eternal happiness.

"Upon reading this petition, nothing further was done in the premises."

"Ordered by the Court here that Peter Deaver be allowed in the next County levy twenty shillings for his trouble in keeping and maintaining a poor child named Ruth Jones since May last to this time.

"Alexander Jones engages with the Court here to keep and maintain a poor child named Ruth Jones from this time until next June Court for and in consideration of £7 current money to be levied in the next County levy."

"The Justices agree to purchase a brass hundredweight which is now at Rock Creek Warehouse which Mr. George Gordon was security for to Prince George's County Court, for £5 currency."

Mr. Samuel Beall, Sheriff, acknowledges to have received from Nathaniel Wickham, Jr., one of His Lordship's Justices, the sum of 30 shillings in discharge of Cornelius Carmack's fine for bastardy."

Sarah Turner was fined £1/10 sh. for bastardy, and Mary Richards was fined £3 for having a "bastard child and not discovering the father of it." Elizabeth Scaggs was fined 240 pounds of tobacco for bastardy.

In the trial of John Plummer, who was presented for not having a trader's license, he was fined £8 current money and ordered by the Court to be committed to the custody of the Sheriff.

In the three indictments for "breach of the peace ignoramus," all three individuals threw themselves on the mercy of the Court and were found not guilty. But they were obliged to pay the fees due the officers of the Court.

Edward White was brought before the Court "for cutting a part of William Winfield's hand off." The case is merely marked "abated."

The suit of John Trammel against Henry Rotten for a debt of 2,204 pounds of tobacco was, after three continuances, marked "abated by death of the plaintiff."

In a suit of Robert and Thomas Dunlop vs. Thomas Ray on an open account, some of the items are stated in sterling, some in current money, and then these amounts are translated into terms of tobacco:
"Reprizeing 2 light hoggsheads of tobacco: 7 sh. current money.
Cash: 5 sh., 6d in sterling, 5 sh. in current money."
The total debt was £9/17/4 sterling and £1/9/6 current money. Ray paid on account "2 hoggshead of tobacco on Rock Creek," weighing 1645 pounds net. Of this, $147\frac{1}{2}$ pounds, at 20 shillings, offsets the £1/9/6 current money. The balance of $1497\frac{1}{2}$ pounds is translated into sterling at 10 shillings per hundred, or £7/9/9.

[Dr.] George Jacob Trautwein sues James Lamar

on account in which some of the items named include:

4 bottles of mouth water	£1/ -/-
Salivating your Negro woman	5/ -/-
Finding of said Negro diet, washing and lodging and attendance from 9 January to 23rd February 1755	3/15/-
	£9/15/-

AUGUST COURT OF 1755

The August Court of 1755 met on the third Tuesday and 19th day of August in the 5th year of His Lordship Frederick's Dominion. The Justices present were: Nathaniel Wickham, Jr., Gentleman, Chief Justice, Thomas Beatty, Thomas Prather, William Griffith, John Rawlins, Joseph Smith, David Lynn, Thomas Cresap, Joseph Wood, Charles Jones and John Smith Prather. Samuel Beall was Sheriff and John Darnall was Clerk.

The Grand Jury was composed of Alexander Beall, foreman, Charles Hedge, James Dyall, George Williams, Thomas Lucas, Peter Rench, Thomas Hogg, John Davis, Jeremiah Simpson, William Wilson, Thomas Harriss, John Veatch, Samuel Rogers, John Johnston (Kittocton) and Richard Simpson.

Some of their indictments included:

Nicholas Brocson [Broxon] "for stealing about 2 yards of linnen cloth" from John Davis.

Evan Shelby "for beating and abusing Charles Cheney."

Elizabeth Keephart "for assault and battery on Margaret Pack."

John Quirk states "that he is conveniently situated on the main road leading to Bladensborough and George Town" and he desires a license to keep a public house. It is granted.

165

HEMPSTEAD COUNTY LIBRARY
HOPE, ARKANSAS

Arthur Charlton presents a petition for a renewal of his tavern license in Frederick Town. This is also granted.

Joseph Belt petitions for continuation of his license for tavern keeping "at George Town, Rock Creek, in the house where he formerly kept tavern." The license is granted.

Daniel Debus petitions for a license to keep a public house in Frederick Town, and it is granted. Michael Jesserang asks for a license to operate a tavern in Frederick Town, but does not call it a renewal. It is granted. Likewise, Conrad Crosh gets a license renewal to keep a tavern in Frederick Town. Richard Smith's petition for a license to operate his tavern "on the Great Road leading to Conococheague" is also granted. Ninian Beall, son of Ninian, asks for a license to keep a public house "at the Sugarland Road," which is granted. Lucy Beall asks for a renewal of her license to keep her tavern in George Town. William Luckett petitions for a license renewal for his tavern at the Mouth of Monocacy. Valentin Shroiner petitions for a renewal of his license to keep his tavern in Frederick Town. Thomas Schlye asks "for a license for selling liquor," presumably in Frederick Town, but makes no reference to his previous license. William Beall seeks a license to keep tavern in Frederick Town. James Christie states that he lives "on the Great Road that leads from Frederick Town to Conococheague" and asks for a license to keep a public house there. All these petitions are granted.

Lewis Jones presents a petition to the Court which states that the Court had previously allowed him 500 pounds of tobacco for his support and he requests a continuation. The Court, however, orders "that the same be rejected, the petitioner having served his time in Prince George's County.

Mary Edwards petitions the Court "that having

been imposed upon by the wives of Matthew and Mark Edwards in bringing to her counterfeit money to carry to buy saddles with, she not knowing anything of their fraudulent design, they having brought the money to her at dark and she not knowing anything of it nor much of the nature of money whether good or bad, begs therefore that Your Worships would be so good as to take it into consideration and acquit your petitioner, a poor prisoner left here destitute of either friends or money, her husband having been gone to Carolina ever since last February and she being intended to follow him before now if she had not been unluckily stopped by passing the abovesaid counterfeit money which she was entirely innocent and ignorant of or of any other felonious or fraudulent action and in hopes of Your Worships' clemency remains as in duty bound will always pray.

"The honest and good behavior of the above petitioner is attested by us the subscribers who have known her these several years: Isaac Eltinge, Arthur Hickman, George Jack, Isaac Baker, Moses Jewell, Robert Lamar, William Hickman, Nehemiah Ogden and Henry Hickman.

"Upon reading which petition, nothing further was done in the premises."

"Ordered by the Court here that John Nicholls be discharged from a presentment for neglect of duty as overseer of the highway, it appearing to the Court that the said John Nicholls was at that time in His Majesty's service and could not attend his duty as overseer.

Samuel Dunn, aged 13 years last February, and Arthur Dunn, aged 12 years last February, are by the Court here bound to Richard Ridgeway until they arrive to the age of 21 years and the said Richard Ridgeway in Court here promises and obliges himself to learn (or cause to be learned) the said Samuel Dunn and Arthur Dunn to read well and to write a plain hand and at the expiration of their times to give them each £15 and freedom dues according to the custom of the country."

Evan Shelby makes oath "that his wife Letitia Shelby (against whom there is a prosecution for cutting down and destroying a bound tree of a tract of land called 'Shelby's Misfortune' belonging to Dr. Charles Carroll) was when he left home Tuesday last sick of the flux and cannot safely attend this Court."

"Ordered by the Court here that Martha Lakin be allowed in the next levy the sum of 600 pounds of tobacco for keeping Elizabeth Ward, an infant, from the time she had [taken] the child to next November Court.

The Justices again established the rates for liquors and accommodations. Each year, usually at the August Court, these rates were set. Since the first schedule of rates was established in 1748, minor changes in some rates, mostly downward, had been made. Some illustrations of the seven-year cumulative reduction in prices are:

	1748	1755
Stabling and good fodder for an horse, per night	1/-	-/10
A sealed quart of maderra wine	4/-	3/ -
Maryland spirits distilled from grain, per gallon	9/8	6/ -
Peach brandy, per gallon	13/4	8/ -

The substantial cumulative reductions in the last two items are quite probably an indication that more grain and fruits were being grown, for which there existed a wider market and on which a greater profit could be realized by distilling than otherwise.

In the trial of Nicholas Broxon [Brocson], laborer, it is charged that he "on March 10, 1755 with force and arms two yards of linnon of the value of 20 pounds of tobacco the goods and chattels of a certain John Davis then and there feloniously took, stole and carried away against the peace of the said Lord Proprietary His good rule and government and contrary to the form of the Act of Assembly in such cases made and provided."

Brocson pleads not guilty and puts himself on the mercy of the Court. For reasons not indicated, the Sheriff is directed to impanel a jury "of twelve good men &c.," who are named as follows: Alexander Beall son of James, Robert Lazenby, Garah Davis, Philip Hawker, James Rimmer, John Harlin, John Williams, William Murdock, Ninian Tanyhill, John Dowden, Valentine Myres and James Whiteacre.

The Jury finds Brocson not guilty.

In a suit of Robert Mundell against Alexander Lamar on an open account, three items are of some interest:

1 yard of blanket	9d
1 lb. of peper	1 sh./8d
2 nutmeggs	3d

A suit of Elizabeth Bowie, executrix of John Bowie, against Benjamin Harris, after three continuances, is marked "abated by marriage of the plaintiff."

Similarly, in a suit of Mary Sprigg, executrix of Col. Sprigg, versus Samuel Beall, Sr., after one continuance the same notation appears: "abated by marriage of the plaintiff."

A married woman could not sue and would have to bring suit in the name of her new husband.

NOVEMBER COURT OF 1755

The November Court of 1755 met on the third Tuesday and the 18th day of November in the fifth year of His Lordship's Dominion. The Justices present were Nathaniel Wickham, Jr., Gentleman, Chief Justice, Thomas Beatty, John Rawlins, William Griffith, Joseph Wood, Joseph Smith, Charles Jones and David Linn.

The Grand Jury was comprised of William Williams, foreman, Samuel Cissell, John Butler, Robert Owen, Mounts Justice, John Sheppard, Benjamin Biggs, Francis Gattrell, Jeremiah Virgin, Handall Bergh, George Darby, Casper Schaaf, Henry Gaither and Thomas Johnson.

The Jury presents Mary Reed "for feloniously steeling from Benj. Christian the body of one osnaberg shirt and two yards of brown sheeten and one pees of soap and one pocket bottel and half a yard of linnin, one towell, a pair of Pockets and pockit flaps, sum slips of sheloon."[23]

They also present Christopher Cook "for felonously stealing two iron wedges from Christon Shoal."

Peter Oler offers the following petition to the Court: "Your petitioner lives on the main road between Frederick Town and York Town. Your petitioner has seen a great deal of inconvenience in the road and bring the road some considerable distance nearer than it now is and a farr better road by your petitioner's house where he now lives and he is willing to make the road good and sufficient for waggons and others on his own cost and charges provided You will be pleased to allow the same to be the County road."
The Justices appointed Thomas Norris and Thomas Harris to lay out the road prayed for and to report to the next Court.

Sundry unnamed inhabitants of Frederick County present a petition "that there is a necessity for a cart road from Potomac River where John Nelson formerly kept ferry to Frederick Town the nearest and best way for travellers to cross the said River in general and leads to the conveniency of a good ford which will be of

---

[23] Shalloon: light cloth for coat-linings and women's dresses.

greater service to the petitioners as well as to the general publick which will have occasion to travel out of Virginia to the said Town. Since Philip Noland has moved his ferry lower down the River there being no road to the said place fit for travellers to pass with cart or waggon where may be a very good road and by farr nearer and your petitioners pray there may be persons appointed to lay out the said road and order an overseer for the same, and your petitioners pray the said road be cleared the nearest and convenientest way and kept in repair a publick road and your petitioners will pray &c. Signed by several of the inhabitants."

The Court appointed "Robert Lamar, Richard Richardson and Daniel Kennedy or any two of them to lay out the road prayed for and to make report thereof to the next County Court."

Sundry inhabitants of Frederick County, unnamed, present the following petition to the Court: "The humble petition of sundry of the back inhabitants that as there is a bridge wanting over the Sideling Hill Creek your petitioners pray that You will grant a sufficient sum of money to build a bridge over the said Creek or otherwise to grant a sum to build a bridge over the Town Creek which will not cost above half the sum as building one over the Sideling Hill Creek and that the Flat which now is at the Town Creek may be removed to the Sideling Creek." [These creeks are between Hancock and Cumberland. Cf. also p. 148.]

The Court appoints "Col. Thomas Cresap to agree with any person to build said bridge over Town Creek for the sum of £25 currency and no more and it is ordered that security be given for keeping it sufficient for ten years."

Peter Oler petitions the Court for a license to keep tavern stating "that your petitioner lives on the road from Frederick Town to York in pensilvania near the pines on Piney Creek."

The Court grants him a license.

171

George Beckwith likewise petitions the Court for a license to keep a house of entertainment, stating that he "lives convenient on the road leading from Frederick Town to Monocasy."

The Court grants him a license.

Margaret Hufman petitions the Court as follows: "Your poor petitioner having three children that were born blind, which are now partly grown up and besides this one of them has got convulsion fitts so extreme bad that your poor petitioner is obliged to keep her almost frequently with her for fear of any accident befalling her, and your petitioner now being reduced so low besides growing old and infirm is rendered incapable of supporting either herself or them, therefore prays Your Worships to grant such a competent allowance for the support of those poor creatures as shall seem convenient."

The Court allows her "2,000 pounds of tobacco for her and her children's support until the next November Court."

Leonard Decose petitions the Court "that your petitioner having received your charity in the year 1753 and inadvertently expecting an annual continuance thereof omitted petitioning Your Worships these two years past from which numbers of difficulties and inconveniences have accrued, being blind, aged and infirm otherways, whereby I was subjected to the charity of Christian people to whom [I] have been very troublesome ever since. Therefore humbly hopes Your Worships will commiserate my case and grant me such allowance as Your Worships may think sufficient for my support the ensuing year and for a reimbursement to those Christian people on whom my support has depended as I would not be understood or even felt to impose on the Court. Give me leave to refer you to the Sheriff for a confirmation hereof."

The Court allowed him "2,000 pounds of tobacco in the next County levy for his support" for the next year.

John Tyson petitions the Court "that by the perswasione of one of the Court took in my care Eleanor Smith an old petitioner in a deplorable condition unable to help herself anyways unless by my family's assistance ever since June to the last of October which she departed this life, having buryed her, having had a good deal of trouble from the first of my taking the said Eleanor Smith are in hopes Your Worships will take it into your consideration to allow your petitioner a reasonable allowance."

The Court allowed him 700 pounds of tobacco in the next levy.

Mary Perry petitions the Court "that your petitioner was born in the said County is gotten a great deal worse than previously and is almost perished for want of both victuals and clothes and prays that Your Worships will take her distressed condition into consideration."

The Court allowed her 400 pounds of tobacco in the next levy.

Owen Humphreys petitions the Court "that your petitioner had the misfortune of one of his boys about 5 years old having his left hand cut off by his brother. For the cure of it, the Doctor charged £5/17 sh. Therefore your petitioner humbly prays Your Worships please make him a further allowance to enable him to pay the Doctor."

The Court allowed him "200 pounds of tobacco in the next County levy besides the Doctor's account which is ordered by the Court to be paid the Doctor."

Frederick Cheese petitions the Court stating that "he is a poor cripple that cannot well subsist without you will be pleased to make him an allowance."

The Court ordered "that the petitioner be allowed £6/5 sh. to pay the Doctor and 600 pounds of tobacco in the next levy for his support."

Daniel Davis in a petition states that "he hath maintained Frederick Cheese, a poor cripple, three months with good meat, drink, washing and lodging and the poor man by his misfortune is not able to make your petitioner recompense for his maintenance humbly prays Your Honors to take it under consideration."

The Court allowed him 300 pounds of tobacco in the next levy.

Thomas Kirk presents a petition that "he now being aged 65 and serving the King and Queen by land and sea these 44 years and living in America above ten years by heat and cold being unable to labor as usual" asks to be made levy free.

The Court grants his petition.

Christopher Cooke presents a petition that he "did bring with him from Halifax in Nova Scotia a woman servant named Mary, widow of John Hart, on condition that she should serve me and family the term of six years, which indenture was made the 4th of December last in Boston by Justice William Skinner and witnessed, by her own free will and consent and the said Mary when we came up to Brother's House told me and my wife before Mr. Cooke that she would not serve me but that she would be sold to some other person, which accordingly I sold her to Mr. Samuel Fleming for twelf pounds currency and she has been with the said Fleming ever since March last until Tuesday the 25th of October 1755 and has made her elopement and is gone to live with Mr. Turnbull, sadler, and says she will not serve Mr. Fleming nor me because I have lost my letter case wherein said indenture and several other papers were and whereas I can prove by several persons I had an indenture who have seen it before I lost it I hope Your Worships will oblige her to serve the remainder of her time that I may have the liberty of disposing of her."

The Court ordered that the petition be rejected.

"Ordered that Dr. Adam Erlewyne for medicine found Elizabeth Rockebern, a poor woman in her illness, as per account proved and produced to the Court, be allowed 640 pounds of tobacco for the same in the next levy."

"The Justices of the Court here appoint the several Constables following to execute the law in relation to the suppressing the tumultuous meetings of Negroes in their several Hundreds and ordered that they be allowed for the same on compliance with the Act of Assembly in that case made and provided:"
William Wallace, Jr., Lower Part Potomac Hundred
Luke Barnhard, Upper Part Potomac Hundred
Henry Gaither, Newfoundland Hundred
Edward Burgess, Lower Part Newfoundland Hundred

From two pages listing roads designated as Main Roads, a few of interest may be noted:
All the Main Roads that lye between Ballenger's Branch and Potomack River that leads to the top of Kittocton Mountain. John Johnson, overseer.
The New Road that leads from top of Kittocton by George Matthews to Ballenger's Branch. Thomas Taylor, overseer.
The Road called the River Road and Touchstone's Road and the road that leads from Alexander Jones' to the top of Kittocton that leads to Frederick Town. James Hooke, overseer.
From Husseys Ford to Smiths Branch. James Cranmer, overseer.
From Smiths Branch to Great Pipe Creek and then to John Digges Works. Bigger Head, overseer.
From Great Pipe Creek to the Temporary Line. Andrew Hole, overseer.
From Major Ogle's Ford to John Biggs' Ford on Monocacy. Charles Springer, overseer.
From the Temporary Line to William Ambrose's. Edward Brawner, overseer.
From Ambrose's Mill to Abraham Miller's mill.

Jacob Miller, overseer.

From Frederick Town to Richardson's and to the new Ford on Monocacy and from Town to Peter Apple's and from Town to Dulany's Mill. Valentine Stickle, overseer.

From Frederick Town to the top of Kittoctin Mountain and the new road from Ballenger's Branch into the road that leads to Conococheague near John Kimbol's. Samuel Fleming, overseer.

From Town to Reynolds Ford and from Town to John Biggs' Ford. Jacob Getsatanner, overseer.

From Town to Jacob Peck's Fulling Mill. Gilbert Kemp, overseer.

The Court appoints Lawrence Owen and John Middaugh "press masters of this County for the year ensuing."

Many accounts sued on are stated in two terms, one of sterling, the other of current funds. One example includes two columns, one of £4/4/- in sterling, the other of £2/7/- current money, but of no connection or equivalence between them.

Edward Dorsey sues Jacob Weller on a promissory note of £30 and secures judgment by the Court.

At this point, on page 1082 of Judgment Record H-2, the record of this November Court of 1755 abruptly ends. No adjournment is noted.

NOVEMBER COURT OF 1757

Following one blank page, the record resumes with a part of the proceedings of the November Court of 1757. No organization of the Court is recorded and the 22 pages of that record contain no items of significant interest.

Missing also are records of the other Courts of

176

March 1756 through March 1758. The present Clerk of the Circuit Court has no information concerning these missing records.

JUNE COURT OF 1758

The Judgment Records for the June Court of 1758 begin on page 1221 of Volume H-2.

This Court met on the third Tuesday and 20th day of June in the eighth year of Frederick's Dominion. The Justices present were: Thomas Beatty, Chief Justice, Joseph Wood, David Lynn, William Luckett, Moses Chapline, Thomas Prather, Joseph Smith, Andrew Heugh, Peter Bainbridge, Thomas Norris and Jacob Duckett. James Dickson was now Sheriff, but John Darnell continued as Clerk.

The Grand Jurors were Samuel Magruder III, foreman, Richard Wells, Frail Pain, John Philips, John Garret, John Wymer, David Jones, Joseph Mayhew, John Dickerson, Jacob Lockman, Joshua Harbin, Samuel Magruder (Kittocton), Frederick Woolhider and James Coffee, summoned out of the several Hundreds of the County.

"We the body of the Grand Jury of Frederick County do present Elias DeLashmeat and James Hook for breach of His Lordship's peace this instant."

Peter Murphy presents an interesting petition in which he states "being a prisoner now almost three years lately acquitted from his confinement the Constable having taken Your Worships' petitioner as a taxable prays Your Worships will exempt your petitioner from being charged and from paying any levy for the future. Your Worships' petitioner is now seventy years of age."

The Court allowed him 300 pounds of tobacco for support until next November Court.

Gasper Hiser petitions the Court "that whereas the Court Martial hath fined your petitioner in the sum of 400 pounds of tobacco for not mustering as the law directs, your petitioner being unacquainted with the said law and likewise being near the age of 57 years, and troubled with a violent pain in his back which disables him for many days together....being but a foreigner hath no English &c. Likewise the Court Martial hath fined John Hiser the son of your petitioner four fines though your petitioner's said son was not of age of 16 years until the 28th day of April last." He asks that these fines be remitted, but the Court rejects his plea.

Vinsill Barlange petitions the Court "that your petitioner being a German born came into this Province in the year 1740 a servant for five years, which time I truly served William Stansbury of Baltimore County and afterwards in the year 1748 in pursuit of labouring business which ever has been what I profest I came to Anteatum in this County....never been troublesome to any person in the neighborhood as all my acquaintances can testify as also that I have paid my part of the County's levies yearly. But, Gentlemen, it hath pleased God in my old age to afflict me with heavy disease and to deprive me of my eyesight. I am decrepit and blind and unable to support life any longer without some help." He asks for assistance, which the Court rejects.

Priscilla Pipsco petitions the Court "that your petitioner being a free woman, is detained in servitude by a certain Daniel Collins contrary to all right and justice and humbly prays that summons may issue for the said Collins....to answer the premises."
The Court issues the summons as requested.

"Ordered by the Court here that Lodowick Davis be allowed £2/11/4$\frac{3}{4}$ in consideration of his servantsman inlisting in His Majesty's service."

George Scott is appointed Cryer of this County Court. "Ordered by the Court that he be allowed the same as Alexander Jones had for cleaning the Court House and beating the drum."

Catherine Honey swears that she attended [Court] eight days "to testify for the Lord Proprietary against Michael Risener."

Elias DeLashmet and James Hook who were presented by the Grand Jury were each fined one shilling and undetermined costs for their breaking of the peace.

In a suit by the Lord Proprietary against Daniel Cresap for "buying an ammunition blanket from Morris Williams a soldier belonging to Captain Alexander Beall's Company" he was discharged upon paying the costs.

A suit on behalf of the Lord Proprietary versus Latitia Shelby "for destroying a bound tree for a tract of land belonging to Dr. Carroll" was marked "struck off after fifteen continuances."

Charles Carroll, who is executor of Dr. Charles Carroll, in turn listed as a merchant at Annapolis, sues Handel Hann on an account and is awarded the amount for which sued.

A suit of Alexander Magruder versus Alexander Jones under which Magruder is granted a judgment and the Sheriff is ordered to attach the assets of Jones shows the following:

4 cows, 3 yearlin[g] heiffers and 2 yearlin bulls	£10/ -/-
2 stears	3/ -/-
4 chains	7/3
1 small walnut table and 1 frying pan	7/-
	£13/14/3

The appraisers for this attachment were Westall Ridgley, Thomas Thrasher, Nathaniel Walker and John Radford, all of whom lived in the Jefferson area, thus giving a clue to the probable location of Jones, whose locale cannot otherwise be established from the land records.

Magruder got the execution order, but Jacob Duckett, Gentleman, "present here in Court in his proper person, pledges himself as security for the debt" and the property is therefore restored to Alexander Jones.

AUGUST COURT OF 1758

The Judgment Record for the August Court of 1758 begins on page 1 of a volume marked "1758-1760, Part I." That Court convened on the third Tuesday and the 15th day of August in the 8th year of His Lordship's Dominion. Present were the Worshipful Thomas Beatty, Gentleman, Chief Justice, Thomas Prather, Joseph Wood, Joseph Smith, Andrew Heugh, William Luckett, Peter Bainbridge, Moses Chapline and Jacob Duckett. James Dixon, Gentleman, was Sheriff and John Darnall was Clerk.

The Grand Jury consisted of Joseph Beall, foreman, Charles Jones RC [Rock Creek?], Richard Ancrum, Stephen Rensberg, Nathaniel Magruder son of Ninian, James Coffee, John Moore of Antieatum, Peter Kemp, John Swearingen, Jr., William Blair, William Shields, Zacharia Magruder, William Duvall, Thomas Fee, James Beall son of Ninian and James Hooke.

The Grand Jurors presented four indictments:
Samuel Deuvall, James Brown, Isabel Willit and John Nichols of Thomas, for "keeping back taxables."
Eve Wall "for feloniously taking 20 shilling bill of the Colona of Vergana [Colony of Virginia?]."
Thomas Ledston for stealing a horse from Elias DeLashmutt.

There are several pages of applications for licenses to keep taverns, but not one of them indicates geographic location and so all are lacking in historical significance.

Benjamin Kelly petitions the Court "that on November last died Mr. Brock Mackbee, his wife and child left behind them a large family of young children, unprovided for and living on the petitioner's land. Your petitioner in regard to the family was at the charge of burying the said Brock, his wife and child in a decent manner and likewise I have been at a great expense in clothing and maintaining them ever since the death of the said Brock Macabee and as to the estate of the said Brock his eldest son by a former wife, Egbert Macbee, have taken all and will not assist in maintaining the children on any account. Your petitioner, being a poor man and having a family of his own cannot afford to maintain the other without being allowed something towards maintaining them."

The Court allowed the petitioner 2,000 pounds of tobacco "for the care and expense he has been at."

A petition of Timothy Killeyhorn states that "being old and past his labor and drove down by the Indians from his habitation whereby he has met with considerable losses and at present in very low circumstances so that he most humbly beggeth the Court to allow him small pension which without he is not able to live, he being obliged last year to sell his shirt off his back for four shillings to pay his levy. He therefore most humbly beggeth, Gentlemen, that you would take his case into your consideration."

The Court allows him 400 pounds of tobacco for his support until next November Court.

Valentine Usleman petitions the Court that he "had a servant inlisted into His Majesty's service for which he never received any satisfaction for, your petitioner therefore humbly prays some allowance for said servant."

The Court rejects his petition.

Charles Howard of Baltimore County petitions the Court "that a certain William Lewis of said County has under his care an orphan named Edmond Howard, aged about 19 years, which is yet unbound by the Court and as the said child is brother to your petitioner he is therefore desirous of having said child bound unto him and prays that the said William Lewis may be summoned to bring the child unto the next County Court to be bound out as the Court shall think fit."

A petition by sundry inhabitants of Little Pipe Creek states "that your petitioners have long labored under a very great inconveniency, viz., of having no road, or at least no direct road from their settlement to Frederick Town. We therefore humbly pray Your Worships to grant us an order in Court to clear a road from where the dividing line of Frederick County and Baltimore County crosses the waggon road that leads from Baltimore Town to this settlement (said road being cleared as farr as said line by order of Baltimore County Court) till it strikes the Conestogoe Road that leads to Frederick Town near George Trucks and as your petitioners humbly conceive the said road will be of great service to travellers in particular who incline to travel the old Indian Road which is rendered almost impracticable now by plantations and want of opening, so it will be of infinite service to your petitioners in general who by means of this road will have much easier access to this Town, to transact their lawful affairs."

The Court appointed William Farquer, William Roberts and Joseph Sparks or any two of them "to goe and view the road and acquaint the several persons that have lands that may be affected thereby to appear at the next County Court and make their objections."

Rates of liquors and other ordinary accommoda-

182

tions vendible in this County for the ensuing year were set as follows:

Hot dyet for a gentleman with a pint of beer or cyder	1/3
Same for gentleman's servant with ditto	-/9
Cold dyet with ditto	-/9
Corn and oats per bushel and so pro rata per Winchester measure	4/-
Stabling and good fodder for a horse per night	-/9
Ditto for 24 hours	1/2
Lodging in a bed per night	-/6
Good small beer per gallon, sealed and so pro rata	1/-
Maryland good strong beer, per gallon	2/-
Peach brandy per gallon	10/8
Cyder per gallon	1/8
Maryland spirits, distilled from grain, per gal.	8/-
Rum per sealed quart	4/-
Bowl of punch with sealed quart of rum and loaf sugar	5/-
Ditto with brown sugar	4/-
Quart of Madeira rum	4/-
Port wine, sealed, per quart	5/-
All European wines not here mentioned per sealed quart	5/-
English strong beer per sealed quart	1/8
French brandy per quart made into punch with loaf sugar	8/-
Good lemons, a piece	-/6
Good limes, a piece	-/2

"Ordered that bench warrant issue for searching Thomas Graves' house."

"Ordered that Mathew Mackbee, aged 15 years, Jeremiah Mackbee, aged 11 years, Mary Mackbee, aged 5 years, and Cazier Mackbee, aged 2 years, be bound to Benjamin Kelly and that the said Kelly learn the boys to read and write and the girl to read and that he give them at the expiration of their freedom [sic] cloathes and every other necessary for orphans."

"The Court agrees with Dr. James Brand for to attend the several County pension[er]s and such other persons as shall be deemed proper objects of charity within this County, recommended by any one Magistrate to the said Doctor's care. As such the said Doctor to agree with any convenient nurse to attend said objects not exceeding ten shilling per week, including board which account shall be legally proved by such persons nursing said pension[er]s or other persons and the said Doctor for his medicines and attendance be allowed £55 per year and that a proportional part thereof be levied next November Court and that he produce to the next August Court an account of the medicines by him expended on account of said pension[er]s at the same price that he supplys others at."

In a suit by His Lordship against Elizbeth Ireland for bastardy, she is fined £3 and William Waugh and Michael Jesserang are bound in £10 each for the fine and to bear the County harmless.

In a suit of His Lordship against Margaret Ward for breach of the peace for beating and abusing John Johnson, she appears in Court and throws herself on the mercy of the Court through her attorney Loyd Buchanan.
The Court fines her 20 shillings.

NOVEMBER COURT OF 1758

The November Court of 1758 met on the third Tuesday and the 21st day of November in the eighth year of His Lordship's Dominion. The Justices present were: Thomas Beatty, Gentleman, Chief Justice, Thomas Prather, Thomas Norris, William Luckett, David Lynn, Joseph Smith, Charles Jones, Joseph

Wood, Moses Chapline, Andrew Hugh and Peter Bainbridge.

The Grand Jury consisted of Thomas Claggett, foreman, Hezekiah Magruder, John Prather, William Kelly, Stephen Rensburg, Samuel Ellis, Conrad Hogmire, William Campbell, Samuel Cissel, Michael Jesserang, Michael Raymer, Edward Crow, Joseph Johnson, Jehu Ogle and Hugh Riley.

They present:
Michael Dowden "for a cheat."
Wensley Bean "for assaulting Robert Constable on October 20th on his own plantation."
Conrad Whinemiller "for stealing a horse belonging to William Duval."
Ann Hilton "for having of a mulatto child."

Constables in present-day Frederick County included Samuel Wickham (upper Part of Monocacy Hundred), William Lewis (Pipe Creek), John Seagar (Burnt House Woods), William Beall (Middle Part, Monocacy), Thomas Tennelly (Lower Part, Monocacy), John Kimboll (Frederick Town), Edward Butler (Kittocton).

Road overseers of interest were:
Meredith Davis for the road "from Monocacy Ferry to Ballenger's Branch and from the main road that leads to the Mouth of Monocacy to the ford commonly called Powell's Ford."
William McCarty for "all the main roads that lie between Ballenger's Branch and Potomac that leads to the top of Kittocton Mountain."
Thomas Taylor for "the new road that leads from the top of Kittoctin by George Matthews to Ballenger's Branch.
John Tucker for "the road called the River Road and Touchstone's Road and the road that leads from Alexander Jones' to the top of Kittocton Mountain that leads

to Frederick Town.

John Huffman "agrees to take John Bligh, an orphan child aged two years next February, to keep the same child to June Court next for £4."

"Bench warrant ordered and issued against [Dr.] George Jacob Troutwine."

"Ordered that Thomas Beatty be allowed £20 for keeping ferry where Thomas Reynolds now lives till next November Court."

Joseph Mayhew, having been appointed pressmaster for the County, petitions the Court that he "thinks himself uncapable, being an old man and much troubled with the sceatick [sciatic] pains" and asks that he be relieved and somebody appointed in his place. The Court discharges him and appoints John Kimboll "in his room."

Sundry inhabitants of the County, who are unnamed, petition the Court that they "conceive a better and nigher road might be made to Fort Frederick for the road to begin out of the road now leading thereto between the Mountains through Curry's Gap by Robert Turner's and by Joseph Holmes, by Dr. Neal's and so into the road by Joseph Volgamot's." The Court appointed Capt. Moses Chapline, Mr. James Smith and Mr. Joseph Tomlinson to lay out the road.

Martin Line petitions the Court that "in the year of God 1753 [he] redeemed a redemptioner as a servant from Garmany then deemed to be ten years of age until he should arrive to the age of 21 years and having no indenture according to law humbly prayeth Your Worships to adjudge the same according as the law directs."
The Court orders that the petitioner "have the effect of his prayer."

186

John Justice petitions the Court "that your petitioner is now almost 80 years of age and is not able to do anything "for the support of his family" and asks to be made levy-free.

The Court rejects his petition.

The Vestry of Prince George's Parish petitions the Court to levy a tax "of three pounds of tobacco per poll on the taxable inhabitants of Prince George's Parish."

The Court grants the petition.

John Pritchett states in a petition to the Court that he had previously been allowed 1,000 pounds of tobacco for the support of himself and his wife and that this had been supplemented by use of a house and a small allowance from Walter Evans, owner of a small tub mill for which the petitioner was caretaker. He states that Mr. Evans has now disposed of his mill and therefore his additional means of support is no longer available. He asks therefore for an increase in his allowance, which the Court rejects.

Esther Matew petitions the Court that she and her granddaughter having been sick for a long time and her granddaughter being born a natural [an idiot] from her birth and she herself being 75 [years old] asks that she be granted further allowance.

The Court allows her 1,600 pounds of tobacco.

Mary Sims petitions the Court "that whereas your petitioner is confined in Frederick County gaol and likely so to be for some time, she therefore prays Your Worships would grant her the liberty of having a small chamber stove fixed into the chimney of the upper room of said gaol which if Your Worships will please to view you will be persuaded it will be of no prejudice to the said chimney's draught or security of the gaol.

"Which petition was read and nothing further done."

187

Richard Coombs petitions the Court "for a license to keep tavern on the road to Baltimore Town near the Burnt House Woods [vicinity of Taylorsville]."

The Court grants him the license.

Timothy Collihorn petitions that "thro the many unhappy vicissitudes incident to humanity he is under a necessity of petitioning for relief....and having had his substance destroyed by the Indians and being old and very infirm" asks for relief.

The Court rejects his petition. (See also below.)

Simon Nicholls presents the following account to the Court, dated November 1757:

Coffin for Lewis Jones	£1/-/-
"My trouble for burying him"	1/-/-
He petitions for reimbursement of:	£2/-/-

and the Court grants him his petition.

A petition by Susannah Apple states that she "was employed by Dr. James Brand for attending and keeping a soldier named Thomas Perkins in his sickness and had a great deal of trouble with him for the space of two weeks." Then he died. She asks that she be allowed for her trouble and the Court grants her 320 pounds of tobacco.

Dr. James Brand presents to the Court an account from Lodowick Young "for making a coffin for one of his patients" in the amount of £2.

The Court grants him 96 pounds of tobacco for the recovery on the bill.

Timothy Calyhorn (see also above) states to the Court in a second petition that "having the misfortune of being drove from my habitation by the Indians" he hopes that the Court will allow him some relief.

The Court rejects his petition.

Joseph Smith and Moses Chapline, who had been

appointed by the Court to view a road desired through a gap in the Mountains called Curry's Gap, state that this road "is a better way from Frederick Town to Fort Frederick than any yet carried across said Mountain."

Sundry inhabitants, whose names are not noted, petition the Court that "their business requires them to pass very frequently over the ferry at Mouth of Monocacy." They state that the cost of the ferry is quite a burden on them and they ask that the Court "change the said ferry from a public to a County one, so that every resident of the said County may freely pass by egress and regress."

The Court orders that the petition be granted.

In an account presented to the Court in a suit of Christopher Lowndes and Company versus William Beall's executor is an item for one tomahawk valued at 2 sh., 6d.

In a suit by William Beall versus Nathaniel Wickham, Sr., the item most frequently appearing in the account is for "shaving, 6d."

In a suit by Thomas Cresap against Barney Hughes and Joseph Simons, whose total amount is £293/13/10, credit is allowed for the defendants in the amount of £200/1/- "for sundry goods agreed for as by invoice which goods according to said agreement were to be delivered at Fort Cumberland."

In a condemnation suit of Abraham Crum versus Michael Danbuscart one item in the appraisal is for "three acres of Indian corn now growing, at 12 sh., 6d per acre."

An order (dated August 23, 1758) out of the Lord Proprietary's High Court of Chancery to James Dickson, Gentleman, Sheriff, ordered him to convene at

189

least three Justices together with himself to sit as a
Court of Elections and to set a date for the freemen of
the County to elect four delegates to the General As-
sembly to be held on the third Tuesday in October at
Annapolis. Present were Thomas Beatty, Thomas
Prather, Joseph Wood and William Luckett, Gentle-
men, Justices, together with the Sheriff. The Court
set Wednesday September 27th as the day for election.
Those elected were Capt. Henry Wright Crabb, Capt.
Joseph Chapline, Edward Dorsey, Esquire and Thomas
Cresap, Gentleman.

This entry, out of chronological order with the
others, was perhaps an afterthought. It is followed by
a notation that the November Court adjourned to the
third Tuesday of March next.

MARCH COURT OF 1759

The March Court of 1759 met on the third Tuesday
and the 20th day of March in the eighth year of Frederick's Dominion. Present were the following Justices: Thomas Beatty, Gentleman, Chief Justice,
Moses Chapline, Thomas Norris, William Luckett,
David Lynn, Joseph Wood, Peter Bainbridge and Joseph Smith.

James Dickson, Sheriff, presented to the Court
his panel of Grand Jurymen and Petit Jurymen. "The
Grand and Petit Jury discharged without either being
impaneled upon account of the smallpox raging in
Frederick Town at this present time."

In the absence of the Grand Jury the Court issued
several orders of attachment and bench warrants and
ordered the Sheriff to pay Michael Miller an extra 500
pounds of tobacco over and above the 700 pounds allowed him last November, the Sheriff to make this
payment "out of the tobacco he now has in his hands."

Another order issued by the Court was to the

effect that "Mr. John Cooke be wrote to to settle with this County for the tobacco due it and in his hands unaccounted for."

Thomas Slighe presents a petition to the Court in which he says "that your petitioner did not intend to keep tavern any longer last August Court but as he now has a mind to keep the same for another year" he asks for a license, which is granted. (See below.)

John Moore, stating to the Court "that your petitioner is very desirous of keeping a public house or house of entertainment near Fort Frederick," applies for a license, which is granted.

In a suit of Ninian Beall versus Edward Burrage on an open account, certain items allowed as credits against the account are as follows:

For weaving 33 yards of linnen at 6d per yard
For weaving 35 yards of cloath at 6d per yard
One-half bushel of hemp seed, 2 shillings

Henry Hill petitions the Court for relief, stating that he is "incapable of getting his living, being upwards of 60 years of age."
The Court allows him 800 pounds of tobacco.

"James Dickson, Sheriff of Frederick County, acknowledges to have received of Joseph Wood 15 shillings currency as a fine of Thomas Sligh for selling liquor without a license."

JUNE COURT OF 1759

The Court reconvened on the third Tuesday and 19th day of June in the ninth year of the Dominion of Frederick. The Justices present were Thomas Beatty, Gentleman, Chief Justice, Charles Jones, David Lynn, William Luckett, Joseph Wood, Thomas Norris, Joseph Smith, Andrew Heugh, Moses Chapline and Peter Bainbridge.

191

Impaneled as Grand Jurors were Charles Harding, foreman, John Johnson, John Wilds, Jacob Foutz, John Carmack, William Powell, John Jones, Benjamin Harris, Van Swearingen, Jr., William Blaire, Stephen Julian, Thomas Hawkins, Frail Pain, Gabriel Ketchentandr, William Carmack, Philip Pindle, William Beatty, William Murdock and Abraham Haff.

David White, aged 12, is bound to John Dears and the said Dears promises "to learn the said White to read, write and cast accounts."

"Henry Gaither allowed £5 for the keeping [of] Ann Hilton's mulatto child from November Court last to this Court."

"Ann Hilton's child named John Hilton being viewed by the Court here, it is adjudged that the said child is a mulatto and ordered to be sold to the highest bidder in consequence thereof. Henry Gaither bought said child for £10 to be paid next November Court; said child born August 2, 1758."

"Ordered that the windows of the office in the Court House be mended and that Mr. Slye make lattices of wire to said windows of the Court House and window shutters and what other necessary repairs is wanting about the Court House and bring his account for the same."

"Ordered that Mr. Dickson pay to Mr. David Lynn 8 shillings, which he paid the printer for advertising the Public Gazette in relation to weights and standards for the use of this County."

Sundry unnamed inhabitants present a petition to the Court asking it to "order the publick main road to be laid out from Christian Shoat's Mill on Bush Creek to Daniel Kennedy's ford on Monocacy."

Elizabeth Hall, servant of John Banks, brings

192

suit against Banks, stating that she "has served her time with John Banks of this County and he has turned her away without giving her anything at all, nor please Your Worships he wont deliver up the indenture, so please Your Worships she hopes that you will all take into consideration for to look into it about her freedom dues and she will in duty bound for to pray for you all, Gentlemen."

The Court ordered a summons for Banks and ordered that Elizabeth collect her freedom dues agreeable to Act of Assembly and her costs.

Unnamed inhabitants of the Andeatum area state to the Court that "ever since the march of General Braddock" there has been a bridge over Andeatum built by the inhabitants at the request of Governor Sharpe. The bridge, although slightly built, has been found of great convenience to the inhabitants and travelers. They request the Court to build a better bridge, and the Court grants the request.

Thomas Kirk was brought into Court accused of stealing a pair of black worsted stockings valued at 20 pounds of tobacco. He protested his innocence and a jury was impaneled which found him guilty. He was sentenced to "be set upon the pillory for 15 minutes and afterwards be set to the whipping post and there receive on his bare back 15 lashes well laid on."

Margaret Wilson was tried in Court, charged with stealing a beehive valued at 50 pounds of tobacco. A jury was impaneled and found her innocent.

In a suit of John Westby versus John Quirk on an open account a few items are valued as follows:

3 packs of cards	3/-
1 spelling book	3/-
1 quire of paper	2/-
1 coffee pot	12/-
1 New Testament	2/6

In a suit by Dr. George Jacob Troutwine against John Trammel for medical services it is shown that the fee for one visit was ten shillings.

James Conn sues Middleton Smith and his wife Rebecca on an account which consists of the following, addressed to Mrs. Rebecca Ramsey as the debtor:

1 hogshead of tobacco, net of 832 lbs.
Cash lent   £4/ 6/-
Making 4 shirts at 3 sh. each   12/-
Washing and mending   6/-

Evidently Smith married Mrs. Ramsey and is now being sued for her debt.

For those who consider the term "Irish Potatoes" as entering our American vocabulary at the time of the 19th Century potato famine and its resultant migration of Irish people to our shores, it is interesting to note in another suit, one century earlier, on an open account:

1 bu. of Irish potatoes   2/-

AUGUST COURT OF 1759

The August Court of 1759 met on the third Tuesday and the 21st day of August in the ninth year of Frederick's Dominion. The Justices present were: Thomas Prather, William Luckett, Thomas Norris, Joseph Wood, David Linn, Peter Bainbridge and Moses Chapline.

The Grand Jury consisted of Arthur Nelson, foreman, Peter Stilly, John Fletchall, Jeremiah Virgin, Stephen Rensberg, Van Swearingen, Sr., Jonathan Hagar, Mark Casner, John Cartwright, George French, George Loy, Garah Davis, Serrett Dickerson, John Shelman, Michael Miller and Walter Smith Greenfield.

"Ordered by the Court that the Clerk write in each lawyer's docket for November Court next that no action without sufficient cause shown shall be continued on the docket beyond the time limited by law for the future."

"Ordered by the Court that if Thomas Sly do not glaze the windows of the Court House before the bad weather that Peter Butler agree with somebody to do it."

Mary Hunt presents a petition to the Court that "having bound her son Richard Johnson an apprentice to Bartholomew Lynham of Frederick Town to learn the art of the tailor's trade, instead of that may it please Your Worships that he keeps him to wash dishes, to clean knives and forks and all manner of drudgery about the house, contrary to the tenor of my agreement and not only so but uses him in the most barbarious manner by whipping him to that degree more like a horse than a Christian, which is a great grief to me that bore him of my body. I beg Your Worships to be so candid as to take some proper method with Lynham to use my child more milder and to learn him his trade according to the tenor of my agreement or else let me have him again."

Seemingly something is missing from the record, since the final entry is that "the Court ordered that he [Lynham] be dismissed with costs." A subsequent entry notes Bartholomew Lynham's application for a license to keep a tavern. This somewhat explains the use Lynham was making of his tailor-apprentice.

Mary Ann March petitions the Court that "she has a son named James Hamilton who was bound an apprentice to Mr. John Adamson of this County to learn the art, trade or mistery of a peruke maker, but contrary to the agreement he keeps said apprentice to the hoe and ax and has not complied with the indenture." Summons were issued for both master and apprentice.

Henry Fiander presents a petition to the Court that "he received a great hurt some years ago by a

195

hogshead of tobacco running over him which disabled him so that he is not capable of doing any hard labor." He asks to be made levy-free in the future and for some allowance for welfare, both of which the Court grants.

Michael Jesserang gives security for his proper keeping of tavern in Frederick Town.

Christian Leatherman, Nicholas Leatherman, John Arnold, Jr., Daniel Arnold and Mathias Syler give bond to the Court in the amount of £20 that "they do build a bridge over Andietum by November Court next and also keep said bridge in good repair for ten years."

Here the Court adjourned until the third Tuesday in November next [1759], although the next entries in the volume marked "1758-1760, Part I" concern the March Court of 1760, q.v.

NOVEMBER COURT OF 1759

For entries pertaining to this Court, we must return to page 1108 of the Judgments volume marked "H-2" (see also above, p. 176). The November Court met on the third Tuesday and 20th day of November in the ninth year of Frederick's Dominion.

The Justices present were: Thomas Beatty, Thomas Prather, Joseph Wood, David Lynn, Andrew Heugh, Thomas Norris, William Luckett, Moses Chapline, Charles Jones and Peter Bainbridge. James Dickson was Sheriff and John Darnall was Clerk.

The Grand Jury consisted of Stephen Newton Chiswell, foreman, John Smith, John Simpson, Samuel Reed, James Coffee, Stephen Julian, Nathaniel Magruder, John Watson, Jacob Brunner, Sr., John Swearingen, George Clem, Jonathan Hagar, William

Williams, William Thomas, Clementious Davis, Abraham Laken and Gilbert Kemp.

Among the presentments by the Grand Jury were the following:

Mary Ann March for "inticing and convaying the servant of John Adamson, her son, and clandestanly binding him to another person to ye damage of said master."

Bartholomew Lynham "for denying a diet when requested and when pay was tendered."

Susanna Striflar petitions the Court "that your petitioner has been now two years past unfortunately married to a servant, one Hans Vindil Striflar of this town who most inhumanly and cruelly treats and behaves toward your petitioner that your petitioner not withstanding the barbarous and severe usage received from her said husband Striflar has from her own nature been always industrous to endeavour to reconcile herself to her said husband in all his humours and has endeavoured by a faithfull discharge of her sacremental vows to make life easy and agreeable to him in every shape and for this purpose by her own labour and industry has often acquired by her own particular services several sums of money which upon her return home the said Striflar, her husband, assisted by his daughters by a former wife has been taken from her and your petitioner stript of everything and turned naked out of doors. This practice has been two after [too often] and frequently repeated to your petitioner and she must be without redress unless Your Worships will in some shape take her case into consideration and grant her such relief as in humanity she ought deservedly to receive."

"Upon reading this petition and consideration thereof had, it is ordered by the Court here that nothing further be done in the premises."

Cornelius Poulson in a petition to the Court states

that having lived in the County upwards of thirty years
and willingly and cheerfully paying his taxes has now
"by the blessing of God" arrived at the age of 65 years.
"He pleads the privilege and benefit of the law made
and provided for the setting the aged levy free" and requests that he be therefore free of taxes.
The Court rejects his petition.

Sundry inhabitants of the precinct between Great
Pipe Creek and the Temporary Line petition that "they
never consented to the new road laid out by Peter Owler as the subscribers find they cannot make a sufficient road in crossing Pin[e]y Creek at that place being
swampy ground and requires four bridges which every
high fresh[et] carried off and as the old road has a good
gravel fording place pray that Your Worships will allow the old road to stand."
The Court rejects the petition.

Another petition by the Pipe Creek inhabitants
states that last year they applied for an order to "clear
a road from Baltimore County near the head of Little
Pipe Creek through their settlement to the old York
Road near George Trucks [cf. above, p. 182]," but
that nothing has been done in response. They state
that "in times of great floods many people are put in
eminent danger at the fords of the two Creeks." They
ask that a bridge be built over the two fords.
The Court grants the request.

The Vestry of Prince George's Parish petitions
the Court to levy two pounds of tobacco on the taxables
of the Parish.
The Court grants the request.

The Vestry of All Saints Parish likewise requests
a levy on the taxables of its Parish, but its requested
amount is ten pounds per taxable. The petition is
signed by "Joseph Wood, Registrar."
The Court orders this levy also made.

In a petition to the Court John Ferguson states that he "has lodged, maintained, found everything, nursed and attended a certain Jane Johnson for the space of fourteen days and then died and as the said John Ferguson found and furnished all materials toward bur[y]-ing said person" he requests some allowance be made to him.

The Court allows him £4/10 in the next levy.

Thomas Lewis presents a petition to the Court in which he states that he "has boarded and nursed Alexander Reed and George Streetton as per Dr. James Brand's agreement with me." He asks for payment.

The Court allows him 1,337 pounds of tobacco.

Josiah Gosling petitions the Court "that your petitioner has a rupt[ur]ed man and almost past his labour and did gitt his damage in King George the First servis on bord the Lenox man of war and was allowed by Chest of Chapham £6 a year pention" and asks for some allowance.

The Court grants him 600 pounds of tobacco in the next levy.

Parenthetically, to the casual observer this Court seemed to have had an unusual number of applications for welfare, relief and pensions.

The Court appoints overseers for various roads in the County, including the following:

From the Mouth of Monocacy to Ballenger's Branch and from Powell's Ford to the said road and from the upper end of Pyburn's old field to the top of Kittocton Mountain and from William Barker's to the upper ford on Monocacy: John Jacobs, overseer.

From Monocacy west bank at Reynold's Ferry to Linginoa Ford: Michael Harmon.

The road called Touchstone's Road and the road that leads from where A[lexander] Jones lived to the top of Kittocton that leads to Frederick Town and the road that leads from the top of ditto by Ses[?] Schaf's place to the top of the South Mountain: William House.

From the road that leads out of the main road by Capt. Bainbridge's to the top of the South Mountain and the new road that goes through Curry's Gap: John George Arnold, Jr.

All the main roads below Beaver Creek in Andietum Hundred and the new road from Curry's Gap to Beaver Creek: Nathan Robinett.

From Smith's Branch to Great Pipe Creek and to Diggs's Works and the new road from Log Cabbin Branch to George Trucks: Paul Woolf.

From Great Pipe Creek to the Temporary Line: Frederick Fryer.

From Major Ogle's Ford to John Biggs' Ford on Monocacy: Gilbert Crum.

From the Temporary Line to Ambrose's Mill: William Elder, Jr.

From Ambrose's Mill to Miller's Mill: Lawrence Creager.

From Frederick Town to Richardson's Mill and to Foutt's Mill and to the ford at Daniel Kennedy's: Francis Pairpoint.

From the upper bridge in Frederick Town to the top of Kittocton and the road from Ballenger's Branch to the road that leads from Frederick Town to Conococheague: Adam Ransberg.

From Frederick Town to Reynold's Ford and to John Biggs' Ford: Christian Thomas.

All the streets and lanes in Frederick Town and the road to the English church and the road to Mr. Dulany's Mill and the road to Rue's ford: John Adam Evertt.

Sheriff Samuel Beall, Jr., petitions the Court as follows: "Your petitioner humbly begs leave to move for your consideration on the most deplorable state and condition of the unhappy prisoners arising from the want of fresh water and a necessary place &c. As he flatters himself from your known humane dispositions no arguments need be urged to engage or excite your compassion for those miserable people. A long detail of the risque of their health and infection that may in all probability arise thereon for want of those necessaries which Nature &c may require need not be run out. Therefore give him leave to hope for your serious reflections thereon and grant such relief as your wisdom shall direct....

"Upon reading which petition....the Court agrees with Thomas Schley to sink a well in the prison yard which is to have sufficient water therein, to wall up said well in a workmanlike manner and put therein a good and sufficient pump, also to build in said yard an House of Office with a sink and an iron grate to the sink and a trough to lead from the pump to the House of Office so as to carry off the filth and to give him for the above services the sum of £30."

Schley, who is here shown as an innkeeper, gives a performance bond for £30. His securities are William Luckett and James Dickson.

"The Court here agrees with Thomas Schley to make one hundred tin or brass badges for the pensioners of this County to be stamped on each badge 'A pensioner of Frederick County, Maryland' for the sum of £5.... Ordered by the Court here that every pensioner of this County ware a badge when given them for the future upon the upper garment on the upper side of the arm constantly. If they do not comply and wear the same their pension to be taken from them."

Daniel Michael was charged with stealing a "cuting knife" of the value of 40 pounds of tobacco. He pled not guilty and demanded a jury trial. A jury was impaneled, consisting of the following: Nathaniel Magruder, Charles Hedge, Aaron Lanham, John Johnson, Rudolf Eltinge, William Patrick, Joshua Harbin, John Johnson, Jr., James Gore, Samuel Plumer, Peter Stilly and Hesekiah Magruder. After testimony from 11 witnesses, including William Dern and William Dern, Jr., each of whom "attended for seven days,"

201

Michael was found guilty. The Record, however, does not state his punishment for so small an offense.

The Court orders that all actions on the trial docket on which judgments have not been entered be continued until March Court next, "it appearing to the Court that Daniel Dulany, Esq., one of the attorneys of this Court, is sick and is unable to attend."

Here the Court adjourned until the March Court of 1760, although the next entries in Volume "H-2," beginning on page 1121, pertain to the June 1758 Court, as detailed above, page 177.

MARCH COURT OF 1760

Entries for the March Court of 1760, which met on the third Tuesday and the 18th day of March in the ninth year of Frederick's Dominion, may be found in the Judgment Record for "1758-1760, Part 2," following the August Court of 1759, i.e., on pages 647-730.

The Worshipful Justices present were Thomas Beatty, Joseph Wood, David Lynn, William Luckett, Peter Bainbridge, Thomas Norris and Moses Chapline, Gentlemen. Nathaniel Beall, Gentleman, was Sheriff and John Darnall was still Clerk.

The Grand Jurymen were John Middagh, foreman, Erasmus Gill, Alexander Magruder, Peter Stilley, Joseph Mayhew, Arthur Nelson, William Carmack, Thomas Whitten, John Greenup, Thomas Beatty, Jr., Henry Clegett, John Dowden, Joseph Perry, Jonathan Hagar and Zachariah Magruder.

They presented:
John Woodard and Luke Woodard "for committing an assault and battery on Ninian Beall Magruder, one of His Lordship's officers in the execution of his office."
Benjamin Macall, Jr., and James Macall "for as-

saulting Richard Talburd on the road and threatening his life."

James Hutchcraft "for passing of split Pennsilvany currency for double the value of it to Catherine Callaghan."

Catherine Cramer "for stealing a hatt belonging to Richard Holland."

Jacob Young "for committing an assault and battery on Catherine Young, his wife, and threatening her life and cocking a pistle at his wife's mother's breast and declaring if she speaks a word he'll shoot her."

In a petition to the Court Sarah Butler states that she "has two Negroes, one named Paul and the other Joice, who are incapable by old age and other infirmities to labor" and asks that they be set levy-free.

The Court grants the petition.

Juliana Benninger presents a petition to the Court in which she states that a certain John Trundle, a tenant farmer, "hath detained Catharine Wolphin, daughter of the said Juliana, illegally although the said Catharine hath demanded of John Trundle [her freedom]. From time to time he has refused to let her depart from him." She asks the Court to proceed according to their sentiments in such a case.

The Court orders a summons to issue returnable in the June Court for John Trundle.

John Shelman presents a petition to the Court in which he states that "on the thirteenth instant at night or after midnight the persons hereafter mentioned, viz., Benjamin Wofford, Charles Turner, Alexander Scott, William Duvall, Philip Turner and Charles Scott did at the house of your petitioner forcibly try to break into his house and when they could not break the door, they did throw stones or something as did break your petitioner's barr window entirely, consisting of four sash panes of glass and seven panes of glass about the same size of upper windows." He petitions the

Court for redress, and the Court issues summons for the parties named, returnable at June Court next.

Sundry inhabitants, unnamed, petition the Court, stating that they live about Toms Creek and that "it would be of much advantage to us to have a road opened from Rankin's Mill in the side of the South Mountain, a path that formerly led to said mill being so stop'd and turned about by new improvements and cast upon such hilly and rough ground that it is almost impossible to take a moderate load either on horseback or waggon to the said mill." They ask that a better road be laid out, and the Court appoints Samuel Carrack and Thomas Wilson to lay out the said road and "give notice to all parties concerned and make report to June Court next."

In a memorandum dated December 15, 1759 Joseph Wood and Thomas Norris state that they "have this day agreed with George Trucks to build a bridge over Little Pipe Creek at the ford nie where he now lives for the sum of £40 current money to be finished by the second Tuesday in August next and to maintain the same for ten years."

A similar memorandum is dated the same day, presumably by the same two people, who state that they have "agreed with Messrs. John Logsdon and James White to build a bridge over Great Pipe Creek at the York ford near George Trucks and to maintain the same for ten years for the sum of £60 and to be finished by the second Tuesday of August next."

Evan Shelby presents a petition in which he states "that the road leading from Chambers Mill to Fort Frederick is greatly wanted for King's stores, etc., to be carried that way. Therefore prays You to order the same to be cleared."
The Court ordered that "Isaac Baker and Thomas Edmonston lay out the road prayed for.... and the over-

seer of Conococheague Hundred to clear the same."

"Ordered by the Court that James Allen deliver Isaac Parsley to Leonard Wayman, he being bound to said Wayman by his mother."

A suit by His Lordship against Catherine Smith "for having a mulatto bastard" was struck off "by order of the Court, defendant being run away."

Another suit in the name of His Lordship against Bartholomew Lynham "for refusing to sell accommodations," was "abated by death of defendant."

In a suit against Ann Cook for bastardy, she was fined £1/10. Reverend Thomas Bacon became security for the payment of the fine. The order was issued by Joseph Wood on March 4, 1760.

Margaret Drapier brings suit against John Preston and wife Mary. She states "that she hath ever been accounted esteemed and reputed amongst good honest and prudent men as well as her neighbors....to be of good name, character, honest behavior and adversation and hath all her life lived and continued untouched and unsuspected of the crime of fornication and incontinancy or such like enormous crime and that because thereof several young men of good name and character had at several times desired to take her to be their wife and in particular one John Ogle of Frederick County, farmer, before the speaking and publishing of the false and scandalous words hereafter mentioned did with great fervancy and protestations of love and sincerity solicit the said Margaret to consent to be his wife." She also states that she was at the time "a sole unmarried, pure, chaste and honest virgin" and that Mary Preston knew all these facts and maliciously undertook to prevent her marriage by stating in hearing of many and good and true that "Margaret hath a bastard son" and "a child who calls her sister to cloak the said Margaret's disgrace." She further states that because of these malicious slanders her suitor abandoned her and her reputation has been ruined to the extent of £130 current money.

Both plaintiff and defendants submit their case to the Court and a jury is impaneled, consisting of William Pritchett, Thomas Hogg, James Henthorn, William Duval, Edward Bucey, Zachariah Magruder, Middleton Smith, Joseph Ray, Joshua Harbin, John Ray, Jr., Charles Harding and Thomas Nickolls, Jr. The Jury finds the defendants guilty and Margaret is awarded £10 current money and 2,052¼ pounds of tobacco for her costs.

Richard Snowden sues Benjamin Harris on an open account, whose items include the following:

2 Dutch blankits	14/-
1 quire of wrighting paper	-/9
3 yards bead ticken [bed ticking]	3/-
1 thimbell	-/2

In another suit on open account, we find these items:

1 linnen wheel	7/6
1 reel	4/-
1 churn	3/-

The following items appear in a suit of William Duval versus Henry Threlkeld:

my two shares of 10,133 lbs. of crop inspected tobacco, clear of casks made on your plantation	1842 lbs.
boarding your coopper as per agreement when making of hogsheads	30 lbs.

Named in a suit of William Quick versus Middleton Smith are these items:

13 lbs. shuger [sugar]	13/-

3 barrels and 4 bu. Inden corn	1/18/-
2 laying hens	1/3
½ bu. flax seed	1/9
3 horse collers	3/-

JUNE COURT OF 1760

The June Court of 1760 convened on the third Tuesday and the 17th day of June in the tenth year of Frederick's Dominion. The following Justices were present: Thomas Beatty, Thomas Prather, Joseph Wood, Charles Jones, David Lynn, Thomas Norris, William Luckett, Peter Bainbridge and Moses Chapline, Gentlemen. Samuel Beall was Sheriff and John Darnall was Clerk.

The Grand Jury was composed of Arnold Nelson, foreman, Joseph Beall, Thomas Lansdale, Hezekiah Magruder, William Knight, William Beatty, John Carmack, William Harrison, Abraham Haff, Joshua Bucey, Richard Anderson, John Fletchall, Stephen Julian, Stephen Ransberg, Abraham Crum, Jonathan Hagar and David Jones.

Among their presentments were:
Patrick Swilevan [Sullivan] for stealing a pocketbook of Stephen Ransberg "with about twenty pounds in itt."
Nathaniel Pigman "for assaulting and beating George Rice."

"Mr. Thomas Johnson and Mr. Hugh West qualify as attorneys of this Court."

"John McCullagh, aged 12 years last April, and Daniel McCullagh, aged 7 years May 13th last, is bound to Matthew Clark and Elizabeth, his wife, till they arrive at the age of 21 years; said Clark is to learn them reading, writing and arithmetic and to give each of them at the age of 16 years a breeding mare with £5 and when free....a decent suit of apparel."

207

"Ordered by the Court here that Samuel Beall, Gentleman, Sheriff, apply to the Clerk of Charles and Ann Arundel Counties to get a copy of the rules of their Courts for which this Court will allow him any reasonable costs he may be at."

"The Court here agrees with Joseph Hardman to dig a sufficient sink twelve foot deep and stone it up and to be six feet in the clear when walled up convenient for to sink the filth that is carried from the prison for which he is to be allowed £8, which the Sheriff is ordered to pay him as soon as the work is compleated."

Patrick Sullivan and Bridget Kelly, alias Sullivan, are brought to trial and a jury is impaneled, which finds them guilty of the theft of Stephen Ransberg's pocketbook. They are ordered to pay to Ransberg 3,996 pounds of tobacco "for fourfold thereof and restore to the said Ransberg the money so stolen and the said Stephen Ransberg in his proper person in Court here remits the fourfold as aforesaid."

The Court then orders that Patrick and Bridget be "set upon the pillory for one half hour and that afterwards they be set to the whipping post and there receive on each of their bare bodies 20 lashes well laid on."

In a suit of Elisabeth Gates versus Samuel Cissell the former recites in her complaint that her son Samuel Gates, an orphan, about eight years ago was bound to a certain Samuel Cecil, who sold the said orphan child to a certain Sabret Cecil, "who does not think himself obliged to give him schooling &c., according to the original order of the Court."

The Court considered the case on its merits and decided that the aforesaid Samuel Gates be absolutely free and discharged from the service of the said Samuel Cissell and that he recover against the said Cissel £6 current money of Maryland together with $164\frac{1}{4}$ pounds of tobacco for his costs and charges.

The action by the Lord Proprietary against Jacob Young for assault and battery was marked "struck off by order of the Court, defendant being run away."

In a suit against Alexander Jones for a debt owed Elias DeLashmutt "the Court values tobacco at 25 shillings currency per hundred."

In a suit against Sarah Needham on an open account several items appear, including:
1 doz. ivory table knives and forks 15/-
½ doz. Delf soup plates   4/3

AUGUST COURT OF 1760

The August Court of 1760 met on the third Tuesday and the 19th day of August in the tenth year of Frederick's Dominion. Justices present were Thomas Prather, David Lynn, William Luckett, Charles Jones, Peter Bainbridge, Joseph Wood and Moses Chapline.

The Grand Jury consisted of Samuel Magruder, foreman, Thomas Gore, Henry Clagett, Orlando Griffith, Henry Gaither, John West, Sr., James Duley, Daniel Sexton, John Harbin, Paul Woolf, George Hinckle, George French, Joseph Mayhew, Jacob Fout, and Valentine Black.

The Jury presents:
Mary Cornwell, "servant of Dr. Charles Neel, Sr., for having a baseborn mulatto child."

The Ministry and sundry inhabitants of All Saints Parish residing beyond the South Mountain state in a petition "that the chapel of late beyond the said mountain is situate in the midst of woods and tho' surrounded by several high roads passing by the same at a moderate distance not accessible by any other than very small incommodious paths to the great inconvenience of the congregation and impediment to the public worship of Almighty God." They ask that the Court order the opening of a "communication from the said chappell to the several parts hereafter mentioned, viz., to the main road near Joseph Helme's to the main road leading from the mouth of Conococheague to the main road leading to White's Mill and to the Fort at William Kelly's upon Antietam and that these may be made public roads."

The Court appoints Joseph Helmes and John Perrin to view the roads as requested and report to the next County Court.

"Mr. Cuthbert Bullet, Mr. Basil Dorsey and Mr. John Hammond qualify as attorneys of this Court."

Mr. Thomas Johnson, Jr., "produces a commission as prosecutor for His Lordship in this Court with which the Court concurs."

"Henry Gaither in consequence of his recognizance taken June Court 1759 brings into Court here the body of Ann Hilton for molatto bastardy upon which it is ordered by the Court that the Sheriff sell the said Ann Hilton to the highest bidder for the term of seven years agreeable to Act of Assembly....and the said Sheriff informs the Court that he has sold the said Ann agreeable to the above order for the sum of £12/10/- current money to a certain Thomas Price of said County, hatter."

A suit of George Gordon against Adam Henry and Sarah, his wife, Executrix of Alexander Beall, reflects a number of customs of the times. Obviously Beall died, naming his wife Sarah as executrix, and Sarah has since married Adam Henry. This is the reason the suit is brought as it is, because a married woman could not sue or be sued except in conjunction with her husband. Apparently there was a long-standing open account due Gordon. The account sued on is headed as follows: "Sundry Articles and

210

Necessaries for Mrs. Elizabeth Halmard provided and paid for by George Gordon of which Capt. Alexander Beall is to pay one-half." The total bill is composed of two parts, one half of £54/18/- or £27/9/- in current money and £35/16/8 in sterling. There is no indication of the relationship of Mrs. Halmard to any of the principals. She was evidently an invalid. Included in the accounts were these items:

2-wheeled chair and harness	£10/ -/-
2 gal. of molassis	8/-
1 suit of cotton for Negro Toby	15/-
strengthening plasters	2/-
dose of salts	1/-
1 blister plaister for her knees	2/6
oil amber and salts	7/-
7 yards Irish linen for shiffts	1/ 2/9
1 pair of spectacles, thimble and thread	3/6
3½ years allowance of rum at 16 gal./yr. to May 1, 1759 (56 gal. at 5 sh.)	14/ -/-
Paid Dr. David Ross for phisick and smith's work	3/13/3
Perygreen Magness' account of rum before she came to The Woodyeard	1/10/-

The above items are a portion of those totalling the £54/18/- current money. Separately stated in sterling is this single item:

3 years & 7 months board for Mrs. Halmard and her maid from 7 November 1755 till May 1759 at £10 sterling/annum as per agreement	£35/16/8

NOVEMBER COURT OF 1760

The November Court of 1760 met on the third Tuesday and 18th day of November in the tenth year of His Lordship Frederick's Dominion.

The Worshipful Justices present were Thomas Beatty, Thomas Prather, Joseph Wood, Charles Jones, William Luckett, Thomas Norris, Moses

Chapline and Peter Bainbridge.

The Grand Jury consisted of Thomas Clagett, foreman, John Simpson, Abraham Lakin, Nathaniel Magruder, Christopher Burkitt, Robert Blackburn, John Pain, Frederick Heifner, James Duley, Thomas Pack, Samuel Cissell, William Thomas, Jr., Thomas Hawkins, William Beatty, Charles Clagett, Archibald Edmonston, Jr., and Hugh Riley.

Among the Grand Jury's presentments, half of which seem to be for baseborn children, is:
John Tutterah "for begetting a baseborn child on the body of Mary Cyder by information of said Mary."

In a petition to the Court Margaret Huffman states that the allowance previously made by the Court has not been sufficient "to maintain her and her poor blind children." She asks for an increase in her allowance.
The Court allows her 3,000 pounds of tobacco in the next levy.

The record lists thirty applications for welfare relief submitted to the November Court. This is a marked increase compared to previous Courts.

George Trucks, who some time ago contracted to build a bridge over Little Pipe Creek for £40, now petitions the Court, stating that he "finds that the aforesaid £40 will not complete it and therefore prays Your Worships to grant him an additional sum of £20."
The Court rejects his request.

John Logsdon and James White, who had contracted to build a bridge over Great Pipe Creek for £60, also ask for £15 additional, which the Court also rejects.

George Orchson petitions the Court as follows:
"On the 18th day of June last I was committed to gaol

on suspition of being a deserter which I am not. I humbly begg you will take my miserable condition into consideration as there is people in town that is willing to pay my fees so that the Sheriff has orders from Your Worships to relief me."

"Ordered by the Court here that the Sheriff sell him at the end of six months if he cannot otherwise satisfy him."

Thomas Connelly similarly petitions the Court "that your petitioner was taken up last June on suspicion of being a disarter and put into prison and there continued until this time. I therefore beg Your Worships will be so good to order that I may be disposed of in some manner to discharge my fees and releave me other ways being almost naked."

"Ordered by the Court here that the Sheriff sell him at the end of six months if he cannot otherwise satisfie him."

Joseph Ferrell petitions the Court that he is "detained unjustly as a servant by a certain Andrew Hugh" and asks that summons issue for Hugh.

The Court orders the summons issued.

A long petition by "sundry inhabitants of the Lower Part of Andietum, living between Shanon Dor [Shenandoah] and Elk Ridge" gives much background concerning life in that area. In the petition they state that "ever since the first setling of the country they have labored under great inconveniency for want of a road through our settlement...." They state that they "have never failed to meet and help clear all roads through the Hundred of no use to us, as we have no road through our settlement into any of the main roads other than small paths leading from one plantation to another, which often meets with obstructions by clearing of fields and moving fences and turning the path into the most mountainous places insomuch that it has become almost impracticable for to pass with loaded horses to

213

any of our mills which are all above us in the Hundred and no conveniency of a durable stream to build amongst us; and also our country product we can in no wise remove to any market for want of a road; and further we are much debar'd from the communion of God's Holy Worship as we have no road to our church which is fifteen miles distant at least from the Lower part of our settlement and only a bad path thither that in the most seasonable time women and children can scarcely be in time to hear a sermon." They ask that "a waggon road be cleared from Fraill Pain's on Potomac to the main road from Frederick Town to Andietum Bridge nere to the hickory tavern."

The Court appoints Moses Chapline, Robert Turner and Nathaniel Robinett to view and lay out the road prayed for.

Sundry unnamed inhabitants from Frederick Town petition the Court that "whereas we have raised money for and being desirous of making post and railing in at the north end of the Court House a bowl alley which is to be extended seventy foot out from said House and at the extent will be between 55 and 60 foot which will be contained by a straight line to the end of said House which is 34 foot broad we request permission to build this bowl alley."

The Court grants the request.

A great number of petitions for the keeping of taverns or houses of entertainment are here omitted because they do not give any more indication of location than the oft-repeated statement, "Where I now live." An exception perhaps is the petition of John Gilbert, who petitions the Court for a license "to keep a publick house of entertainment on Piney Creek in said County near the Temporary Line and on the road that leads from Frederick Town to Lancaster." This license was granted by the Court.

A petition of Daniel Dulany states that he owns a

tract of land called "Dulany's Lott" and that the boundaries are uncertain and asks for a commission to establish these boundaries. The Court appoints Messrs.
Joseph Wood, Thomas Norris, James Dickson and
Stephen Ransberg.

The Rev. Mr. Thomas Bacon, Minister of All
Saints Parish, presents a petition on behalf of himself
and numbers of other well disposed persons in the
Parish, stating that "he most humbly sheweth that your
remonstrant with deep concern and inward grief hath
observed profaneness and immorality to abound among
the said public times; and in particular during the sitting of this present Court the voice of riot, drunken-
ness, swearing and sporting with the great and fearful
name of Almighty God has been elevated in our streets
by day and by night to an uncommonly audacious pitch
to the vast scandal of Christianity, the heavy sorrow
of the sober and well-inclined and the open insulting
and contempt of the dignity of the magistracy solemnly
assembled for the administration of justice and the
conservation of peace and good manners in the community; that public and notorious vices such especially
as proclaim a disregard to all decency good government and religion call loudly for a due exertion of the
civil power which is entrusted to the magistrate for
this very thing; that as the Minister of God," he is
obliged to call this situation to the attention of the
Court and that he hopes the Court will put "into strict
and effectual execution without favor or malice that
Act in particular for punishing blasphemors, swear-
ers, drunkards and Sabbath breakers which is directed
to be read four times a year in every parish church
throughout this Province."
"Upon reading which remonstrance and consideration thereof had, it is ordered by the Court here that
nothing more be done in the premises."

Dr. Charles Neale binds himself in the amount of
£30 current money that "he will bring to the next

County Court a certain Mary Cornwell who now is servant to the said Neale after she is free in order that
she may be sold for seven years for having a mulatto
bastard child."

"Mr. Thomas Jennings qualifies as attorney of
this Court."

There are 19 rules covering the better part of
four pages and governing the conduct of attorneys,
Sheriff, Clerk and others before the Court of 1760,
which may be of interest to the legal historian. (Cf.
"1758-1760, Part 2," p. 1072 et seq.)

"The Court appoints Major Joseph Wood to lay out
a new road from John Biggs' Ford to Israel's Creek
near Albaugh's plantation."

A new list of Constables includes the following:

Thomas Clagett	Potomac Hundred, Lower Part
Samuel West	Potomac Hundred, Upper Part
John Waters	Newfoundland Hundred
Jeremiah Simpson	Rock Creek Hundred Middle Part
Arthur Hickman	Sugarland Hundred
William Norris of Ben.	Sugar Loaf Hundred
John Greenup	Linginoa Hundred
Thomas Beatty, Jr.	Mannor Hundred
John Carr	Monocacy Hundred, Upper Part
James White	Pipe Creek Hundred
Michael Hodgkiss	Burnt House Woods Hundred
Thomas Goodson	Piney Creek Hundred
Charles Hedge	Monocacy Hundred, Middle Part
John Kimbol	Frederick Town Hundred
Arthur Nelson	Monocacy Hundred, Lower Part
Samuel Magruder	Kittocton Hundred, Lower Part
Henry Boteler	Andiatum Hundred, Lower Part
Michael Miller	Andiatum Hundred, Upper Part
Exekial Chaney	Marsh Hundred
William Beard	Salisbury Hundred

Thomas Edmonston	Conococheague Hundred
Edward Perrin	Linton Hundred
Prob Mounts	Old Town Hundred

"The Court here appoint the several Constables following to execute the law in relation to the suppressing of the tumultuous meetings of Negroes in their Hundreds: Thomas Clagett, Samuel West, John Waters, Samuel Israel Godman and Jeremiah Simpson."

Overseers for roads in present Frederick County designated as Main Roads by the Court of November 1760 included:

The New Road that leads from the top of Kittocton by where George Matthews lived to Ballenger's Branch: Jacob Coleman, overseer.

From Monocacy West Bank at Reynolds Ferry to Linganore Ford: Michael Haman.

The road called Touchstone's Road and the road that leads from where Alexander Jones lived to the top of Kittocton that leads to Frederick Town and the road that leads from the top of ditto [Catoctin] by Caspar Schaaf's place to the top of the South Mountain: Nathaniel Walker.

From Frail Pain's to Harpers Ferry and the new road when laid out from Pain's into the main road leading to Conococheague: Thomas Hogg.

From the road that leads out of the main road by Captain Bainbridge's to the top of the South Mountain and the new road that goes thro Curry's Gap: [Name of overseer was not recorded.]

From Reynolds Ford to Smith's Branch and from the Glade to the east side of Isral's Creek: Christian Vought.

From Great Pipe Creek to the Temporary Line: Valentine Rinehart.

From Major Ogle's Ford to John Biggs' Ford on the Monocacy and from Biggs' Ford to the Glade: George Devel[biss].

From Isral's Creek near Albaugh's to Linganore

217

Chapel [near Unionville]: William Albaugh.

From Frederick Town to Richardson's Mill and to Foutt's Mill and to the Ford at Daniel Kennedy's: Jacob Fought.

From the Upper Bridge in Frederick Town to the top of Kittocton and the road from Ballenger's Branch into the road that leads from Frederick Town to Conococheague: Joseph Mayhew.

All the streets and lanes in Frederick Town and the road to the English church, the road to Mr. Dulany's Mill and the road to Rue's Ford: Sampson Lazarus.

Pagination here jumps from page 1099 to page 2000!

In a suit on a debt which had been continued through several Courts, on each occasion when the Sheriff had been instructed to bring the defendant into Court he had defaulted. In this Court the ruling by the Court is "that the said Sheriff, to wit, Samuel Beall, for default as aforesaid be amerced, [24] forfeit and pay to His Lordship the sum of £3/6/6 current money, the damages aforesaid as also $227\frac{3}{4}$ pounds of tobacco plus one shilling current money for costs."

MARCH COURT OF 1761

The March Court of 1761 convened on the third Tuesday and the 17th day of March in the tenth year of Frederick's Dominion. Justices present were Thomas Beatty, Joseph Wood, Charles Jones, David Lynn, Moses Chapline and Peter Bainbridge.

The Grand Jurors were William Beall, foreman, Stephen Ransburg, Peter Stilley, Martin Casner, James Henthorn, Charles Harding, Thomas Appleton,

---

[24] Fined by the Court arbitrarily, rather than as prescribed by law.

Benjamin Veatch, William Patrick, Joseph Mayhew, George French, Conrad Hogmire, Peter Pinkle, Charles Swearingen, David Jones and David Jones. Jr.

The Jury presents Richard Dean "for stealing one shirt, some knives and forks and one blanket from Edward Grimes — and we also present said Grimes for compounding the said fellony in consideration of the said Dean's returning the said goods and giving his note for 30 shillings."

Thomas Mason, Gentleman, qualifies as an attorney of the Court.

"Ordered by the Court here that John Carr be appointed Constable in the room of Jacob Weller for Upper Part of Monocacy Hundred."

Sundry unnamed inhabitants petition the Court for a road "to begin at the Province line and cross Monocacy Creek about a mile from said Line at a place called Elder's Bottom, it being the best ford for waggons that is near us on said Creek, from thence as straight a course toward Baltimore Town as the ground will admit."

Inhabitants of the upper part of the County in a petition state "that whereas the road leading from the mouth of Conococheague Creek to Pittsburgh is very much frequented and used by persons travelling from the lower settlements of this Province and others, inhabitants of Virginia, there being a road out from Friend Cox's ferry into the aforesaid road for the conveniency of such who travel to Pittsburgh or other [of] His Majesty's forts and whereas the Town Creek is seldom passable in the spring and fall of the year and very often in the summer, such travellers are there stopped and detained suffering hunger and cold for eight or ten days to the great loss and detriment of such who carry provisions to supply His Majesty's

219

forces by which means the army is often reduced to scarcity." They ask that a bridge be made over Town Creek "and for as much since the Warr the inhabitants are very few not being returned to their former dwellings and therefore unable to build it at their own expense."

The Court rejects the petition.

Hugh McDaniel petitions the Court that he "was on the 17th day of last July taken up and put into gual [jail] on suspicion of being a deserter and there has been continued until this time which is eight months and as nothing of the kind has appeared, I hope Your Worships will be pleased to order that I may be disposed of in some manner to discharge my fees and free me from gaol."

"Ordered by the Court that the Sheriff discharge the petitioner upon his paying all fees due from him."

"Joseph Hardman gives into Court here the following account:

Building a gallows	£2/-/-
Making a coffin and diggin a grave for John Harrison	1/-/-

The Court orders the account paid in the next levy.

Mathias Ringer and John Markley, who state that they are security "for a certain Jacob Coller [Culler] upon administration granted him on the estate of Christian Gaugh, deceased," suspect that the estate is declining and ask that Coller be summoned to countersecure them. The Court orders such a summons for Coller, returnable to the next Court.

John Childs states that he had served out his time with his master John Edwards and had never received from Edwards his freedom dues although he had several times asked for them. "He living a great way off and therefore his trips to Edwards cause him great hindrance of his business and loss of his time," he asks for and the Court grants a summons for Edwards.

The basis for a suit of Michael Kirkpatrick vs. John Craigg is a bill dated in 1753 for "2 men and 2 horses, 13 days driving of cattle from Salsburry to Fort Cumberland, to be paid 3 sh., 6d per day for each man and horse going and returning home, £4/11/-."

In a suit of John Cook against Frederick Garrison, an account dated June 1758 lists these items:

The hyer of one horse ten months
   which you pretended to press for
   His Majesty's service but with-
   out authority   £12/ -/-
One pair of harness you took with
   the horse   5/-

John Gray McDaniel sues George Jewill on an account involving the following items:

Building of one house   £6/ -/-
Building of one house   2/ -/-
Macking of one small coffon   5/-
Macking of one large coffon   10/-

Appointed to review and fix the boundaries of Daniel Dulany's parcel "Dulany's Lott" (see above, page 215) were Joseph Wood, Thomas Norris, James Dickson and Stephen Ransberg. It was customary to post a notice on the church door concerning the hearing, in effect a summons to any one who knew anything about the property to appear at the scheduled meeting to be held near where they thought the boundaries lay. In this particular case, all they wanted to know was the survey's starting point.

John Kimbol stated that he was 63 years of age or thereabouts, that there had stood for many years a white hickory tree at the mouth of a branch commonly called Addison's Branch emptying into the Monocacy, about three-quarters of a mile on a straight course from Reynold's Ford on the main road that leads from

Frederick Town to Lancaster. He had been twice present when this land was run.

Thomas Beatty stated that he was 58 years of age and he testified that about thirty years ago [±1731] he had been told the same hickory tree was the starting point. "Deponent further sayeth that some small time after one Robert Owens laid out 1,000 acres of said tract of land for one Susannah Beatty and began at the aforesaid hickory tree."

JUNE COURT OF 1761

The June Court of 1761 met on the third Tuesday and the 16th day of June in the 11th year of Frederick's Dominion.

The Worshipful Justices present were Thomas Beatty, Thomas Prather, Joseph Wood, Charles Jones, David Lynn, Peter Bainbridge, Thomas Norris, William Luckett and Moses Chapline.

The Grand Jurors were Robert Lamar, foreman, Archibald Edmonston, David Carlysle, Joshua Bucey, Joseph Wheat, Joseph Mayhew, John Carmack, Peter Stilley, John Swearingen, Stephen Julian, Thomas Conn, Abraham Haff, Ninian Edmonston, George Moore and James Gore.

The Grand Jury presents:
Richard Powell "for daming the Father, Son and Holy Ghost, by information of Mordecai Maddin."

Sundry inhabitants stating that they live between Piney and Great Pipe Creeks petition for permission "to clear a road from the Temporary Line down by Peter Erbs' mill into the new road near the head of Little Pipe Creek."

The Court appoints John Logsdon and Richard Wells to view the road prayed for and report at the next Court.

A petition by Henry Cock asks the Court that a servant named Henry Bush, "about forty years of age, who has lived with your petitioner and his father ever since his childhood just for his vituals and cloaths which he is hardly able to earn, he being almost a natural fool not knowing many times what he doth," be made levy-free.

The Court rejects this petition.

Thomas Clayland states to the Court, "About two years ago Stephen Jarbeo, unknown to your petitioner, carried off a child of his then about 9 years of age, which child he' keeps.... much against your petitioner's inclination. Your petitioner has often sent for his child (being lame himself), but he refuses to let her go. And as the said Jarbeo is a professed papist, your petitioner has the greatest reason to believe he will bring her up in that religion, which gives him the greatest concern and unhappiness." He asks the Court for return of his daughter, which the Court rejects.

Mary Fouts in a petition states "that the road from Frederick Town to Fouts Mill is very bad, especially in the winter season as it being for the best part of the way very low ground and withall very much out of the way and very inconvenient for said Town's inhabitants to go to said mill." She asks that a new road be laid out, but the Court rejects her petition.

James Keith qualifies as an attorney of the Court.

In a suit on an account by Jacob Sennett versus Abraham Teagarden, a number of items appear:

1 feather bed and bolster	£2/4/4½
1 new frying pann	8/6
1 pewter gill cup	1/-
8 lbs. of sugar at 1 sh./lb.	8/-
½ cord of wood	1/-

William Hall sues James Gorrell, stating in his

complaint that he "was legally intituled to a convict servant named James Cook who was bound and obliged by Act of Parliament to serve for the term of seven years next after his arrival in the Province, which term of seven years is not yet expired and that the said James Gorrell did deprive him of his said servant by sending the servant out of this County as he the said Hall apprehends as a soldier and he further states that he has never since been able to obtain possesion of his servant."

Upon presentation of the case, Joseph Wood and David Lynn, Justices of the Court, become manu-captors for Gorrell. This seems to indicate that he was a man of some parts, particularly when the case was moved by writ of certiorari to the Provincial Court and taken out of this Court.

Abraham Crum sues John Shelman stating that on March 27, 1760 Shelman assaulted him. He asks for damages. A jury is impaneled, finding Shelman guilty and awarding Crum £12/10/- current money and $1831\frac{1}{4}$ pounds of tobacco plus 6d currency for costs.

Edward Trafford and son sue Benjamin Hopkins on an account in which two of the items are:

1 pack of cards   1/-
6 gun flints   -/5

Dr. George Steuart sues Nathaniel Wickham on a note of £103/13/4, which Dr. Steuart through his attorney Thomas Johnson, Jr., states is in default.

Three cases were transferred to this Court, one from Anne Arundel County, one from Baltimore County and one from Prince George's County.

AUGUST COURT OF 1761

The August Court of 1761 convened on the third Tuesday and the 18th day of August in the 11th year of

Frederick's Dominion. Present were the Worshipful Thomas Beatty, Peter Bainbridge, Thomas Prather, Charles Jones, David Lynn, Joseph Wood, Moses Chapline, Thomas Norris and William Luckett, Gentlemen.

The Grand Jury consisted of Thomas Lansdale, foreman, Jonathan Hagar, John Gregg, Thomas Powill, Weaver Barnes, Stephen Julian, Charles Williams, John Cartwright, Richard Chaney, William Erwin, Joseph Mayhew, Jacob Bruner, John Howard, Samuel Cissell, Archibald Edmonston, Jr., William Dyall and Carlton Tannyhill.

Most of the Grand Jury's indictments were for bastardy. Two were for felony without further explanation.

Catherine Clapsaddle petitions the Court that "your petitioner, the wife of Daniel Clapsaddle, living on Conewago in the Province of Pennsylvania, was travelling from thence to Antieatum to see her friends and for want of a pass was apprehended and taken to Justice as a runaway and was committed to goal as such where she still continues. Your petitioner therefore most humbly prays Your Worships will take her deplorable condition into serious consideration and grant her relief."
"It is ordered by the Court here that the petitioner be discharged from the custody of the Sheriff on paying all fees."

John Shriver in a petition to the Court states that "he has lived about a year and a half with a certain John Lingenfelter as an apprentice by indenture which is of no effect as your petitioner has been informed and by means of said Lingenfelter's using your petitioner very ill has left said Lingenfelter, though was obliged to go without cloaths, therefore hopes Your Worships will compel said Lingenfelter to let your petitioner

225

HEMPSTEAD COUNTY LIBRARY
HOPE, ARKANSAS

have his cloaths."

"Ordered by the Court that summons issue immediately for John Lingenfelter, who comes and answers the complaint, after the hearing of which the said apprentice is ordered back to his master."

Richard Coombs applies for a license to keep a tavern on the main road that leads from Frederick Town to Baltimore, and it is granted.

John Orme asks for a license to keep a public house at George Town, and it is also granted.

Ewell Swearingen applies for a license to keep a public house in Frederick Town, which is granted.

Aaron Phipps petitions for a license to keep a public house at the mouth of Conococheague where he lives, and that is granted.

Thomas Schley applies for a renewal of his license to keep a public house where he now lives. It is granted.

John Darnall, Clerk of the County, and Peter Butler, Deputy Clerk, present certificates from Joseph Wood that they have taken the proper oaths of office.

Sundry inhabitants, unnamed, present a petition to the Court "that your petitioners are in very great want of a road from Conococheague to cross the mountain to Baltimore Town to transport their wheat to market and we humbly conceive that there may be a good waggon road from Stoner's Mill and cross the mountain at a place called Smith's Gap and to intersect a road already laid out and cleared from George Trucks' to Baltimore which must be of infinite service to the inhabitants of Conococheague as well as several on the other side of the mountains by reason of it going by Stoner's Mill aforesaid and near Ambrose's, Smith's, Sixes' and Digges' Mills."

The Court orders that Major Joseph Wood, Captain Thomas Norris and Joseph Doldrige [Doddridge]

226

view the road which the petitioners want and report to the next Court.

By an interlined notation, the following petition is indicated as having been presented in the June Court, but is recorded here:

Sundry inhabitants of the Upper Hundred of Monocacy state in a petition that they have "labored under much hardship and disadvantage for want of a good road to the nearest landing, viz., Baltimore Town. We humbly request that Your Worships grant us an order for opening and clearing a road from the Temporary Line along a gap in the mountain to John Lillie's Mill and from thence a straight course to Baltimore Town until it falls in with a road lately opened from George Truxes [Trucks] to said Town."

The Court orders that "Thomas Willson, John Friend, Joseph Doldrige and John Roberts view the proposed layout and report to August Court next."

Thomas Norris and Joseph Doldrige who were appointed to view a proposed road "through the mountains do say that by viewing the same that a road may be made from Stoner's Mill across Mount Missery and by Gasber Smith's from thence near Ambrose's Mill, from thence near Captain Ogle's late dwelling place, then to Ogle's ford on Monocacy, then to strike the new road from George Trucks' to Baltimore County line."

"Court concurs with the report and orders that Major Joseph Wood lay out the same."

Thomas Stevenson, who was tried in Court for stealing "one caster [beaver] hatt valued at 140 pounds of tobacco," was found guilty and was sentenced to be put in the pillory for five minutes and "afterwards to be set to the whipping post and there receive on his bare body ten lashes."

John Baptist Munrow sues Abraham Teagarden for one silver watch purchased in 1760 and valued at £9.

NOVEMBER COURT OF 1761

The November Court of 1761 convened on the third Tuesday and the 17th day of November in the 11th year of Frederick's Dominion.

The Worshipful Justices present were Thomas Beatty, Thomas Prather, Peter Bainbridge, David Lynn, Joseph Wood, Moses Chapline, William Luckett, Thomas Norris and Charles Jones.

The Grand Jurors were Zachariah Magruder, foreman, James Walling, Sr., James Walling, Jr., Samuel Cissell, James Duley, John Stull, James Coffee, John Holland, Hugh Riley, John Fletchall, Benjamin Beall son of Benjamin, John Shepherd, Andrew Link, Charles Hoskinson and Ephraim Davis.

There was none of the usual presentments, but four women were charged with bastardy in suits by the Lord Proprietary. Three of them were dismissed by order of the Court.

Francis Kenedy states to the Court in a petition that his brother Daniel Kenedy is now deceased, "having left several small children whom is under Your Worships' care (they being orphans). Therefore your petitioner prays You to grant him liberty of finding out and putting said children to such persons as he shall think proper."
The Court rejects the petition.

James Russell in a petition states that "a certain Herbert Wallace unjustly detains him in servitude by unjust and fraudulent measures and contrary to the rules of equity and justice." He asks the Court either to dismiss him from service or to require Wallace to show good basis for his detention.
The Court orders summons issue for Wallace and the petitioner returnable at March Court next.

A petition from sundry unnamed inhabitants states that "they are desirous of having an old main road open from the widow Griffith's to the top of Kittocton Mountain and a new one laid out and cleared from the top of Kittocton Mountain to the Winchester road where it intersects Kittocton, the north side of it which road will be very beneficial to sundry persons."

The Court appoints Elias DeLashmutt, James Hook and William Luckett to view the proposed road and report to the March Court.

A petition by sundry inhabitants who are unnamed states that previously the Court had ordered in response to an earlier petition several gentlemen to view the route proposed, but the gentlemen had never done so. They state that they have therefore more or less taken matters into their own hands and "at our own cost, great labour and expense built, cleared and made a good waggon road from Jacob Pullman's bordering on the Temporary Line to James Pattission's to Lodowick Raines' to John Lilly's Mill to Samuel Carrick's to Joseph Fare's to John Strine's on Tom's Creek and to Thomas Willson's on Monocacy and thence intended as straight as may be until it comes into the great waggon road that goes to Patapsico (alias Baltimore Town). We also declare to Your Worships that Gentlemen from Cumberland County [in Pennsylvania] who hath an order from London to clear a road as straight as possible a considerable distance to join the aforesaid road at the Temporary Line and viewed our road aforesaid and approve thereof without any exception but delays the event of their proceedings to the happy accomplishment and fulfilling this Your Worships' order."

"Ordered by the Court that Messrs. Thomas Norris, John Firor and William Shields view and lay out the road and make report thereof to March Court next."

Sundry inhabitants in Frederick Town state in a petition that "the bridges over the Creek which runs through Frederick as well as the causeway from one of said bridges is in want of repair and in a few years there will not be timber without being brought a considerable distance to repair them if they continue to be of wood and it is evident at present that in the winter and bad seasons they are scarce passable." They request the Court to appropriate a sum of money by a levy on the taxable inhabitants of said County "to build stone bridges where the wooden ones now are and a causeway where necessary."

The Court orders that "Messrs. Christopher Edelin, James Dickson and John Cary treat with workmen to build said bridges and report to the March Court next."

John Dorsey and Samuel Swearingen present a petition to the Court in which Dorsey states that he was lately in possession of a certain convict servant man named John Noon whom he had sold to Swearingen for his unexpired term and that Noon ran away and was gone for eleven months. They were at £5 expense in recovering him. They ask the Court to assess punishment for the servant.

"It is adjudged by the Court that the said John Noon serve his present master Samuel Swearingen three years after the expiration of his first servitude and pay him £20.

Joseph Belt petitions for a license to keep a public house in Georgetown, which the Court grants.

Peregrine Mackaness petitions for a license to keep a public house "at George Town at the mouth of Rock Creek," which the Court grants.

All of an unusually large number of petitions for relief from the County, 37 in total, are granted. Not all are new petitions; some ask for renewal of their allowance or pension.

"The Vestry of All Saints Parish petitions the

Court to assess eight pounds of tobacco per poll on the taxables of this Parish."

The Court grants the petition.

The Vestry of Prince George's Parish offers a similar petition, which is also granted.

Dr. James Brand, the visiting physician of the County, presents an account as follows:

Board and attendance of John Perce, a County patient, from March 22nd to May 12th at 10 shillings per week	£3/11/5

Arthur Charlton presents a bill to the Court:

For five days' house rent &c &c	£5/ -/-

Joseph Hardman presents the following account:

Cleaning the prison yard by the Court's Order and omitted to be charged last year	£1/ -/-

Joseph Hardman presents another account as follows:

For John Batman for his services, his board and 'tendance 10 weeks at 10 sh. per week	£5/ -/-
Coffen, sheat, burall [burial]	15/-
Doctor	18/-

Dr. Orlando Griffith presents the following account on behalf of John Francis, deceased:

Attendance in sickness, 30 days	£2/ -/-
Finding a coffin	10/-
Finding a sheet and muffler	10/-
Digging a grave	5/-

Moses Chapline presents the following account:

Viewing and laying out the road from the Conococheague Road that leads from Frederick Town to the mouth of said Creek, to Potomac River near John Paines at 10 sh. per day	£2/-/-

231

Horatio Sharpe, Esq. [Governor of Maryland] gives into Court here the following account, dated 1761 and addressed to the inhabitants of Frederick County: "Seal dedimus protestatem [see footnote, page 279] to qualify all officers, civil and military: 90 lbs.

A petition by sundry inhabitants for a "ferry over the Mouth of Monocacy."

"Ordered by the Court that the ferry be kept up as formerly and that William Luckett be allowed £35 till November Court next."

John Kimboll, John Watters, Jeremiah Simpson, Samuel Israel Godman and Samuel West state to the Court under oath that they have "complied with the Act of Assembly for suppressing the tumultuous meeting of Negroes." The Court allows them each 400 pounds of tobacco in the next levy.

"The Inspectors of George Town Warehouse report that there is remaining in the said Warehouse 7,425 pounds of transfer tobacco which is sold to Samuel Beall, Gentleman, at 13/3d per 100 pounds."

"Ordered by the Court that the Sheriff set John Bell in the stocks for half an hour for his indecent behavior to the Court."

By taking the proper oaths of office, the following qualify: Samuel Beall as Sheriff, Thomas Bowles and Clementius Beall as Undersheriffs.

The Court orders that "Messrs. Charles Jones, David Lynn and William Luckett view the Warehouse at Rock Creek and agree with persons to make such repairs as are needed and to take such measures as they think proper to secure such tobaccos as are now in danger."

"The Court appoints Thomas Reynolds as Cryer

for the Court for the future and allow him £4 per annum for his cleaning the Court House and beating the drum."

"Ordered by the Court that the Sheriff summons to each County Court to be hereafter held a Grand Jury Man out of each Hundred and mention the same to the person when summoned."

"Ordered by the Court here that the new warehouse that George Gordon lately built be deemed and taken to all intents and purposes as the former warehouse is."

"Ordered by the Court that two Constables be appointed to tend each County Court for the future."

"Ordered by the Court that Peter Butler agree with some person to put up shelves convenient in the office in the Court House....and to get four constables' staffs made out of white hickory or oak."

In a long listing of roads and their overseers, again (cf. p. 217) no overseer is shown for the road from the one "that leads out of the main road by Captain Bainbridge's to the top of South Mountain and the new road that goes thro Curry's Gap."

Adam Henry and Sarah, his wife, sue Joseph Hays on an agreement made before the marriage of Adam and Sarah, while she was sole [unmarried]. The agreement noted that for one year "the said Joseph should have the fifth bushel of all grain growing on the plantation of the said Sarah and the fifth bushel of hempseed and the fifth hundredth of the hemp and the fifth part of the cyder to be made on the same plantation, the grain to be divided on the threshing barn and the said Joseph should attend the orchard and pay for trimming the trees thereof and likewise help to break the said hemp." The suit claims that Hays failed to fulfill his part of the bargain. He is tried before a

233

jury consisting of Joseph Beall, Michael Raymor, John Dowden, Ninian Beall Magruder, George Burkitt, Peter Stilley, William Patrick, William Beall, Thomas Nicholls, Jr., James Gore, Benjamin Davis and John Springer, who find for the defendant.

MARCH COURT OF 1762

The March Court of 1762 met on the third Tuesday and the 16th day of March in the 11th year of Frederick's Dominion. The Worshipful Justices were Thomas Beatty, Thomas Prather, Peter Bainbridge, Thomas Norris, Joseph Wood, Moses Chapline, David Lynn and William Luckett, Gentlemen.

The Grand Jury included Josias Clapham, foreman, Joseph Lazear, William Downey, George Burkitt, John Harling, Christian Vought, George Becraft, John Orr, William Teagarden, James Smith, Peter Stilley, John Shelman, Joseph Mayhew, Samuel Carrick and Jonas Brown.

Margaret Huffman in a petition to the Court states "that a certain Dr. Stork had set forth in the Pennsylvania Gazette of his restoring to sundry blind people their eyesight and that she was desirous of having her three children's sights restored."
The Court ordered that "nothing more be done in the premises."

Christian Yesterday [Easterday] petitions for a license to keep a public house, which the Court grants.

Godfrey Brown presents a bill to the Court for making a bookshelf in the Court House   £2/2/6

Jacob Gardenhouer presents a bill for making a coffin for John Pearce, a County patient   £1/-/-

Sundry inhabitants petition "for to have Henry

Braddock before this Court in order to give security or leave this Province as he has been guilty of felony which might be prejudicial to them, the subscribers."

The Court ordered that "nothing more be done in the premises."

"The Rev. Thomas Bacon produces to the Court his induction as rector of the parish church of All Saints and qualifies himself by taking the several oaths to Government &c."

"Ordered by the Court that summons issue for Isabella Willet to show cause why she sells the children of a mulatto woman living with her."

JUNE COURT OF 1762

The June Court of 1762 convened on the third Tuesday and the 15th day of June in the 12th year of Frederick's Dominion. Present were the Worshipful Thomas Beatty, Thomas Prather, Peter Bainbridge, William Luckett, David Lynn, Joseph Wood, Thomas Norris and Moses Chapline.

The Grand Jurymen were Arthur Nelson, foreman, Joseph West, Jr., John Perrin, Andrew Grim, James Walling, Jr., John Stull, Peter Beaver, Joshua Hickman, Leonard Wayman, William Aldrige, Charles Clagett, David Davis, Benjamin Bigges, John Badams, Thomas Johnson, John Jacobs and George Easter.

They present Michael Young "for taking of hemp out of a mill, the property of Christian Kemp."

John Logsdon and James White appear before the Court stating that they had agreed to build a bridge over Great Pipe Creek and keep it in repair for ten years for £60 and state that since they built the bridge "a flood of ice swept the bridge quite away." They now ask that they be allowed to return such part of the

235

money "as they should think fitt."

The Court orders "that they build the bridge anew or return the money by November Court next."

Elizabeth Allen in a petition to the Court states that having served her whole term of servitude to Francis Gartreal "upon application to him for three barrels of Indian corn as part of freedom dues, he positively refuses such payment or anything in lieu thereof." She asks the Court to intercede in her behalf and the Court orders that summons issue for Gartreal, returnable in the August Court next.

James Barnard petitions the Court on behalf of Steward Kennedy "an orphan, son of Daniel Kennedy, deceased, who was taken from his grandmother from school by Francis Kennedy, his unckle. He therefore prays Your Worships to order that the child may be returned in order that he may be kept to school and when able be put to a good trade."

The Court orders summons issue for Francis Kennedy.

Joseph Hutson in a petition to the Court states "that Rebecca Hutson, his wife, was an indentured servant to Thomas Davis and sold to Jeremiah Spiers and sold again to Benjamin Warford and the time of servitude is expired, but none of her said masters will give her a freedom due."

The Court orders that summons issue for Benjamin Warford.

In a suit by the Lord Proprietary against Susannah Corwin for bastardy, the Clerk marks the judgment as "acquitted per verdit." The Court held that she was not guilty and dismissed her with the payment of the necessary fees for which a certain Peter Creager became surety.

"Ordered by the Court here that John Adams and

236

Honor, his wife, be discharged from the custody of the Sheriff and that their fees be charged to the County."

"Jacob Fout, aged 17 years October next, is here bound to Mathias Need until he is of age, said Need to learn him the trade of a farmer and when free to give him £5 in lieu of his freedom dues and to learn him during his servitude to read, write and cast accounts as far as the rule of three."

"The Court agrees with John Shelman to make two windows in the Court House at the back of the chair by August Court next to finish them completely and two small places to write on for the sum of £7."

"The Court appoints Christopher Edelin, Casper Shaaff and Thomas Schley or any two of them to agree with workmen to build two wooden bridges over the Creek that runs through Frederick Town where the old ones formerly stood and make return thereof to August Court next."

Robert McRea and Company sue "John Kidd, late of Frederick County, Gentleman, otherwise called John Kidd, late Lieutenant in the Maryland Troops," on a debt, and judgment is found for the plaintiff.

Jeremiah Duvall and Eleanor his wife in a suit against William McCoy claim "my part of a prize in a lottery at Frederick Town, the whole being $20 and the one moiety being my part by agreement as a share in it which he [McCoy] has received and refuses to pay is £3/15/-." The plaintiffs state that when Eleanor was sole, she entered into the oral agreement to share in this lottery. McCoy refuses any payment to either her or her husband.

A jury is impaneled who find for the plaintiffs in the full amount of the suit. (The jury consisted of Joseph Beall, John Bruner, John Harlan, James Duley, Charles Davis, Zachariah Magruder, Joseph Ray, Carlton Tannehill, William Carmack, Thomas Davis, Elisha Williams and Ninian Beall Magruder.)

A suit by the deacons of Marble Town Church versus George Beatty ended in a judgment of £45 and 294 pounds of tobacco costs in favor of the plaintiffs.

AUGUST COURT OF 1762

The August Court of 1762 met on the third Tuesday and the 17th day of August in the 12th year of His Lordship's Dominion. The Justices were Thomas Beatty, Thomas Prather, Peter Bainbridge, David Lynn, Joseph Wood, Charles Jones and Thomas Norris.

The Grand Jurymen were Samuel Magruder III, foreman, George Tucker, John McIntyre, Thomas Lane, Leonard Everly, Archibald Boarland, Charles Hedges, Samuel Calwell, Stephen Richards, Thomas Beatty, Jr., Mathew Lane, William Norris, Alexander Waddle, William Barrick and Herbert Wallace.

Not one of more than two dozen applications for tavern licenses mentions the location of the tavern. But the names of the applicants included Christian Yesterday, George Truck, Joseph Belt, John Gilbert, Ninian Beall, John Orme, Joseph Helmes, Samuel Swearingen, Aaron Phipps, William McClellen, Henry Leek, Robert Gregg, Conrad Grosh, Arthur Charlton, William Luckett, Thomas Reynalds, Jacob Young, John Lingenfelter, Thomas Davis, Michael Jesserang, Felty Shroiner, Andrew Black, Daniel Shultz, Thomas Schley, Adam Henry, Rachel Dowden and Benjamin Light.

John Clegatt presents a bill to the Court "for expenses for support of Sarah Graham's bastard mulatto child from the 29th of November last to the 18th of August of 1762 in the amount of £8/1/-.

John Weaver presents an account to the Court for "4 Constable stafes for the Constables in Frederick Town, ordered by Peter Butler, 10 shillings."

Christopher Edelin, Thomas Schley and Casper Shaaff state to the Court that "they were appointed to agree with workmen to build two bridges over the Creek that runs through Frederick Town" and they certify that they have "agreed with Mr. Samuel Perry to build the said bridges by November Court next for the sum of £39, the cost to include keeping the bridges in good repair for 10 years."

Unckle Unckles petitions the Court to have Susannah Youngblood, the daughter of John Youngblood, bound to him.
The Court postpones action until the next Court.

Mary Tomlinson, aged 13 years next April, is bound to Francis Cost until she becomes 16 years of age, and Cost is to "learn her to read and when free to give her a heifer and a decent suit of apparel."

James Farrell, an orphan aged two years last March, is bound to Peter Stilly until he becomes 21 years of age. "Stilly is to give him 18 months schooling after he arrives at the age of 10 years and when free to give him a new decent suit of apparel, a mattox, an ax and a weeding hoe."

Michael Divelbiss, an orphan aged 14 years, is bound to Michael Raymore.

"Rebecca Hedges makes choice of John Willson as her guardian."

"Ordered by the Court that the Sheriff carry down Michael Peck, who was committed to him for the murther of George Jacob Poe, and Mary Peck, his wife, who was committed as an evidence."

In the suit of the Lord Proprietary against Sarah Graham for bastardy, she "submits and acknowledges the child to be begot by a Negro. The child set up to the highest bidder and sold to John Clegatt for £8/1/- for 31 years."

In a suit against Mary Cromwell for bastardy, the following notation is entered in the record: "Sold to Dr. Charles Neale for having a mulatto bastard for the sum of £11/10/- and the said Mary Cromwell is ordered to serve the said Charles Neale 7 years."

Elizabeth Allen sued Francis Gartrill for freedom dues (see above, p. 236). "It is ordered by the Court here that said Gartrill pay unto the said Elizabeth three barrills of Indian corn or £1/17/6 in lieu thereof."

"Henry Snuke, late of Frederick County, farmer, otherwise called Homony Suck of Lebown [Lebanon?] in the County of Hunterdon and Provance of West iersey [New Jersey], yeoman, was summoned to answer unto Joseph Bennett in a plea that he render unto him the sum of £5 of West New iersey money of the value of £5 Maryland currency."

In a suit of James Dickson against Robert Lamar, Dickson is awarded judgments of £10/14/1½ sterling and £2/13/8¾ currency.

NOVEMBER COURT OF 1762

The November Court of 1762 met on the third Tuesday and the 16th day of November in the 12th year of Frederick's Dominion. The Justices present were Thomas Beatty, Joseph Wood, William Luckett, Thomas Norris, David Lynn and Charles Jones.

The Grand Jury consisted of John Middagh, foreman, Peter Stilley, David Davis, Abraham Haytor, William Galson, Alexander Waddle, John Riely, John

Garrett, Thomas Johnson, William Harrison, George Clem, George Beall, Nathaniel Magruder, John McIntire and Andrew Grim.

Negro Coffee, a slave of Henry Wright Crabb, was tried for stealing from Crabb's meat house 25 lbs. of bacon valued at 10 shillings sterling. Coffee pled innocent, a jury was impaneled and he was found guilty.
The Court orders that the said Negro "be taken from the bar of the Court here and carried to the prison from whence he came, from thence to the common place of execution and there to be hanged until he is dead." The Court values him at £75. (N.B. Such amounts were customarily paid to the master.)

Francis Dade qualifies as an attorney of the Court.

"Ann Cook, servant to the Rev. Thomas Bacon, is ordered by the Court to serve her said master two and one-half years for fine, fees and other charges for having two baseborn children, the time to commence from the time her former servitude ended."

"Ordered by the Court that the Clerk make known to His Excellency [the Governor] that Negro Coffee.... was found guilty for house-breaking and sentence of death passed upon him accordingly and the Court are sorry that they cannot recommend him to His Excellency for mercy."

"Ordered by the Court that Thomas Bowles, Christopher Edelin and Casper Shaaff agree with workmen to make good the pump in the prison yard, to put in good order the stocks and pillory and to enclose the poarch before the Court House door and well cover the same."

"The Vestry of All Saints Parish petitions the Court for to assess eight pounds of tobacco per poll on the taxables of said Parish toward defraying parocal charges of said Parish. Read and granted."

241

"The Vestry of Prince George's Parish petitions the Court for to assess three pounds of tobacco per poll on each taxable of said Parish. Read and granted."

Elias DeLashmutt applies for a licence to keep a public house, which is granted.

Constables Samuel West, Jeremiah Simpson, John Kimbol, John Fletchall, Hezekiah Magruder and Nathaniel Walker were granted 400 pounds of tobacco each "for suppressing the tumultuous meetings of Negroes."

"Ordered by the Court that attachment issue to possess Charles Hedges for the ballance of Joseph Hedges estate."

MARCH COURT OF 1763

The March Court of 1763 met on the third Tuesday and the 15th day of March in the 12th year of Frederick's Dominion. The Worshipful Justices present, including a number of new Justices, were: Thomas Beatty, Peter Bainbridge, Joseph Wood, Charles Jones, David Lynn, William Luckett, Thomas Norris, Thomas Price, James Dickson, Josiah Beall, Kensey Gittings, James Smith, William Blair and Evan Shelby.

Thomas Prather, Gentlemen, was Sheriff but John Darnall was still Clerk.

The Grand Jurors were Ninian Riely, foreman, John Swann, Jacob Casner, John Nickolls, Michael Kirkpatrick, Ephraim Skiles, Benjamin Johnson, Joshua Harbin, John George, William Collier, Joseph Benton, Thomas Glenn, William Breshears, William Teagarden and Andrew Grim.

"Samuel Chase is admitted as an attorney of the Court."

242

"Matthias Ringer and William Dern, Jr., appointed Constables to attend this Court."

"Court appoints William Ducker Constable of George Town Hundred....and that he be allowed for suppressing the tumultuous meeting of Negroes in said Town."

Charles Hedge was appointed guardian of Rebecca Hedge, with Peter Stilley, Mathias Ringer and Peter Balser as his securities.

"Ordered by the Court that Major Joseph Wood and Captain John Middagh agree with workmen to build a bridge over Israel's Creek near Mr. Beatty's, the undertaker to keep said bridge in good order for ten years."

Catherine Snider is bound to Frederick Whitman who agrees to teach her to read and at the end of her service to give her a decent suit of apparel and a new spinning wheel.

Sundry inhabitants petition for an order to lay out a road "from the Governour's Road to the Cave and from thence to Ambrose's Mill across the South Mountain and to fall into the road leading to Petapsicoe at George Truckses on Pipe Creek."

Samuel Plumb in a petition to the Court states that "whereas there is no licensed ordinary or public house kept between Fort Frederick and the upper limits of this province on Potomac River, which is not only disadvantageous to travelers but also very inconvenient and pernicious to the back inhabitants inasmuch as travelers are often stopped by high waters and obliged to trouble housekeepers for necessaries who are not able to supply such needs gratis or even for money so that many often suffer and your petitioner residing on the waggon road near Evertts Creek a place much used for encamping by pack horse men and cattle drivers most humbly craves license for the vending and selling of liquors."

The Court grants his petition.

Robert Wood in a petition to the Court states that "he is desirous of keeping a publick house of entertainment at his dwelling on the main road that leads from Frederick Town to Lancaster."

The Court also grants his petition.

Indicative of the Clerk's evolving tendency to omit details included in earlier recordings of similar cases is the following: "Evan Shelby against Thomas Johnson: Judgment confessed for £13/12/6 and costs." No more is stated.

JUNE COURT OF 1763

The June Court of 1763 met on the third Tuesday and the 21st day of June in the 13th year of Frederick's Dominion.

The Justices present were Thomas Beatty, Joseph Wood, David Lynn, Peter Bainbridge, William Luckett, James Dickson, Kensey Gittings, Thomas Price, Evan Shelby, James Smith, Samuel Postlethwait, William Blair, Charles Jones and Joseph Smith.

The Grand Jurors were Samuel Dorsey, foreman, William Biggs, Leonard Wayman, Adam Burns, John Briscoe, William Leach, Jr., Joseph Perry, Lawrence Oneal, Moses Williamson, Thomas Hogg, Christopher Burkitt, Martin Casner, John Forest Davis, Isaac Dawson and Mathias Oats.

"The Court approves of Nicholas Fink and John Jones as securities for the ballance of Morris Millhouse's estate."

"The Court orders that a certain person committed by the name of Emanuel to the Sheriff's custody as a runaway be discharged, he appearing to be disordered in his senses."

Thomas Beatty, Sr., gives bond to the Court in the amount of £20 for "keeping the bridge built by him over Israel's Creek in good order and repair for ten years." His two sureties are Thomas Beatty, Jr., and Charles Beatty.

Samuel Swearingen states to the Court that he apprehends that it is in the power of the Court "to rent any part of the lotts belonging to the County for the use of the Court House and prison so as to be no detriment to the said Court House and prison." He therefore asks that the Court lease to him the lott next to Mr. Gordon under mutually agreeable arrangements.

The Court agrees to rent him the lot for four years, he "paling it in with good locust posts ten feet asunder with three rails between the posts and good pales.... and to leave it at the end of four years in good tenantable order." No money consideration is mentioned.

Leonard Weaver presents a bill to the Court "for mending, repairing and taking up the pump in the prison yard, being seven days at 5 sh., per day."

Thomas Bowles, Christopher Edelin and Casper Shaaff report to the Court that they have agreed with Jeremiah Adamson "to enclose the porch before the Court House, to cover it with round jointed shingles and to board it as it was before and with gates; to build new stocks, whipping post and pillory and to find every necessary thereto for a price of £30 to be completed without delay."

"Wednesday appointed for the Clerk to attend in the Court House agreeable to Act of Assembly."

245

AUGUST COURT OF 1763

The August Court of 1763 met on the third Tuesday and the 16th day of August in the 13th year of Frederick's Dominion. The Worshipful Justices present were Thomas Beatty, Peter Bainbridge, Charles Jones, William Luckett, David Lynn, Joseph Wood, James Dickson, Evan Shelby, James Smith, Kensy Gittings, William Blair, Gentlemen.

The Grand Jury included Erasmus Gill, foreman, William Beckwith, Abraham Holland, Richard Carter, Henry Butler, James Piles, Unckle Unckles, Joseph Sparks, Posthumus Clagett, Jacob Durner, Hugh Terrence, John Hinton, William Barrick, Peter Derr and Alexander Waddle.

Negro Lie, a slave of James Conn, was tried and found guilty of "stealing a meal bagg and some flower." He was sentenced to be taken to the whipping post, given 39 lashes on his bare back and delivered back to his master.

Thomas McMullen, a white man, was tried for stealing a rifled gun and found guilty. He was sentenced to 15 lashes and set 15 minutes in the pillory.

"The Court agrees with James Brand to attend the County patients as usual."

"Ordered by the Court that Thomas Bowles agree with a workman to plaster the inside of the prison wall and to underpin the porch before the Court House door and lay the poarch with flagg stone."

"Ordered by the Court that Samuel Ford and Mathias Baker, Jr., apprentices to Godfrey Brown be discharged from the said Brown."

A number of unnamed inhabitants "of Tawneys

Town and inhabitants thereabouts" ask the Court to consider the appointment of a magistrate and suggest Mr. Abram Hayter be recommended to the Governor.

They state that they are so distant from the Court that they would like a Justice more nearly in their community. The Court decided there was nothing more to be done in the premises.

A new list of prices and accommodations included the following:

Hott dyett for a gentleman with a pint of beer or syder	1/6
Cold dyett for ditto ditto ditto	1/-
Hot dyet for a gentleman's servant with beer or syder	1/-
Cold dyet for a gentleman's servant ditto ditto ditto	-/9
Lodging in a bed per night with clean sheets	-/6
Corn or oats per quart Winchester measure	-/2
Stabling and good fodder or hay for a horse per night or 24 hours	1/-
Pasturage for a horse 24 hours or under	-/6
Cane spirits per quart, sealed	7/-
French brandy per quart, sealed	8/-
Good West India Rum per quart	4/-
New England or Philadelphia Rum per quart	3/-
Peach brandy per quart, sealed	2/-
Spirits distilled from grain, per quart	2/-
Good Madaria Wine per quart	5/-
Good Port wine per quart	5/-
All other European wines per quart	5/-
English strong beer per quart	1/-
Good Maryland strong beer per quart	-/6
Good syder per quart	5/-
Good small beer per quart	-/3
Good lemons, a piece	-/6
Good limes, a piece	-/2

In a suit for trover[25] the plaintiff agrees to take dollars at 7/6d or Pennsylvania money.

NOVEMBER COURT OF 1763

The November Court of 1763 met on the third Tuesday and the 15th day in the 13th year of Frederick's Dominion. The Worshipful Justices present were Thomas Beatty, Peter Bainbridge, Charles Jones, David Lynn, William Luckett, Joseph Wood, Thomas Price, James Dickson, Samuel Beall, Josiah Beall, Evan Shelby, James Smith and Samuel Postlethwait.

The Grand jurors were Archibald Edmonson, Jr., foreman, James Walling, Jr., Joseph Pridmor, Casper Smith, John McIntire, Robert Lee, James Ford, James Harbin, Edward Gaither, Benjamin Perry, Jr., John Banks, Stephen Julian, John Wilcoxon, John Lackland and John Shepherd.

The Grand Jury presented Robert Blackburn, John Charlton, Henry Charlton, Pointer Charlton, Thomas Charlton, William Dunwoody, James Dunwoody and William Watson "for committing a riot." Blackburn, who was evidently the instigator of the riot, was fined £1. The others were fined 6d each.

Samuel Annan who was presented for stealing a "wach" pleaded guilty and was sentenced to receive 39 lashes on his bare back and to stand a quarter of an hour in the pillory and to pay 2,000 pounds of tobacco for the goods stolen.

William Allison, an orphan, was bound to John Ford "to learn the trade of a house carpenter.... and Ford is to send him a year and a half to school and when free to give him a decent suit of apparel and a sett of tools such as is necessary to carry on the trade

---

[25] Recovery of damages against a person who had wrongly converted goods of another to his own use.

or mystery of a house carpenter."

"Elizabeth Boyd swears in Court here that John Cook was the father of her baseborn child."

Jane Dempsey, who sued Henry Fout for her freedom, was ordered set free and Fout was ordered to pay the costs incurred.

The Court established Cumberland and Fort Frederick as new Hundreds. They appear in a new list of Constables, as follows:

Aaron Lanham	Potomac Hundred, Lower Part
Samuel West	Potomac Hundred, Upper Part
Aquilla Duvall	Newfoundland Hundred
Samuel Selby, Jr.	Ibid., Lower Part
Allen Bowie	Rock Creek Hundred
John Fletchall	Sugarland Hundred
Richard Northcraft	Sugar Loaf Hundred
Samuel Dorsey	Linganore Hundred
William Beatty	Mannor Hundred
Mordecai Beall	Monocacy Hundred, Upper Part
John Helmes	Monocacy Hundred, Middle Part
Carlton Tannehill	Monocacy Hundred, Lower Part
Richard Brown	Pipe Creek Hundred
Daniel James	Burnt House Woods Hundred
John McKinley	Piney Creek Hundred
William Kimboll	Frederick Town Hundred
Nathaniel Walker	Kittocton Hundred, Lower Part
William Humbert	Kittocton Hundred, Upper Part
James Winders	Andieatum Hundred, Upper Part
John Banks	Andieatum Hundred, Lower Part
Isaac Dawson	Marsh Hundred
James Little	Salisbury Hundred
Peter Pinkleu	Conococheague Hundred
Elias Stillwell	Linton Hundred
James Crabtree	Old Town Hundred
Joseph Mounts	Cumberland Hundred
William Ducker	George Town Hundred
Caleb Litton	Fort Frederick Hundred

The Court appointed road overseers, including the following:

From the Mouth of Monocacy to Ballinger's Branch and from Powell's Ford to the said road and from the upper end of Pyburn's old field to the top of Kittockton Mountain and from William Barker's to the upper ford on Monocacy and from the widdow Griffith's as the old road formerly went to the top of Kittockton: Elias DeLashmutt, overseer.

The new road that leads from top of Kittockton by where George Matthews lived to Ballinger's Branch: Mathias Pooley.

The road called Touchstone's Road and the road that leads from where Alexander Jones lived to the top of Kittockton that leads to Frederick Town and the road that leads from the top of Kittockton by Casper Shaaff's place to the top of South Mountain: Conrad Crown [Crone].

From Frail Payns to Harper's Ferry and the new road when laid out from Payns into the main road leading to Conococheague: Jacob Brunner.

From Fort Frederick to intersect the old road near the malt house where William Wells lives: George Easter.

From Fort Frederick upwards to go the road the Governour cleared till it intersects the old road: William Yeates.

From Reynold's ford to Smith's Branch and from the Glade to the east side of Israel's Creek: Peter Derr.

From Frederick Town to Reynold's ford and to John Biggs' ford: Frederick Havenor.

From Major Ogle's ford to John Biggs' ford on Monocacy and from Biggs' ford to the Glade: William Barrick.

From Ambrose's mill to Miller's mill and the new road from Captain's Creek to Honey Creek and from the mountain to Captain's Creek: Conrad Keller.

All the streets and lanes in Frederick Town and the road to the English Church, the road to Mr. Dulany's mill and the road to Rue's ford: Jacob Bare.

Francis Edwards petitions the Court stating that "being upwards of 100 years of age, he is now and has been quite blind for several years and having a wife upwards of 90 are both helpless." He asks for an allowance from the County, which is granted.

Samuel Wedge and his wife Jene state in a petition to the Court "that your petitioners are desirous to have one of their children bound unto Baltis Fout as they are not able to maintain the said child."
The Court grants the petition.

The Vestry of All Saints Parish petitions the Court "to assess this year seven pounds of tobacco per poll on the taxables of this Parish." The petition is signed by Joseph Wood, Reg[istra]r.
The Court agrees to make such a levy.

Joseph Helmes states to the Court in a petition "that a certain John Flinn came to the house of your petitioner with a most grievous disorder of a cancer in his face and that he was at great cost and charges that I was obliged to hire several people to attend him while alive and that I likewise gave him decent burial and that the poor man had nothing of his own to make satisfaction for the above charges." He presents an account as follows:
For attendance and expenses from
  the 26th of September to the 19th
  of October   £10/-/-
The Court allows him £7/10/-.

Unckle Unckles in a petition to the Court states that he "has had in his charge for this 7 or 8 years past a certain Henry Miller, an orphan child that cannot in any shape be of any help to himself and cannot so much as go anywhere but as he is carried by another person or so much as help himself to eat but so as he is fed by another person." Henry is 17 years of age now and difficult to care for. He therefore asks for

some maintenance help from the County.
The Court rejects the petition.

"Frederick County, December 13, 1763: The inspectors of R[ock] Creek Warehouse represent to the Court that two of the old warehouse wants to be repaired and the prizes is out of order."

Arthur Charlton presents the following bill to the Court:

March 6th: sitting as Court in my room and
    finding firewood   £5/ -/-
November 6th: for six days ditto ditto ditto   7/10/-
    The Court orders the bills paid.

Bills, each for 187 pounds of tobacco, were also presented to the Court by the following:

By Andrew Heugh, Coroner, dated March 26, 1762, "fee for a jury of inquest on the body of Pearce Tracey, drownded at the upper falls of Potowmack the 24th instant."

By Joseph Wood, for "an inquisition held on the body, of an infant, a bastard of the body of one Elizabeth Boyd."

Also by Joseph Wood, for "an inquisition held on the body of John Stull, about $2\frac{1}{2}$ years old, son of Peter Stull."

By Joseph Smith, dated January 28, 1763, for "holding an inquisition on view of the body of Thomas Field, dead by misadventure."

By William Luckett, dated July 7, 1763, for "a jury of inquest on the body of a drownded Negro belonging to Garah Davis."

The Court orders all of them paid.

Seven Constables are each allowed 400 pounds of tobacco "for suppressing the tumultuous meeting of Negroes: Joseph Price, Jeremiah Stimpson, Thomas Conn, John Fletchall, Thomas Lansdale, Aquilla Duvall and Nathaniel Walker."

252

MARCH COURT OF 1764

The March Court of 1764 met on the third Tuesday and the 20th day of March in the 13th year of Frederick's Dominion. The Justices present were: Thomas Beatty, Peter Bainbridge, David Lynn, William Luckett, James Dickson, Thomas Price, Samuel Beall, Jr., Josiah Beall, Joseph Smith, William Blair and Kensey Gittings.

The Grand Jurors were Erasmus Gill, foreman, Hezekiah Magruder, William Cecill, William Kelly, Posthumous Clegatt, Benjamin Ricketts, Richard Gartrell, William Bright, Thomas Hawkins, Edward Owen, Jr., Alexander Waddle, Michael Dowden, Andrew Rench, Joshua Bucey, John Barwick, Conrad Hogmire and John Reynolds.

The Grand Jury presented James Hook "for beating David Ryan and William Smith."

Negro Toby, the slave of Benjamin Hall, was tried, charged with murder, "not having the fear of God before his eyes, but being moved and seduced by the instigation of the devil on the 25th day of December, 1763 with force and arms in and upon Eli Linchcom did shoot....him slightly below the bottom of his ear." Linchcom died instantly. A jury was impaneled which found Toby guilty. The Court ordered that he "be carried to the prison from whence he came, thence to the common place of execution and there to be hanged by the neck until he is dead....The Court values the Negro to £50."

"Edmund Key produces his commission as His Lordship's Attorney General."

"Ordered by the Court here that the Clerk acquaint His Excellency, the Governor, that Negro Toby, slave of Benjamin Hall, was capitally corrected for murdering a certain Eli Linchicum and that they recommend the said slave to His Excellency's clemency."

The Court appoints Richard Morris Constable of Old Town Hundred to replace James Crabtree "who has left the Province."

Mary Harris states in a petition to the Court that about a year ago she bound her son James Harris to John Campbell as a servant to learn the "art, trade, or mystery of a weaver." She further states that Campbell has since been committed to the County Gaol for "divers sums of money and is likely to stay there for some time." She therefore asks that her son be discharged from his said master.
The Court grants her petition.

George Buchanan states in his petition that he had a boy by the name of Benjamin Riddle bound to him for four years and four months as an apprentice. The boy is the son of Jane Gregg and "sometime last October the boy went to his father-in-law's [stepfather's] burial and was unlawfully detained by his mother." She still detains him and he feels he should have the services of his apprentice and asks the Court to take it under consideration.
The Court orders Jane to deliver her son to Buchanan.

Joseph Farrell states to the Court that he has a daughter about 7 years old and about four years ago "he let the child go to live with a certain John Abington and intended to have bound her to him until she was 16 years of age. But as the child has neither clothes to wear nor to sleep in and Abington refuses to let her return to her father," he asks the Court for some relief.
The Court orders summons issue for Abington to appear in the June Court.

254

Sarah Swearingen, widow, states that her "late husband kept a ferry over Potomac between this town and Winchester since which there has been a new town erected near where your petitioner lives and her husband died possessed of lands on this side of said river convenient for the road to pass through said new town of Meclenburgh." She asks that a road be laid out "from Christian Orndorff's mill to the new landing."

The Court appoints a committee to view the road and make a report.

John Semple states to the Court that he is establishing an iron works at the head of Shanandoah Falls on Potomac River and he asks that "a road be opened along the River side from Ore Hill to Harper's Road to serve as a portage past the falls of Shanandoah so that all commodities may be transported to and from the back country to tidewater at small expense." He asks that he be permitted to lay out the road.

The Court appoints a committee to view the site.

Casper Myer states that he is the owner of part of "Tasker's Chance' which is now known as "Long Acre" and that the boundaries are in decay. He asks for a commission to reestablish them.

The Court grants his request.

JUNE COURT OF 1764

The June Court of 1764 met on the third Tuesday and the 19th day of June in the 14th year of Frederick's Dominion. The Worshipful Justices present were Thomas Beatty, Peter Bainbridge, William Luckett, Charles Jones, David Lynn, James Dickson, Thomas Price, Samuel Beall, Jr., Kensey Gittings, William Blair, Joseph Smith, Enoch Innis and Evan Shelby, Gentlemen.

The Grand Jury was comprised of William Dent, foreman, Jacob Miller, John Matthews, Robert Wood,

Jacob Myers, John Young, Edward Butler, Jr., Thomas Hogg, Daniel Robins, Casper Smith, Thomas Lane, Archibald Edmonston, Jr., William Thompson, Jonathan Markland and Henry Gaither.

"William Paca qualifies as an attorney of this Court."

"Ordered by the Court that Thomas Bowles agree with workmen for sundry repairs about the Court House and prison."

In a petition to the Court, John Carmack states "that as he now keeps a house of entertainment for travellers on the main road that leads from Frederick Town to Baltimore" he now asks that the Court "allow the road to be turned through his plantation by his door which will not alter the distance above 40 rods and.... will save him the trouble of making gates to pass through the plantation much to his disadvantage."

The Court appoints John Middagh and William Beatty to view the proposed road and report to the August Court.

The Reverend Mr. Alexander Williamson, Rector of Prince George's Parish, petitions the Court to build roads from his house "in such a manner as may be most convenient for his attending his duty."

The Court rejects his petition.

William Luckett and James Dickson report that in obedience to the order of the Court they have viewed a proposed road "from Mr. Sample's iron works at Oar [Ore] Hill to Harpers Ferry.... along the River side on the head of the Shannadore Falls to Harpers Ferry." They "are of the opinion that it would be impracticable to lay out such road by reason of large rocks being in the way of the road for a considerable distance and that there can be no road laid out from his iron works to Harpers Ferry unless it runs into a draught of the

River Potomac and that should a road be laid out agreeable to the petition there are not a sufficient number of taxables either to lay out or to support it."

The Court orders that nothing further be done.

A number of suits involve Thomas Beatty and Company including one against Jacob Keller on a debt of £16 in which the plaintiff got judgment by default.

AUGUST COURT OF 1764

The August Court of 1764 met on the third Tuesday and the 21st day of August in the 14th year of Frederick's Dominion. The Justices present were Thomas Beatty, Peter Bainbridge, David Lynn, Charles Jones, William Luckett, James Dickson, Thomas Price, Samuel Beall, Andrew Heugh, William Blair and Joseph Smith, Gentlemen.

Thomas Prather, Gentleman, was Sheriff and John Darnell was Clerk.

The Grand Jury consisted of John Orme, foreman, John Cook, John Ray, Jr., Benjamin Kelly, Richard Gatrell, Samuel Biggs, Thomas Veatch, Samuel Plummer, William Winchester, Peter Hedges, Jacob Miller, John Stull, Christian Orndorf and George Tucker.

They presented "Samuel Price for the sin of fornication committed on the body of Sarah Reynolds, she being pregnant by the said Samuel Price as by the information of the said Sarah Reynolds."

In a suit against Sarah Howard for bastardy, the record indicates that she refuses "to discover the father" and therefore is fined £3.

"William Beatty and Carlton Tanyhill appointed to attend as Constables to this Court."

"Sarah Graham comes into Court and confesses that she had a mulatto bastard child which said child is sold for the benefit of the County to John Clagett until she arrive to the age of 31 years for the sum of 20 shillings."

A petition by sundry inhabitants of the County states that "there is a great want and need of a bridge to be made on the new road leading to Swearingen's Ferry and to the mouth of Connogojigue over Kittockton Creek between Samuel Magruder's and Philip Fink's as there has several people in great danger and almost lost at said fording these last freshes [freshets]." They ask that such a bridge be built.

"The Court orders that Messrs. Joseph Smith and Peter Bainbridge agree with workmen to build a bridge over Kittockton Creek near Samuel Magruder's."

A petition of Raphael Taney (who laid out Taney-town in 1762) upon behalf of himself and sundry inhabitants states that "the inhabitants of Conococheague have cut a road to the Gap of Kittockton Mountain near Mr. William Blair's and your petitioners conceive it will be greatly beneficial to the public to have a road continued from the said Gap of the Kittockton Mountain through Taney's Town as far as Baltimore Town whereby a communication will be opened to great part of the back country, the inhabitants whereof are now subject to great difficulties in the transportance and sending of their commodities and the trade of those parts consequently impeded."

The Court ordered that this matter be postponed until the November Court.

Lettice Grimes in a petition to the Court states "that being born of a white woman intituled to a freedom at 31 years of age and is now nearer 40 years of age and your petitioner's mistress refuseth to give her a discharge," she asks the Court to intervene in

258

her behalf. The Court orders a summons issued for Isabella Willett, returnable in the November Court next.

NOVEMBER COURT OF 1764

The November Court of 1764 met on the third Tuesday and the 20th day of November in the 14th year of Frederick's Dominion. The worshipful Justices present were Peter Bainbridge, David Lynn, Charles Jones, William Luckett, William Blair, Thomas Price, Samuel Beall, Josiah Beall, Andrew Heugh, Kensey Gittings, Joseph Smith, James Smith and Joseph Warford.

The Grand Jury included Archibald Edmonston, foreman, Robert Owen, John Lackland, John Wilcoxon, Ninian Edmonston, Benjamin Perry, Arthur Nelson, William Beckwith, Peter Stilley, Charles Hedges, Jacob Brunner, Jacob Myers, John Oliver and Michael Paul.

They presented "James Levinston, Major of Fort Cumberland, for unlawfully imprisoning a certain John Banks, one of the Deputy Sheriffs of Frederick County, he, the said John Banks, being there in the execution of his office."

Major James Levinston was also presented for "risgaing [rescuing] Richard Trotter from the custody of Thomas Prather, Sheriff of Frederick County, he the said Richard Trotter being arrested by the said Sheriff to answer unto the Lord Proprietary concerning certain trespass, contempt and misdemeanors."

The Court orders that Lettice Grimes be discharged from the services of Isabella Willett.

Thomas Prather is discharged by a writ of discharge from the office of Sheriff and George Murdock is appointed in his stead.

"Lydia Grimes, a mulatto girl, is sold to Col. Samuel Beall until she arrives to the age of 31 years, she being now adjudged to be ten years of age, for 5,000 pounds of tobacco to be discharged at 12/6d per hundredweight."

"The Court orders "that Mr. David Lynn take a mulatto child named Lucy, a supposed daughter of Lettice Grimes, and bring her to March Court next to be sold for the benefit of the County."
"Lettice Grimes, a mulatto, is sold for 2 years and 4 months to Col. Samuel Beall for 1,600 pounds of tobacco for the use of the County, being convicted for mulatto bastardy."

"John Kimbol and Joseph Volgamot appointed press masters for the ensuing year."

"John Beatty brings into Court here John Michael Gimbect and Maudlon Gimbect, servants to him, to be adjudged for their absconding from his service, the said John Michael three days and the said Maudlon 18 days. The Court orders that each of them shall serve 5 days for every one day they absconded and shall each of them serve one month for the expenses that attended the said John Beatty in going and enquireing after them."

The Vestry of All Saints Parish petitions the Court to assess for the present year eight pounds of tobacco per poll; and the Vestry of Prince George's Parish likewise requests a levy of five pounds of tobacco per taxable for defraying necessary expenses. In each case the Court orders "that the same be allowed and levyed."

A petition from Thomas Kindrick to the Court

states that he is in his 92nd year and is completely disabled. The Court grants him 1200 pounds of tobacco for the ensuing year.

Esther Matew appears again, asking for renewal of her pension, which is granted.

David Lynn states in a petition to the Court that he "is possessed of a crop note for a hogshead of tobacco sold at August Court. He therefore prays you will allow him in the levy the sum which the said hogshead sold for." The Court allows him £2.

Arthur Charlton presents to the Court an account "for three days in November Court at 25 shillings per day, £3/15/-."
The Court orders it paid.

Sundry inhabitants of the upper part of Monocoque Hundred petition for a road "to lead from the upper part of this County near Marsh Creek to cross Monococque Creek near John McKorkles and to the most direct way to Tawney Town and from thence the most direct way by the mouth of the Meadow Branch into the road already laid out to Baltimore Town." They state that it would be a great accommodation for them to go "to meeting, mill and market."

Sundry inhabitants of Frederick Town petition the Court "that they find it would be very necessary to have a new, good brich [bridge] builded over Carrells Creek near Usslemans on the main road leading from Frederick Town to Annapolis."
The Court orders the bridge built at a price not to exceed £15.

Lawrence Huff in a petition states that "some time ago he bound his son as an apprentice to William Price to learn the trade of a hatter. He now finds the said Price unable to keep and maintain him or instruct him in any way agreeable to his contract." He asks that his son be released, but the Court rejects his petition.

Leonard Weaver presents the following bill to the Court: For "mending the prison pump and cleaning the well, £2/5/-."
The Court orders him to be paid 200 pounds of tobacco.

Six men are allowed 400 pounds of tobacco each for "suppressing the tumultuous meetings of Negroes:" Nathaniel Walker, Aquilla Duvall, Samuel West, John Fletchall, Thomas Clayland and William Kimbol.

Andrew Heugh presents an account to the Court dated July 11, 1764 for a "fee for jury of inquest on the body of Richard Pipisico, an Indian, who was found dead in Captain George Beall's wheat field yesterday, the 10th instant, 187 pounds of tobacco."

Joseph Wood presents a bill for an inquisition on the body of Eli Linchcome, "about 11 years old, son of Joseph Linchcome, who was shott by Negro Toby, belonging to Benjamin Haul [Hall], Jr., 187 pounds of tobacco."

Charles Beatty presents the following account to the Court:
<table>
<tr><td>Putting one head in the County drum</td><td>7/6d</td></tr>
<tr><td>One cord for ditto</td><td>2/6</td></tr>
</table>

Dr. James Brand presents the following account:
<table>
<tr><td>Board of Isbel Miller from July 7th to September 19th at which time her legg was cut off</td><td>£5/ 5/10</td></tr>
<tr><td>Cash paid for new linen for Isbel Miller's stump</td><td>4/ 2</td></tr>
<tr><td>Board and extraordinary attendance of those in the family upon Isbel Miller from the</td><td></td></tr>
</table>

time of cutting her leg off to
the 23rd of November 6/ 4/2
The wooden leg for Isbel Miller 12/6

William Offutt presents the following bill to the Court:

Board and attendance of Isobel
Miller in her sickness from
April 21st to July 5th, 1764 £4/15/-
My son's carrying a letter to
Dr. Brand 7/-
A Negro fellow and two horses
with Isobel Miller to Freder-
ick Town 1/ 2/6
The boys and horses expenses at
Mr. Lucketts 3/-

Robert Jackson presents an account to the County for burying Manasses O'Cain, a "pentioner" of Frederick County:

For a coffin 12/6
For a sheet 12/-
10 quarts of liquor at the burying 10/-
"waggon and horses haling the
corps to the grave" 7/-
Digging the grave 5/-

Francis Street presents a bill dated July 2, 1764:
For digging a grave and burying
Richard Pipsico, an Indian
found dead in Capt. George
Beall's wheatfield on the 10th,
instant 7/6

The Court orders Messrs. Joseph Smith and Peter Bainbridge to agree with workmen "to build a bridge over Kittockton Creek for a price not to exceed £30.

The March Court of 1765 met on the third Tuesday and the 19th day in the 15th year of Frederick's Dominion "and adjourned until the first Tuesday in May and then adjourned until the 17th of June."

The Justices were Thomas Beatty, Peter Bainbridge, William Luckett, Charles Jones, David Lynn, Thomas Price, James Dickson, Nathaniel Beall, Joseph Smith, Andrew Heugh, Enoch Innis, Evan Shelby and Joseph Wauford.

The Grand Jury was made up of Nicholas Haymond, foreman, Abraham Lakin, Daniel McCoy, Edward Boteler, John Brunner, Jacob Sturrum, Ephraim Davis, William Burgess, Henry Clagett, John Kimbol, William Beatty, Charles Springer, Mathias Ringer, John Harlin, Elias DeLashmutt, Stephen Julian and Allen Bowie.

The Rev. Mr. Thomas Bacon states in a petition to the Court that "a certain John Brown, laborer, a free mulatto," bound himself on the 11th of January 1764 to Bacon's service, but about May 1st Brown ran away and was gone until the beginning of January 1765. He further states that as a result of Brown's absence he was "under many difficulties and was obliged to hire hands at extraordinary rates." Brown returned but was immediately seized with smallpox and "was supported by your petitioner and used with great tenderness notwithstanding which he ran away a second time on the 26th of February, 1765. He was brought home two days after but behaving very ill and attempting to run away again. Your petitioner secured him in jayl, where he now lies until the Court should judge concerning him."

The Court orders that Brown serve his master one year from this time in satisfaction of his runaway time.

"On motion by Edmund Key, Esquire, Mr. John Rogers is admitted as an attorney of this Court."

"Ordered by the Court that Mr. Charles Beatty lay out a road from a corner of the new street by Mr. John Kimbol's by a straight line to the corner of Jacob Huff's fence and make a report to the June Court next."

"The Court appoints Lodowick Young Constable of Salisbury Hundred in the room of John Rench."

"The Court appoints Samuel Magruder Constable of the Lower Part of Kittockton Hundred in the room of Nathaniel Walker, deceased."

"On motion by Edmund Key, Esquire, Mr. James Brice is admitted as an attorney of this Court."

Twenty pages of abbreviated cases, ten to a page, follow. Then the Court adjourns to the 18th of June.

JUNE COURT OF 1765

The June Court of 1765 met on the third Tuesday and the 18th day of June in the 15th year of His Lordship's Dominion. This was one day after the readjourned March Court.

Justices present were Thomas Beatty, Peter Bainbridge, William Luckett, Charles Jones, David Lynn, James Dickson, Thomas Price, Andrew Heugh, James Smith, William Blair, Samuel Beall, Jr., and Evan Shelby. It is a slightly different list from that of the previous day.

The Grand Jury, wholly new, was made up of Abraham Hayter, foreman, Norman Beall Magruder, Anthony Ricketts, Michael Murphy, John Baptist Loveless, Richard Beall, Edward Thomas, Thomas Johnson, Jr., Thomas Hogg, Mathias Ringer, William

Durbin, David Shriver, Philip Greenwald, John Reynalds, Thomas Sumers and Charles Harding.

The Jury presents:
George Hutsel "for not keeping the main road good and passable between Frederick Town and Monocacy at Reynolds Ford and likewise from Frederick Town to Biggs' Ford by the evidence of Thomas Beatty, William Beatty and Charles Beatty."

Thomas Annan for stealing from Mary Wilson three pecks of hemp seed valued at 12 shillings current money.

James Goff for stealing "£2, 12 sh., 6d paper money, the property of James Martin."

"Ordered by the Court that summons issue returnable to the August Court for James Conn and to bring with him William Sibus to answer what shall be objected against him and in the meantime to use the said servant well."

"Ordered by the Court that Mary Burton be allowed 56 pounds of tobacco in the next levy for a taxable overcharged to her this year."

Richard Keen, an orphan aged 15, is bound to Lodowick Weltner to learn the art, trade and mystery of a breeches maker.

"Ordered by the Court that the Clerk give Alice Fouran a certificate under the County seal how she came by a loss of part of her ears."

Isabella Miller now petitions the Court "that she is not in a capacity to get her living having lost one of her leggs by a mortification also in danger of loosing the other leg by the same effect, therefore begs Your Worships will take her pitiful case into your consideration."

The Court allows her 600 pounds of tobacco.

Elizabeth Harrie states in a petition to the Court that her husband Richard Harrie, who for some years past has been allowed 800 pounds of tobacco from the County "died in the hard weather last winter at which time the whole allowance was disposed of, that your petitioner has two small children to maintain and is notwithstanding unwilling to become burdensome. She has therefore bound out one [child] and shall the other as soon as it comes from the breast, that your petitioner was charged 20 shillings for a coffin and the other expense attending the funeral amounted in the whole to 30 shillings currency." She asks to be allowed 30 shillings "so that she may begin in the world clear of debts."

The Court allows 240 pounds of tobacco.

Richard Waller states to the Court that he was appointed by one of the Justices to serve a warrant on John Young for a debt due to Thomas Waller, Sr., and another due William Manford, both of which he served and Young "willingly coming along with me was interrupted by two certain persons, namely George Becraft and Jacob Nickolls." He asks that the Court take appropriate action.

Warrants were issued against Becraft and Nickolls returnable at the August Court.

In a suit by Richard Norwood versus Jacob Schley, Norwood states that he entered into an agreement with Schley whereby Schley, as a gunsmith, was to make for Norwood a gun "for to shoot shot well" and that there was a definite warranty that if the gun didn't perform properly he would either return the money or make a new gun. He claims that neither has occurred.

A jury was impaneled, including Joseph Beall, Robert Owen, Charles Davis, Nathaniel Crawford, William Burgess, William Duval, John Stull, William Shields, Peter Pinkley, Richard Watts, John Harlin and Charles Hedges. They found for the defendant.

There now follow in the record some thirty-two pages with abbreviated case summaries, about ten to the page, most of them concerning debts but yielding little historical information.

AUGUST COURT OF 1765

The August Court of 1765 met on the third Tuesday and the 20th day of August in the 15th year of Frederick's Dominion. The Justices present were Thomas Beatty, Peter Bainbridge, William Luckett, David Lynn, Charles Jones, James Dickson, Thomas Price, William Blair, Samuel Beall, Kensey Gittings, Andrew Heugh, James Smith, Joseph Smith, Enoch Innis, Joseph Warford and Evan Shelby.

The Grand Jury consisted of Abraham Haytor, foreman, Conrad Hogmire, Ralph Hilleary, Stephen Richards, Frederick Kemp, Peter Kemp, Stephen Julian, Mathias Ringer, Charles Hedge, Elias De-Lashmutt, Philip Rodenpiller, George Bare, Edward Tansey, Robert Smith, Alexander Waddle and Carrolton Tannyhill.

In the suit of the Lord Proprietary versus George Becraft "for rescuing John Young from the Constable" Becraft was fined £2/10/-.

Robert Crosson states in a petition that he was bound to Capt. Evan Shelby for a period of three years which he has served, that he has served 20 days additional and that Shelby refuses not only to return the indenture to him but also to give him his freedom dues. He asks for relief in the matter.
The Court orders that a summons issue for Shelby returnable in the November Court.

Jeremiah Adamson states to the Court that in the March Court last he agreed with the commission appointed by the Court to build a bridge over Carrol's

Creek near Valentine Whistleman's for £15 and that "he finished according to agreement." He asks for his money.

The Court orders the Sheriff to pay him.

Sundry inhabitants petition the Court to order a road from Andrew Livingstone's mill "to the main road that leads from Frederick Town to Antiatum."

The Court orders Samuel Buzard and Andrew Arnold to view the road.

Sundry inhabitants "in and about Fort Cumberland" petition the Court to build a bridge over Town Creek, usually called Town Gut, "on the main road leading from Fort Frederick to Fort Cumberland, which during the winter season cannot be crossed without great danger, many having narrowly escaped drowning and one person really so."

The Court orders that Col. Thomas Cresap and Charles Prather "agree with workmen to build a bridge over Town Creek and to maintain the same ten years at a price not to exceed £40."

Mary Harmon in a petition to the Court states "that when I arrived into Maryland, Captain John Dorsey of Elk Ridge bought me from on board of the ship I arrived in at which time I had a son about three years old and on coming home to my said master and living with him about two years he contracted a bargain with me for my son for and during the time of his arriving to the age of 21 years, it being at the same time provided in the said agreement made with my master that at my master's decease my son should be free which happened long before my son arrived to the age of 21 years, soon after which time I took my son away and bound him to a trade which I thought for the benefit of my son, but soon afterwards John Dorsey, son of my old master, came and violently took him away and continues so to keep him in his service giving him no learning neither any trade and as I am thus be-

reaved of my child contrary to any bargain I ever contracted with my old master through the pretensions of
his son I humbly pray Your Worships to take this my
case under your consideration and release my son to
me from John Dorsey or otherwise bind him to some
trade that may appear to Your Worships most necessary for instructions to him to gett his livelyhood when
grown to the years of majority."

The Court orders a bench warrant issue for John
Dorsey returnable immediately "and that he be pro-
tected from all other arrests within the jurisdiction of
this Court during the setting of this Court."

An account from Mathias Need refers to one
drumhead, 8 shillings.

John Michael Widmeyer states to the Court that
Jacob Bennett, deceased, had "sundry medicines in
his shop and your petitioner had no satisfaction for the
same" and he petitions the Court that they pay for:
             "A purge and viel, drops,
                 ointment and tea"   12/6
The Court rejects the bill.

On motion made by Edmund Key, Esquire, the
following are admitted as attorneys of the Court:
James Tilghman III, Thomas Stone, Arthur Bordley
and Benjamin Nicholson.

"Ordered by the Court here that the Sheriff take
Ann Campbell who was servant to Benjamin Becraft
(and the said Becraft refusing to enter security for her
and relinquishes his right of her servitude, she being
fined £3 for bastardy) and sell her to the highest bidder
for the fine aforesaid and fees due to the officers of the
Court."

The Court orders that Sarah Medcalf "be bound to
Joseph Hedge, son of William, until she arrives to the
age of 16 years, she being now adjudged to be four

years and nine months old."

"Ordered by the Court here that Lucy, a bastard child aged 5 years begot on the body of Lettice Grimes, a free-born mulatto woman, by a Negro, be put up to public sale by the Sheriff and sold for the benefit of the County agreeable to Act of Assembly until she arrives to the age of 31 years."

"Whereupon a certain Samuel Beall became the purchaser for 3,000 pounds of tobacco to be discharged at 12 sh. 6d per c., payable next levy."

"Ordered by the Court here that the proceedings relating to Thomas Selby for prophane swearing delivered at November Court last be quashed and that the Sheriff do not collect the fines of the said Thomas Selby."

"Ordered by the Court here that George Lynham be boarded at William Waugh's until November Court next for 50 shillings to be levied in the next levy."

"Ordered by the Court here that scire facias[26] issue against Samuel Perry returnable to the next Court to show cause why he should not forfeit his recognizance for keeping and maintaining Frederick Town bridges in proper repair which he neglects to do."

One Sarah Roscal sues Jeremiah Spiers for her freedom. The Court orders "that Spiers discharge the woman from his service and pay fees."

Ann Dempsey sues John Hyde Sanders for her freedom, and the Court orders that Sanders discharge Ann "from his service."

---

[26] Judicial writ founded on some matter of record, requiring a person to show cause why the effect of such record should not occur.

HEMPSTEAD COUNTY LIBRARY
HOPE, ARKANSAS

An earlier Court had ordered that Messrs. Christopher Edelin, John Cary, Casper Shaaff and Charles Beatty "or any three or two of them view and lay out a road from Frederick Town to the Honorable Daniel Dulany's Mill and make report."

They now report that they have "laid out the road from the lower end of the street where Henry Shover lives to the corner of Lawrence Prangle's [Brengle's] fence to pass by his house from thence to the corner of Casper Shaaff's fence and from thence along the old road to Mr. Dulany's Mill."

John Carmack and Stephen Richards previously appointed to view a road "from the plantation formerly belonging to James Dickson on the Annapolis Road and striking in the Baltimore Road about half a mile above John Carmack's plantation....give as their opinion that the situation above mentioned is very convenient and commodious for a public road." It is their further opinion "that if said road was to turn out of the Annapolis Road by William Beatty's instead of James Dickson's plantation, it would be much nearer and more convenient in many respects than where it was proposed."

The Court orders that the road be laid out as suggested by the committee.

"Ordered by the Court that Messrs. Michael Cresap and Daniel Parsley view and lay out a road and make amendments on the road that leads from Sideling Hill Creek to Isaac Collier's and make report thereof to the next Court."

"Wednesday appointed for the Clerk to attend in the Court House agreeable to Act of Assembly."

Some 25 or 30 pages of abbreviated case notations, averaging 8 or 10 cases per page, follow. At the end of that the Court adjourned to the November Court next.

NOVEMBER COURT OF 1765

The November Court of 1765 met on the third Tuesday and the 19th day of November in the 15th year of Frederick's Dominion. The Justices present were Thomas Beatty, Peter Bainbridge, William Luckett, Charles Jones, David Lynn, Thomas Price, James Dickson, William Blair, Samuel Beall, Josiah Beall, Andrew Heugh and Joseph Smith.

The Grand Jury was composed of the following: Arthur Nelson, Foreman, Henry Gaither, Samuel Watson, James Kelly, John Eason, Mathias Ringer, Charles Hedges, Henry Fouts, George Moore, John Badham, John Bruner, Andrew Grim, Thomas Lane, Jacob Casner, William Knight and William Dickensheet.

George Murdock, Gentleman, was Sheriff and John Darnall was Clerk.

This session of the Frederick County Court is considered locally as the most significant event in the history of the County because of the repudiation by the Court of the hated Stamp Act. This action by the Court was memorialized in 1904 by the local chapter of the Daughters of the American Revolution with a bronze plaque in the second-floor corridor of the Court House. Each year this memorialization is renewed by the Society at its November meeting by inviting the Clerk of the Circuit Court to read to it the text of the Court record. The entry in the Judgment Record and Minutes of the Court embodying the repudiation follows:

"By Frederick County November Court Anno Domini 1765 ordered that the following Resolution and Opinion be recorded:
"Upon application of Michael Ashford Dowden, bail of James Veatch in discharge of himself which the Court ordered to be done, and an entry of the surrender

to be made accordingly, which John Darnall, Clerk of the Court, refused to make, and having also refused to issue any process out of his office, or to make the necessary entries of the Court proceedings, alleging that he conceives there is an Act of Parliament imposing stamp duties on all legal proceedings, and therefore that he cannot safely proceed in exercising his office without proper stamps;

"It is the unanimous Resolution and Opinion of this Court that all the business thereof shall and ought to be transacted in the usual and accustomed manner without any inconvenience or delay to be occasioned from the want of Stamped Paper Parchment or Vellum, and that all proceedings shall be valid and effectual without the use of Stamps, and they enjoin and order all Sheriffs, Clerks, Counsellors, Attorneys, and all officers of the Court to proceed in their several avocations as usual, which Resolution and Opinion are grounded on the following and other reasons:

"1st. It is conceived that there has not been a legal publication yet made of any Act of Parliament whatever, imposing a Stamp Duty on the Colonies. Therefore this Court are of the opinion that until the existence of such an Act is properly notified, it would be culpable in them to permit or suffer a total stagnation of business, which must inevitably be productive of innumerable injuries to individuals and have a tendence to subvert all principles of Civil Government;

"2nd. As no stamps are yet arrived in this Province and the inhabitants have no means of procuring any, this Court are of the Opinion that it would be an instance of the most wanton oppression to deprive any person of a legal remedy for the recovery of his property for omitting that which it is impossible to perform.

"Ordered that John Darnall, Clerk of this Court, be committed to the custody of the Sheriff of this County for a contempt of the authority of this Court, he having refused to comply with the aforegoing order of this Court relative to the execution of his office in issuing process and making the necessary entries of the Court's proceedings, and that he stand committed for the above offence until he complys with the above mentioned order.

"John Darnall, having submitted to obey the aforesaid order of this Court in regard to the due execution of his office, the Sheriff is ordered to release him out of custody, he paying charges."[27]

All entries in the Judgment Records of the Court were made under the date of the Court's convening. Repudiation Day is celebrated in Frederick County on November 23rd, which would have been the fifth day of the session and would have fallen on Saturday in 1765. The date was established by proclamation of Governor Frank Brown in 1894 which made Repudiation Day a half-holiday in Frederick County. There is nothing in either the Court Minutes or the Judgment Records which fixes the date of the Court's action. But in its issue of December 16, 1765 the Maryland Gazette reported that a celebration of the event, which included a mock funeral, was held in Frederick and that the legend on the "coffin" proclaimed that the Stamp Act "expired" on November 23, 1765.[28] Obviously the aroused citizens considered the Stamp Act definitely repudiated.

Notwithstanding all of the foregoing, a careful reading of the Court's Resolution and Opinion indicates that it repudiates only John Darnall's action. Simply stated, the Court disagrees with Darnall's refusal to execute legal documents without stamps affixed thereto and orders him jailed for such refusal. It bases its action on the fact that it has had no official notification regarding the Stamp Act and that no stamps are avail-

---

[27] This entry is recorded in the Judgment Records, Liber M, pp. 579-580.
[28] J. Thomas Scharf, History of Western Maryland (Philadelphia, 1882), p. 542.

able. Therefore, to prevent stagnation, it orders all legal business to proceed as usual without stamps.

While the Resolution and Opinion did not repudiate the Stamp Act itself or forbid the use of stamps if they were available, the Court's action was more courageous and forthright than that elsewhere. In many parts of the Province public and private business was at a standstill because no stamps were available. However, the scope and effectiveness of the Court's action was never put to a test. While there were stamps aboard a ship offshore at Annapolis, they were not brought ashore because of the violent opposition. And the Act itself was repealed a few months later on the 18th of March, 1766.

Two things suggest the possibility that the action of the Court may not have been entirely spontaneous. The first of these is that during the days of the session preceding the entry of the Resolution and Opinion the routine business of the Court was carried on with no hint of what was to occur later. Three bench warrants were issued, two men were certified as inspectors of the Rock Creek Warehouse, seventeen cases were heard in the name of the Lord Proprietary, as well as sundry other actions. Almost certainly some of these would have required stamps within the purview of the Stamp Act. Yet this single case of Michael Dowden, which was not routine and therefore could have been prearranged, was the basis for the Court's action.

The second thing which suggests lack of spontaneity is the reasoned formality of the record. Its tone is unlike the usual judgment entry, as evidenced in all of my previous quotations, and the prefatory order to record the "Resolution and Opinion" is not found elsewhere in records of this Court.

This reasoned formality, considered in conjunction with the clause "no stamps are yet arrived in this

Province," suggests the possibility of more than local interest in the matter. The suggestion arises from use of the word "Province," rather than the word "County," by a County Court of strictly limited jurisdiction. The word "Province" suggests the involvement of someone of wider than county interest in the preparation of the Court's Resolution and Opinion.

If there was stage-setting involved, it may possibly have been in part, at least, for the benefit of John Darnall, who had been Clerk of the Court since the beginning in 1748. Darnall was quite definitely a part of the Proprietary establishment. His father was an agent of Lord Baltimore and Attorney General of the Province.

Whatever his personal attitude may have been — and there seems to be no evidence as to that — Darnall's official position left him little choice. Moreover, his son-in-law, James Dickson, was one of the twelve sitting Justices and may quite possibly have interceded with his colleagues to permit Darnall to be "forced" to disobey the Stamp Act. However, this episode had no apparent effect upon his clerkship, for he continued in that office at least until the June Court of 1767. He died in January 1768.

In connection with the entire proceeding, it is interesting to note that of the original twenty-three Justices commissioned in 1748, only one, Thomas Beatty, was sitting on the November Court of 1765.

And so, with this historical climax and the unanswered questions contained therein, I bring these readings from the Frederick County Court's Judgment Records to an end. In some small measure I hope these excerpts have portrayed something of the customs and mores of the times: This was the life.

APPENDIX A

Frederick County Court Records
Colonial Period

Judgment Records:
>   Court House, Frederick: 1748-1755, 1758-1771,
>   1780-1783 (photostatic copies, except 1763-
>   1766 originals)
>   Hall of Records, Annapolis: 1748-1771, 1780-
>   1783 (originals, except 1763-1766 on micro-
>   film)

Minutes:
>   Court House, Frederick: 1763-1768 (originals)
>   Hall of Records, Annapolis: 1750-1786 (originals
>   except 1763-1768 on microfilm)

Dockets:
>   Hall of Records, Annapolis: 1748-1784 (originals)

APPENDIX B

PROCLAMATION ESTABLISHING THE COURT OF
FREDERICK COUNTY, MARYLAND
December 12, 1748

"This day, to wit, the 13th day of December Anno Dom. 1748 Nathaniel Wickham, Junior, Gentleman, produces the following commission of the peace and Dedimus Potestatem[29] which was publicly read in these words, to wit:

"Charles, Absolute Lord and Proprietary of the Province of Maryland and Avalon, Lord Baron of Baltimore, &c., to Benjamin Tasker, George Plater, Edmund Jennings, Charles Hammond, Samuel Chamberlain, Philip Thomas, Daniel Dulany, Edward Lloyd, Benjamin Young, Benjamin Tasker, Junior, Richard Lee and Benedict Calvert, Esquires, Nathaniel Wickham, Junior, Thomas Owen, Thomas Cresap, Thomas Beatty, Joseph Chapline, Henry Munday, Thomas Prather, George Gordon, Joseph Ogle, William Griffith, John Rawlings, of Frederick County, Gentlemen, Greeting. Know ye that we have assigned you and every of you jointly and severally, as Justices to keep our peace within our County of Frederick and to do equal law and right to all the King's subjects, rich and poor, according to the laws and customs and directions of the Acts of Assembly of this Province so far forth as they provide and when they are silent, according to the laws and statutes and reasonable customs of England as used and practiced within this Province for

---

[29] Latin, we have given power. A writ or commission issuing out of chancery empowering the persons named to perform certain acts.

conservation of the peace and quiet, rule and government of the King's subjects within our said County; and to chastise and punish all and every person or persons offending against the said Acts, laws and statutes and customs or any of them according to the directions thereof and to call before you or any of you all those who in our County aforesaid shall threaten to do bodily harm to any of the King's subjects or to burn their houses or otherwise break our peace and misbehave themselves; to find sufficient security of the peace and good behavior to us and the said subjects, and if they shall refuse to find such security that then you cause them to be committed into safe custody until they shall be delivered by due course of law from thence. Also we have assigned you and every three or more of you of whom we will you the said Benjamin Tasker, George Plater, Edmund Jenings, Charles Hammond, Samuel Chamberlain, Philip Thomas, Daniel Dulany, Edward Lloyd, Benjamin Young, Benjamin Tasker, Junior, Richard Lee and Benedict Calvert, Esquires, Nathaniel Wickham, Junior, Thomas Owen, Thomas Cresap, Thomas Betty [sic], Joseph Chapline, Henry Munday[30] or one of you always to be one of our Justices to inquire by the oath of good and lawful men of our County aforesaid by whom the truth of the premises may be the better known of all and all manner of felonies, petty treasons, murders, rapes upon white women, willful burning of any dwelling house or outhouse contiguous to and used with any dwelling house or any other outhouse wherein there shall be any person or any goods or merchandise, tobacco, Indian corn, or fodder, and all other capital offenses done or perpetrated by any Negro or other slave and likewise all consulting, advising and conspiring of Negroes and other slaves to rebel or raise any insurrection or to

---

[30] Omitted, but included in the listings above and below were Thomas Prather, George Gordon, Joseph Ogle, William Griffith and John Rawlings.

murder or poison any person or to ravish any white woman or to attempt to burn any dwelling house or outhouse contiguous to or used therewith and of all trespasses, engrossings, regratings, forestallings and extortions whatsoever and of all other misfeasances and offenses whatsoever of which Justices of our peace lawfully may or ought to inquire by whomsoever or howsoever in our County aforesaid done or committed or which may hereafter happen to be done or committed and also of all those who in our County aforesaid in riotous manner have gone or rode or shall hereafter presume to go or ride with armed force against our peace to the disturbance of the King's subjects and of all such who in our County aforesaid have lain or shall hereafter presume to lay in wait to maim or kill any of the King's subjects and also of all ordinary [tavern] keepers and other persons who have offended or hereafter shall presume to offend in the abuse of weights or measures against the Acts of Assembly for the common good and profit now in this Province made and used; and also of the Sheriffs, Bailiffs, Constables and other offices who have or shall hereafter misbehave themselves in the execution of their offices or have been remiss or negligent in the execution thereof or shall hereafter happen so to be within our County aforesaid and of all and every the articles, matters and things whatsoever, howsoever or by whomsoever in our County aforesaid done or committed or that shall hereafter happen to be done or committed concerning the premises or any of them; and to inspect all indictments before you or any of you taken or to be taken or before our late Justices of the peace within our said County had and taken and not yet determined and process thereon against all or any person or persons so indicted or which shall hereafter happen to be indicted within our County aforesaid to make and continue until they shall be taken or surrender themselves or be outlawed and to hear and determine all and every the felonies, petty treasons, murders, rapes upon white women, willful burning of any dwelling house or outhouse contiguous to and used with any dwelling house or any other outhouse wherein there shall be any person or any goods or merchandizes, tobacco, Indian corn or fodder and all other capital offenses done or perpetrated by any Negro or other slave and likewise all consulting, advising and conspiring of Negroes and other slaves to rebel or raise any insurrection or to murder or poison any person or to ravish any white woman or to attempt to burn any dwelling house or outhouses contiguous to or used therewith, trespasses, forestallings, regratings, riots, indictments and all other the matters aforesaid according to the laws, customs and directions of the Acts of Assembly aforesaid so far forth as they provide and where they are silent according to the laws, statutes and reasonable customs of England as used and practiced within this Province and the said delinquents and every of them to chastise and punish by fines, ransoms and amerciaments, forfeitures and otherwise according to the laws, customs and directions of the Acts of Assembly aforesaid so far forth as they provide and where they are silent according to the laws, statutes and reasonable customs of England as used and practiced within this Province. But we will not that you proceed in any of the cases aforesaid to take life or member except of Negroes and other slaves but that in every such case you send the prisoners with their indictments and the whole matters depending before you to our Justices of Assize nisi prius[31] and goal [gaol] delivery at the next Court of oyer and terminer[32] to be held for our said County be it whensoever or wheresoever to be holden there to be tried; and we command you and every of you diligently to intend the keeping the peace Acts of Assembly, laws, customs and statutes aforesaid and

---

[31] Court held for trial of issues of fact before a jury and one presiding judge.
[32] Court empowered to "hear and determine" cases of felonies and misdemeanors.

all and every the premises and that at your County courts you make inquisition and hear and determine as aforesaid doing therein what to justice appertains according to the laws, customs and directions of the Acts of Assembly aforesaid so far forth as they provide and where they are silent according to the laws, statutes and reasonable customs of England as used and practiced within this Province. And further we do constitute, ordain and appoint you, the said Benjamin Tasker, George Plater, Edmund Jenings, Charles Hammond, Samuel Chamberlain, Philip Thomas, Daniel Dulany, Edward Lloyd, Benjamin Young, Benjamin Tasker, Junior, Richard Lee and Benedict Calvert, Esquires, Nathaniel Wickham, Junior, Thomas Owen, Thomas Cresap, Thomas Beatty, Joseph Chapline, Henry Munday, Thomas Prather, George Gordon, Joseph Ogle, William Griffith, John Rawlings, or any three or more of you as aforesaid to issue out writs, precepts, processes and attachments and hold plea of all actions popular and all actions personal of what sort soever wherein the demand doth not exceed the sum of £100 sterling or 30,000 pounds of tobacco and all actions personal now depending before you and after judgment, execution to award in all such cases and actions aforesaid according to the laws, customs and directions of the Acts of Assembly aforesaid so far forth as they provide and where they are silent according to the laws, statutes and reasonable customs of England as used and practiced within this Province in which said actions so to be tried we do constitute, ordain and appoint you the said Benjamin Tasker, George Plater, Edmund Jenings, Charles Hammond, Samuel Chamberlain, Philip Thomas, Daniel Dulany, Edward Lloyd, Benjamin Young, Benjamin Tasker, Junior, Richard Lee and Benedict Calvert, Esquires, Nathaniel Wickham, Junior, Thomas Owen, Thomas Cresap, Thomas Beatty, Joseph Chaplain, Henry Munday, Thomas Prather, George Gordon, Joseph Ogle, William Griffith, John Rawlings and none others to be judges. Also by these presents we do command

283

the Sheriff that at the several Courts to be held for our said County he give his attendance and cause to come before you or any three or more of you as aforesaid such and so many good and lawful men of his bailiwick out of each and every hundred thereof by whom the truth of the matter in the premises may be the better known and enquired of; lastly you shall cause to be brought before you at your said Courts all writs, precepts, processes and indictments to your Courts and jurisdictions belonging that the same may be inspected and by due force of law determined. Witness our trusty and well-beloved Samuel Ogle, Esquire, Lieutenant General and Chief Governor of our said Province of Maryland, this 12th day of December in the thirty-fourth year of our Dominion &c., 1748."

Half of the aforesaid Justices were directed to swear in the other half and then the latter half was to swear in the former. This done, the proceedings were to be certified to "our High Court of Chancery with all convenient speed."

Date		Dulany, Daniel	Wickham, Nathaniel Jr	Munday, Henry	Griffith, William	Rawlins, John	Prather, Thomas	Beatty, Thomas	Cresap, Thomas	Chapline, Joseph	Gordon, George	Dowel, Dr. James	Magruder, Nathan	Parker, Hugh	Clagett, John	Alexander, Nathaniel	Needham, John	Beall, Josiah/Josias	Beall, Alexander	Crabb, Henry Wright	Wood, Joseph	Smith, James	Webb, William	Smith, Jo-eph	Linn, David	Prather, John Smith	Jones, Charles	Heugh, Andrew	Luckett, William	Bainbridge, Peter	Chapline, Moses	Duckett, Jacob	Norris, Thomas	Price, Thomas	Dickson, James	Gittings, Kensey	Blair, William	Shelby, Evan	Postlethwait, Samuel	Beall, Samuel	Innis, Enoch	Warford, Joseph	Beall, Nathaniel
1748	Dec.	X	X	X		X	X																																				
1748/49	Mar.	⊗	X	X	X	X	X	X	X	X																																	
1749	June	X		X	X	X	X		X																																		
	Aug.	⊗	X	X		X	X	X	X	X																																	
	Nov.	⊗	X	X	X	X		X		X			X																														
1749/50	Mar.	⊗		X	X	X																																					
1750	June	⊗	X	X	X	X	X	X	X	X				X	X	X		X	X	X	X	X	X																				
	Aug.		X	X	X	X	X	X	X	X				X		X		X	X		X	X	X																				
	Nov.		X	X	X	X	X	X	X	X				X		X		X	X	X	X	X	X	X																			
1750/51	Mar.	⊗	X		X	X	X	X		X				X		X		X	X		X																						
1751	June		X		X	X	X	X		X				X		X		X		X	X	X																					
	Aug.		X		X	X	X	X		X				X		X					X	X	X																				
	Nov.	⊗	X		X	X	X							X		X	X	X		X	X	X																					
1751/52	Mar.	X		X	X		X							X		X	X	X	X																								
1752	June	X		X	X	X		X						X		X	X	X	X																								
	Aug.	⊗		X	X	X		X						X		X	X																										
	Nov.	X		X	X	X								X		X	X	X	X	X																							
1753	Mar.	⊗		X	X	X		X								X	X	X	X	X	X																						
	June	⊗		X	X	X										X				X	X		X	X																			
	Aug.	X		X	X		X			X						X				X	X		X	X																			
	Nov.	X		X	X	X										X				X	X	X	X	X																			
1754	Mar.	X		X	X	X	X													X	X	X																					
	June	X		X	X	X	X	X												X		X	X																				
	Aug.	⊗		X	X	X	X													X		X	X	X	X																		
	Nov.	⊗		X	X	X	X													X		X	X	X	X	X																	
1755	Mar.	⊗		X	X	X	X													X		X	X	X	X																		
	June	⊗		X	X	X	X													X		X	X	X	X																		
	Aug.	⊗		X	X	X	X	X												X		X	X	X	X																		
	Nov.	⊗		X	X		X													X			X	X	X																		
1758	June						X	⊗												X		X	X		X	X	X	X	X	X	X												
	Aug.						X	⊗												X		X	X		X	X	X	X	X	X													
	Nov.						X	⊗												X		X	X		X	X	X	X	X	X	X		X										
1759	Mar.							⊗												X		X	X		X	X	X	X	X	X	X		X										
	June							⊗												X		X			X	X	X	X	X		X												
	Aug.						X													X		X			X	X	X	X	X		X												
	Nov.						X	X												X		X	X		X	X	X	X	X		X												
1760	Mar.						X													X		X			X	X	X		X		X												
	June						X	X												X		X	X		X	X	X		X		X												
	Aug.						X													X		X	X		X	X	X		X		X												
	Nov.						X	X												X		X	X		X	X	X	X		X													
1761	Mar.						X													X		X			X	X	X		X		X												
	June						X	X												X		X			X	X	X	X		X	X												
	Aug.						X	X												X		X	X		X	X	X	X		X	X												
	Nov.						X	X												X		X	X		X	X	X	X		X	X												
1762	Mar.						X	X												X		X			X	X	X		X		X												
	June						X	X												X		X			X	X	X	X		X	X												
	Aug.						X	X												X		X			X	X		X		X		X												
	Nov.						X													X		X			X	X	X		X		X												
1763	Mar.						X											X		X	X		X	X	X	X	X	X	X	X	X	X											
	June						X													X	X	X	X		X	X	X	X	X	X	X	X	X										
	Aug.						X													X	X	X	X		X	X	X	X	X	X	X	X											
	Nov.						X											X		X	X		X	X	X	X	X	X	X	X	X										X	X	X
1764	Mar.						X											X			X	X			X	X	X	X	X	X	X	X									X		
	June						X													X	X			X	X	X	X	X	X	X	X	X							X	X		
	Aug.						X													X	X	X	X	X	X	X	X	X	X									X	X	X	
	Nov.						X											X		X	X	X	X	X	X	X	X		X		X						X	X	X	X	X
1765	Mar.						X													X	X	X	X	X	X	X	X		X	X						X	X	X	X	X
	June						X											X		X	X	X	X	X	X	X	X		X	X	X						X	X		
	Aug.						X													X	X	X	X	X	X	X	X		X	X	X		X				X	X	X	X	X
	Nov.						X											X		X	X	X	X	X	X	X		X	X						X	X	X		X

⊗ = Chief Justice

285

NB: Variations in the spelling of place names have been grouped, where practicable, in a single entry. Because the wide variation in spelling of personal names may or may not be significant, they have not been consolidated and the reader is therefore cautioned to look for all possible spellings.

Banks, John 115, 192, 193, 248, 249, 259
  John Jr. 47, 115
Bar, Frederick vii, 1, 53, 55
Bare, Jacob 250
  George 268
Barick, Peter 62
Barker, William 199, 250
Barlange, Vinsill 178
Barnard, James 236
  John 105
Barnes, Weaver 142, 225
Barnet, Thomas 69
Barnett, Alexander 77
Barnhard, Luke 175
Barns, Thomas 35, 36
Barrack, William 132
Barret, Alexander 43
Barrett, Alexander 139
Barrick, Christian 123, 140
  John 52, 61
  Peter 52, 115, 126, 140
  William 238, 246, 250
Barrisford, John 126
Barton, Benjamin 49
  Jacob 60, 145
  Joshua 49
Barwick, John 253
Bastardy 8, 13, 15, 17, 31, 34, 41, 43, 44,
  55, 63, 64, 67, 68, 69, 71, 72, 75,
  77, 81, 84, 92, 99, 101, 108, 117,
  118, 122, 138, 144, 150, 153, 158,
  159, 163, 164, 184, 185, 192, 205,
  209, 210, 212, 216, 225, 228, 236,
  238, 240, 241, 257, 260, 270, 271
Batman, John 231
Baxter, George 124
Beach, Nathan 17
Beall, Alexander 55, 65, 71, 84, 91, 98,
  99, 107, 115, 117, 125, 133, 138,
  142, 165, 169, 179, 210, 211, 285
  Alexander of James 169
  Archibald 53, 131
  Basil 9, 116
  Benjamin of Benjamin 228
  Clementius 232
  George 69, 118, 241, 262, 263
  George Jr. 135, 154
  Henry 103
  Isaias 86
  Jacob of Ninian 180
  James 21, 142
  John 148
  Joseph 53, 180, 207, 234, 237, 267
  Joseph of Ninian 61, 72, 102, 103
  Josiah 47, 99, 100, 107, 119, 121, 126,
    155, 242, 248, 253, 259, 273, 285
  Josias 55, 71, 77, 84, 91, 98, 285
  Lucy 142, 166
  Mordecai 249
  Nathaniel 93, 101, 121, 202
  Nathaniel Jr. 155
  Nathaniel Sr. 45, 264, 285
  Ninian 53, 96, 102, 118, 191, 238
  Ninian of Ninian 15, 40, 47, 74, 78, 105,
    125, 166
  Richard 85, 100, 102, 103, 113, 115,

Beall, Richard (contd.) 121, 134, 260, 265
  Robert of Ninian 123
  Samuel 121, 133, 142, 143, 149, 154,
    163, 165, 218, 232, 248, 260, 271,
    273, 285
  Samuel Jr. 200, 253, 255, 265
  Samuel Sr. 121, 160, 169
  Sarah (see also Henry) 210
  William 71, 156, 166, 185, 189, 218, 234
  William of Ninian 15
Beaman, Richard 47, 75
Bean, John 6, 61
  Wensley 185
Beany, Jacob 58, 101
Beard, John 103, 105, 133
  William 216
Beatty, Charles 245, 262, 265, 266, 272
  Edward 3, 38
  George 34, 238
  John 260
  Susanna 222
  Thomas ix, 1, 4, 8, 15, 24, 34, 37, 40,
    45, 47, 48, 54, 63, 65, 71, 72, 77,
    80, 88, 107, 133, 138, 142, 143, 145,
    152, 155, 160, 165, 169, 177, 180,
    184, 186, 190, 191, 196, 202, 207,
    211, 218, 222, 225, 228, 234, 235,
    238, 240, 242, 243, 244, 246, 248,
    253, 255, 257, 264, 265, 266, 268,
    273, 277, 279, 283, 285
  Thomas Jr. 202, 216, 238, 245
  Thomas Sr. 245
  William 192, 207, 212, 249, 256, 257,
    264, 266, 272
Beaver, Peter 235
Beaver Creek 200
Beaver Dam Branch 109
Beck, Jacob 106
Beckwith, Basil 107
  George 172
  William 246, 259
Becraft, Benjamin 21, 52, 142, 270
  George 52, 62, 112, 113, 114, 234, 267,
    268
Beech, Elizabeth 101
Bell, John 74, 114, 232
Bell Town 97
Belt, Jacob Jr. 124
  Joseph 55, 102, 142, 153, 166, 230, 238
  Joseph Jr. 21, 81, 115
Beney, Jacob 78, 101, 111, 144
Bennet's Creek 120
Bennett, George 58, 59, 126, 146
  Jacob 70
  Joseph 240
Benninger, Juliana 203
Benton, Joseph 242
Beresford, John 105
Bergh, Handall 170
  John 149
  Peter 149
Bernard, Staffel 13, 14
Bess, Negro girl 42
Betty, Thomas 280
Bewsie, Edward 18
Big Tonoloways Creek 7

287

288

Gittings, Kensey 242, 244, 253, 255, 259, 268, 285
   Kensy 246
Glade Creek 217, 250
Glenn, Thomas 242
Godman, Samuel Israel 232
   Samuel Isral 217
Goesler, Henry 101
Goff, James 266
Goodson, Thomas 216
Gordon, George 1, 3, 8, 15, 17, 21, 31, 34, 40, 43, 47, 54, 60, 61, 66, 68, 70, 71, 90, 95, 121, 122, 163, 210, 211, 233, 279, 280, 283, 285
   George Jr. 3
   Mr. 245
Gore, James 64, 66, 201, 222, 234
   Thomas 209
Gorrell, James 223, 224
Gosling, Ezekiel 135
   Josiah 150, 199
Gow, James 113
Graham, John 136
   Sarah 238, 240, 258
Grand Jury 1, 8, 9, 15, 17, 31, 33, 40, 41, 47, 49, 50, 55, 66, 69, 71, 72, 77, 78, 84, 91, 92, 93, 98, 99, 100, 101, 107, 115, 117, 119, 122, 123, 126, 129, 133, 138, 142, 144, 145, 152, 155, 160, 169, 170, 177, 179, 180, 190, 192, 194, 196, 197, 202, 207, 209, 212, 218, 219, 222, 225, 228, 234, 235, 238, 240, 242, 244, 246, 248, 253, 255, 257, 259, 264, 265, 268, 273
Grant, Isabel 157
Graves, Thomas 183
Gray, Joseph 125
   William 8, 31, 35, 40
Great Bennet's Creek 73
Great Pipe Creek 4, 62, 63, 109, 117, 132, 175, 198, 200, 204, 212, 217, 222, 225, 235
Greenfield, Walter Smith 194
"Green Spring" 109
Green Town (Grinton?), Yorkshire 26
Greenup, John 202, 216
Greenwald, Philip 265
Greenwood, Elizabeth 99
Gregg, John 202, 216
   Nathan 69
Griffith, Dr. 231
   Dr. Joseph 83
   Dr. Orlando 18, 36, 209
   Mr. 24
   Widow 229, 250
   William (Justice) ix, 1, 8, 11, 15, 17, 24, 31, 54, 65, 71, 77, 84, 98, 100, 106, 115, 119, 122, 125, 133, 134, 138, 142, 143, 144, 145, 152, 155, 160, 165, 169, 279, 280, 283, 285
   William (merchant) 98, 106
   William (Captain) 24, 88, 149
Grim, Andrew 235, 241, 242, 273
Grimes, Edward 219
   Lettice 258, 259, 260, 271

Grimes (contd.)
   Lucy 260, 271
   Lydia 260
Gripe, Jacob 147
Groom, Chr. 107
Grosch, Conrad (see also Crosh) 143
Grosh, Conrad 238
Gump, George 97, 132
Gyles, Elizabeth 73
   William 73

Habeas corpus 69, 93
Haff, Abraham 192, 207, 222
Hagar, Jonathan 31, 35, 47, 55, 66, 121, 133, 145, 155, 160, 194, 196, 202, 207, 225
Hale's "History of the Pleas of the Crown" 3
Halifax, Nova Scotia 174
Haling's (River) 133
Hall, Benjamin 253
   Benjamin Jr. 262
   Clement 38, 39
   Elizabeth 38, 192, 193
   Mary 41, 69
   Sary 66
   William 223, 224
Hall of Records, Annapolis v, 278
Halligan, Patrick 25
Hallom, John 142
Hallum, John 55, 93, 103, 104
Halmard, Elizabeth 211
Haman, Michael 217
Hamilton, Dr. 135, 146
   James 195
Hammond, Charles 279, 280, 283
   John 210
   Jonas 15
Hampton, Stephen 72, 116
Hancock, Md. 14, 114, 171
Hann, John 51
Harbin, James 248
   John 209
   Joshua 177, 201, 206, 242
Hardee, Robert 161
Harden, Simon 2, 159
Harding, Charles 192, 206, 218
   Elias 101
   John 49
   Moses 126
Hardman, Joseph 24, 49, 60, 78, 101, 208, 220, 231
Hare, Elizabeth 158
Harlan, John 63, 71, 95, 237
Harlin, John 169, 264, 267
Harling, John 234
Harmon, Mary 269
   Michael 199
Harper, Robert 148
Harper's Road 255
Harpers Ferry 217, 250, 256
Harrie, Elizabeth 267
   Richard 267
Harris, Benjamin 12, 13, 98, 113, 129, 169, 192, 206
   James 254
   Mary 254

Litton, Caleb 131, 134, 249
Livingstone, Andrew 269
Lloyd, Edward 279, 280, 283
Loan Office 150
Lockman, Jacob 177, 285
Log Cabin Branch 200
Logsdon, John 204, 212, 222, 235
  Thomas 107
London 130, 229
Long, Frederick 101, 111, 112
  John 14
"Long Acre" 255
Lonsdale, Solomon 26
Loveless, John Baptist 265
Lowestaber, Jacob 162
Lowndes, Christopher 65, 136, 189
Loy, George 119, 194
Lucas, Thomas 17, 165
Lucket, William 66
Luckett, William 2, 23, 24, 49, 56, 76,
  78, 85, 101, 107, 123, 124, 150, 166,
  177, 180, 184, 190, 191, 194, 196,
  201, 202, 207, 209, 211, 222, 225,
  228, 229, 232, 234, 235, 238, 240,
  242, 244, 246, 248, 252, 253, 255,
  256, 257, 259, 263, 264, 265, 268,
  273, 285
Lumme (Lummy), Elizabeth 76
Lynham, Bartholomew 195, 197, 205
  George 271
  Dr. Philip 89, 93, 128, 136, 140, 144
Lynn, David 160, 165, 177, 184, 190, 191,
  192, 196, 202, 207, 209, 218, 222,
  224, 225, 228, 232, 234, 235, 238,
  240, 242, 244, 246, 248, 253, 255,
  257, 259, 260, 261, 264, 265, 268,
  273

Macabee, Brock 181
Macall, Benjamin Jr. 202
  James 202
Macbee, Egbert 181
Maccabee, Elizabeth Ann 150
McCain, John Brook 126
McCarty, William 185
McCay, Daniel 35, 36
McClellen, William 238
McCoy, Daniel 264
  William 237
MacCubbin, William 131
McCullagh, Daniel 207
  John 207
McDaniel, Hugh 220
  John Gray 221
McFaddin, John 110
McGuire, Philip 110
McIntire, John 241, 248
McIntyre, John 238
Mackaboy, Lucy 31
Mackaness, Peregrine 230
Mackbee, Brock 181
  Cazier 183
  Jeremiah 183
  Leucey 99
  Lucy 110
  Mary 183

Mackbee (contd.)
  Mathew 183
McKenna, Arthur 54
McKinley, John 249
Macklochland, James 81
McKorkle, John 261
Mackquier, Philip 99
McMullen, Thomas 246
Macnaul, Mary 43
McRea, Robert 237
Maddin, Mordecai 222
Madding, John 21
Magess, Elizabeth 139
Magness, Perygreen 211
Magruder, Alexander 98, 102, 103, 107,
  119, 135, 179, 180, 202
  Hesekiah 201
  Hezekiah 185, 207, 242, 253
  Nathan 21, 40, 55, 65, 71, 77, 84, 91,
  107, 122, 285
  Nathaniel 66, 92, 102, 103, 113, 135,
  196, 201, 212, 241
  Nathaniel Jr. 107, 112, 155
  Nathaniel of Ninian 8, 31, 180
  Ninian 98, 101
  Ninian Jr. 1
  Ninian Beall 202, 234, 238
  Norman Beall 265
  Samuel III 1, 40, 163, 177, 209, 238,
  258, 265
  Samuel (Kittocton) 177
  Samuel Wade 135
  Zacharia 180
  Zachariah 102, 103, 113, 202, 206, 228,
  238
Mahue (Mayhew), Joseph 77
Mallerce, Mathew 84
  Matthew 86
Malloro, Mathias 67
Manard (Maynard), Thomas 16
Maneyeard, Thomas 41, 50
Manford, William 84
Man(n)or Hundred, (Monocacy) 6, 60, 61,
  131, 216, 249
Manson, James 103
Manyard (Maynard), Henry 77
  Thomas 31, 55, 92
Marble Town Church 238
March, Mary Ann 195, 197
Mark, Robert 67, 114
Markland, Jonathan 69, 84, 256
  Mathew 107, 114, 122
  Matthew 102, 145
Markley, John 220
Marlborough, Md. 129
Maroney, Henry 81, 140, 144
  Rachel 140
Marsh Creek 261
Marsh Hundred 7, 61, 110, 131, 216, 249
Marshall, William 62, 74, 89, 151
Martin, Edmond 7
  James 266
  John 6
  John Jr. 49, 133
  Louisa 133
  Mary, Queen of England viii

Neal (contd.)
James 63, 64, 67, 68
Sarah 55, 64
Neale, Charles 120
Dr. Charles 215, 216, 240
James 66
Neall, Jonathan 12
William 12
Need, Mathias 237, 270
Needham, John 40, 47, 54, 55, 59, 61, 65, 66, 71, 77, 91, 98, 99, 100, 107, 285
Sarah 209
Neel, Dr. Charles Sr. 209
Sarah 41
Negroes viii, 58, 61, 86, 127, 150, 175, 217, 232, 242, 243, 252, 262, 280, 282
Nelson, Arthur 15, 139, 155, 194, 202, 207, 216, 235, 259, 273
Arthur Jr. 11, 71
Arthur Sr. 11
John 41, 107, 170
John Sr. 11
Nelson's Ferry (near Point of Rocks) 11
Nelson's "Justice" 3
"New Facts and Old Families" vii, 109
New Style Calendar x, 106
Newell, William 96
Newfoundland Hundred 6, 18, 31, 61, 175, 216, 249
Lower Part 58, 61, 131, 150, 175, 249
Upper Part 92, 131
Newkirk, Mary 123
Nicholls, John 21, 50, 60, 61, 94, 167
Simon 188
Thomas 157, 161
Thomas Jr. 234
Nichols, John of Thomas 180
Nicholson, Benjamin 270
Martha 160
Nickolls, Jacob 267
John 242
Thomas 21
Thomas Jr. 206
Nisi prius 282
Noland, Paul 92
Pearce 72
Philip 171
Nolands Ferry 62
Noon, John 230
Norris, Benjamin 108
Capt. Thomas 226
Elizabeth 77
John 6
John III 66
Thomas 170, 177, 184, 190, 191, 194, 196, 202, 204, 207, 211, 215, 221, 222, 225, 227, 228, 229, 234, 235, 238, 240, 242, 285
William 78, 102, 110, 113, 238
William Jr. 126
William of Benjamin 216
Northcraft, Richard 249
Norwood, Richard 267
Nowles, Mary 92

Oar (Ore) Hill 256
Oaths (Swearing) 16, 41, 55, 60, 72, 215, 271
Oats, Mathias 244
O'Cain, Manasses 263
Odell, James 53
Thomas 133
O'Donnel, Neale 54
Offutt, James 129
James Jr. 6
Thomas Jr. 16
William 126, 262
William of William 129
Ogden, Nehemiah 167
Ogdon, Nehemiah 75
O'Gillion, Neal 19
Ogle, Capt. 227
Jehu 185
John 142, 205
Joseph 3, 63, 80, 82, 279, 280, 283
Mr. 108, 109
Gov. Samuel viii, 284
Ogle's Ford, Major 117, 132, 175, 200, 217, 227, 250
Ohio Company 136
Old Style Calendar ix, x
Old Town, Md. 156
Old Town Hundred 217, 249, 254
Oler, Peter 170, 171
Oliver, John 259
Oneal, Lawrence 244
Oneall, William 131
Onsell (see also Unsell), Frederick 119
Onselt, Frederick 52
Orchison, George 212
Ordinary: see Taverns
Ore Hill 255, 256
Orme, John 226, 238, 257
Orndorf, Christian 257
Orndorff, Christian 255
Orr, John 234
Osborn, Thomas 41, 100
Osnaburg (Osnaberg, Oznabriggs) 29, 170
Overseers, Road ix, 4, 24, 25, 31, 55, 60, 62, 71, 72, 74, 76, 77, 88, 92, 93, 95, 99, 111, 116, 117, 120, 121, 128, 131, 132, 133, 147, 148, 149, 150, 151, 167, 175, 176, 185, 199, 204, 205, 217, 250
Owen, Edward 1, 31, 42, 53, 69
Lawrence 66, 78, 102, 121, 131, 138, 176
Robert 66, 77, 170, 267
Capt. Thomas x, 29, 30, 53, 54, 279, 280, 283
Owens, Edward Jr. 253
Robert 222, 259
Owens Creek 109
Owler, Peter 198
Oyer and terminer 282
Oznabriggs: see Osnaburg

Paca, William 256
Pack, Margaret 165
Thomas 212
Pain, Flayl 62

300

303

Wetsel, Martin 118
Wheat, Joseph 131, 140, 222
   William 69, 121
   William Sr. 107
Whetsel, Martin 89
Whinemiller, Conrad 185
Whipping Post ix, 13, 22, 44, 94, 103, 121,
   129, 150, 193, 208, 227, 245, 246,
   248
Whistleman, Valentine 269
White, David 192
   Edward 155, 164
   James 204, 212, 216, 235
   John 145
   Margaret 41, 64
   Samuel 107
Whiteacre, James 169
White's Mill 210
Whitman, Frederick 243
Whitten, Thomas 135, 202
Whitwall, Robert 135
Wickham, Col. Nathaniel Jr. viii, ix, 1,
   3, 4, 8, 15, 17, 24, 30, 31, 37, 39,
   40, 45, 47, 54, 61, 65, 68, 71, 77,
   80, 84, 91, 98, 100, 103, 106, 115,
   117, 119, 122, 125, 132, 138, 142,
   143, 144, 152, 154, 155, 160, 163,
   165, 169, 279, 280, 283, 285
   Nathaniel 224
   Nathaniel Sr. 189
   Nathaniel III 63
   Samuel 185
Widmeyer, John Michael 270
Wilburn, William 3, 8, 31, 55
Wilcoxen, John Jr. 139, 140, 144
Wilcoxon, John 69, 248, 259
Wilds, John 192
Wilkinson, Jane 26, 27
   Mathew 26, 27
Willet, Isabella 235
Willett, Isabella 259
William III, King of England viii
Williams, Baruch 74
   Basil 115
   Charles 21, 225
   Elenor 80, 86
   Elisha 238
   George 165
   Hilleary 97
   James 169
   Joseph 102, 135, 138, 159
   Morris 179
   Richard 44, 64
   William 41, 91, 113, 169, 197
   Rev. William 54, 70, 83
   William of Thomas 66, 69, 77
Williamson, Rev. Alexander 256
   Moses 244
Willit, Isabel 180
Wills Creek 156
Willson, John 239
   Thomas 227, 229
Wilson, George 66, 69, 77
   Joseph 7, 8, 66, 69, 107, 145
   Lancelot 119
   Lawrence 100

Wilson (contd.)
   Margaret 193
   Mary 266
   Phyllis 41
   Robert 114
   Thomas 131, 204
   Thomas of Toms Creek 51
   Wadsworth 69
   William 119, 122, 145, 165
Winchester, William 257
Winchester, Va. 255
Winchester Measure 183
Winchester Road 229
Winders, James 249
Windfield, William 155
Winfield, William 164
Winford, John 145
Winright, Esther 133
Winters, Ann 71
   George 160
Wise, Francis 16, 17, 119
   Melker 118
   Rebecca 8
Witton, Thomas 79
Wofford, Benjamin 203
   William Jr. 150
Wolphin, Catharine 203
Wood, Bennet 122
   Charles 37, 38, 115, 155
   Charity 122
   David 153
   Jacob 122
   Jennett 122
   Joseph 1, 3, 4, 5, 31, 63
   Joseph (All Saints) 22, 56, 88, 91, 198,
    251
   Joseph (Constable) 7
   Joseph (Israel's Creek) 25, 55, 63, 71,
    73, 77, 78
   Joseph (Justice) 115, 119, 122, 125, 133,
    138, 142, 143, 145, 152, 154, 155,
    160, 165, 169, 177, 180, 185, 190,
    191, 194, 196, 202, 204, 205, 207,
    209, 211, 215, 218, 221, 222, 224,
    225, 226, 228, 234, 235, 238, 240,
    242, 244, 246, 248, 252, 262, 285
   Joseph (Linganore) 47, 88
   Juda 122
   Major 216, 226, 227, 243
   Philip 25, 26, 27, 39
   Robert 122, 244, 255
   Stephen 122
Woodard, John 202
   Luke 202
Woods, Joseph 56
Woolf, Paul 132, 200, 209
Woolhider, Frederick 177
Worfford, James Jr. 123
Worthington, John 130
Wray, Rebecca 41
Wyatt, Edward 2
Wymer, John 177

Yates, Thomas 109
Weates, William 250
Yesterday (Easterday), Christian 234, 238